A History of
Lincoln

A History of
Lincoln

Richard Gurnham

PHILLIMORE

First published in 2009 by Phillimore & Co Ltd
This edition in paperback 2013
The History Press
The Mill, Brimscombe Port
Stroud, Gloucestershire, gl5 2qg
www.thehistorypress.co.uk
© Richard Gurnham 2013

Printed and bound in Great Britain by
Marston Book Services Limited, Oxfordshire

CONTENTS

To Jeannie, David,
Paul and Rebecca

LIST OF ILLUSTRATIONS

Frontispiece – The Brayford Pool and Lincoln Cathedral by John Carmichael.

Acknowledgements

In writing this book I have leant heavily on the work of those who have written and published previous histories of the city. Anyone who attempts to write a history of Lincoln today owes a particularly large debt to the pioneering research undertaken by Sir Francis Hill. As my brief and very select bibliography suggests, almost every chapter of this book (the last is the obvious exception) owes a great deal to Sir Francis's four-volume history of the city. It is perhaps a fitting tribute to Sir Francis that his name is included today on the 18th-century obelisk that stands now in St Mark's Square as a memorial to those who have brought honour to the city. More recently, Ian Beckwith's *The Book of Lincoln* and Michael Jones's *Lincoln: History and Guide* have provided very readable, short, single-volume histories. With this work I have attempted to write a rather more detailed account but one, I hope, that is equally readable.

I owe a special thank you to Michael Jones, the City Archaeologist. I have relied heavily on his expertise, particularly for the early chapters, and he has kindly read through the first few chapters of the book and let me use some of the illustrations for these (Figs 11-13, 15, 34-6). In finding pictures to illustrate the book I have incurred many debts. I am grateful to the Rev. John Wilford and the committee members of FLARE (the Friends of Lincoln Archaeological Research and Excavation) for allowing me to use a number of the drawings by the late David Vale, which do so much to bring the past to life (Figs 2, 6, 10, 14, 16, 39, 61) and to Canon Alan Nugent, subdean of the cathedral, for permission to use David Vale's drawing of the cathedral after the earth tremor of 1185 (Fig. 41), and photographs of the interior (Figs 45, 48-51). I am also very grateful to the generous support of Mr Eric Croft, who has let me use more than 30 postcards of 19th- and 20th-century Lincoln, many of which are rare and valuable, to illustrate the later chapters (Figs 103, 105-7, 110, 114, 116-18, 120-8, 130-3, 138, 142-3, 147-8, 156-9, 162-3, 166). I am also grateful to Mr Ray Hooley, the former Librarian for Ruston and Hornsby, who has kindly let me use a number of photographs relating to Lincoln's history as a centre of engineering (Figs 111-13, 115, 149-50, 151-5, 161 and 168), and to Lincoln City Library for pictures from the Local Studies Collection (Figs 4, 98, 135-7, 139-41, 165) and to Ms Julie Bush of the Collection for allowing me to reproduce some of the photographs, paintings and drawings held by the city museum service (including the front cover, the frontispiece and Figs 1, 3, 7, 86, 94-5, 97, 99, 108, 119). It is also a pleasure to acknowledge here the help I have received from Tom Green, particularly regarding some of the more controversial aspects of the first centuries of post-Roman Lincoln, and from Peter Brown, formerly with the *Lincolnshire Echo*, who has helped me with the chapters on Lincoln's more recent history.

Finally, it is always a pleasure to acknowledge the support and understanding I have enjoyed from my family. Once again my wife, Jeannie, has had to put up with a semi-absent husband. Also, together with my son, David, Jeannie has taken many of the photographs of Lincoln that appear in this book and I have also once again relied heavily on my family as proofreaders and advisors on style and readability.

ONE

The Roman City of Lindum Colonia

THE CONQUEST OF THE CORIELTAUVI

When the first Roman soldiers reached the Celtic British settlement at Lincoln in about A.D. 45-6 they found a community of farmers and fishermen living close to the margins of the River Witham and the Brayford Pool. The name they would later give to the first Roman settlement, Lindum, derived from the Celtic 'lindo', the Celtic name for a lake or pool. Both the river and the lake were much wider than they are now and at least part of the existing Celtic settlement was established on small islands in the river and lake. Very little is known about the settlement, but a glimpse of the lives of the people who lived here before the Roman invasion was gained during excavations in 1972 at the site of a former warehouse in the High Street, about 490 feet from where the Witham now enters the Brayford Pool. Here, on what would have been a sandy island in the lake in the first century B.C., archaeologists found late Iron-Age pottery and evidence of Iron-

1   *The late Iron-Age settlement at Lincoln (a reconstruction).*

Age houses: a hearth, post holes, and a circular ditch that was probably a drainage gully for a roundhouse.

It would hardly have been surprising if the arrival of the 5,000-strong IXth Hispana Legion ('Hispana' for the battle honours won in Spain) struck fear into the hearts and minds of the Celtic inhabitants beside the lake. The Roman army brought overwhelming forces and its reputation for military effectiveness and resourcefulness preceded it. News of the invasion by a Roman army of more than 40,000 men, led by Aulus Plautius, and of its victory over the Celtic British tribes on the banks of the Medway near Rochester in A.D. 43, probably reached the people of the area not long after the event. The Celtic tribe to which the people of the settlement belonged was part of a federation of tribes known as the Corieltauvi, whose capital was at Leicester (known to the Romans as *Ratae*) and whose territories occupied most of the area now known as the East Midlands. The tribe that had led the resistance to the invading force (and whose actions had partly provoked it), the Catuvellauni, may have been their enemies and were certainly rivals for territory. The Corieltauvi had not fought at the Medway and may not have been altogether sorry to see a dangerous rival defeated. Following further battles and the subsequent fall of Colchester, the Catuvellaunian capital, the King of the Corieltauvi was probably one of the tribal leaders who made his submission to the Emperor Claudius, while the Catuvellaunian King, Caratacus, fled into hiding in Wales.

Rather than hunt down Caratacus straight away, Plautius decided first to secure the lowlands. While he led the IXth Legion towards Lincoln, the XIVth Legion made its

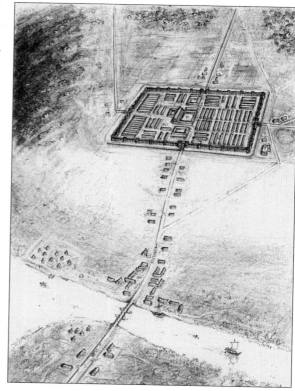

way from Colchester through the Midlands towards Leicester, following the line of the Watling Street. The IInd Legion struck out westwards, first towards the Isle of Wight and then further westwards towards the great fort of Maiden Castle. Plautius probably reached Lincoln by following the existing native trackway – Icknield Street – along the edge of the limestone scarp, having already established a secure base for the legion further south at Longthorpe, near Peterborough, on the eastern edge of Corieltauvian territory. Excavations at Longthorpe suggest that a large fortress was established here soon after the occupation of Corieltauvian territory had begun.

2   *The legionary fortress at Lincoln from the south (reconstruction).*

Exactly where the first Roman camp was established is not known, and there may have been two, both on the hilltop to the north of the river and in the valley below, not far from the crossing point of the river. Firm evidence of a Roman military base south of the river has yet to be found, but the work of archaeologists at the High Street site in 1972 revealed traces of one, or perhaps two, structures that could have been contemporary with the earliest period of military occupation. Pottery found at the site dated from the earliest conquest period. At this stage, before the building of a bridge over the Witham, this island site would have been of strategic importance. It was here, perhaps, that the river crossing was guarded. The most compelling evidence, however, for an early fortress south of the river remains the discovery in the mid-19th century of early Roman tombstones in this area. It has been suggested by some experts that the absence of surnames on the tombstones indicates that they probably date from the reign of Claudius (A.D. 41-54). Confirmation of the existence of an early military cemetery was discovered in the Monson Street area by an excavation in 1982, very close to the convergence of the two major Roman roads, Ermine Street and Fosse Way, which were probably also completed in this earliest period.

For some years the camp, or camps, at Lincoln remained among the most northerly outposts of the Roman Empire. Until his retirement in A.D. 47, Plautius worked to ensure the creation of a deep military frontier zone to act as a protective shield for south-east Britain. A line of fortresses was erected, running from Exeter in the south to Lincoln in the north, with the Fosse Way built to link the two, and then continuing along Ermine Street to the Humber. Legionary detachments were permanently stationed near the front line, together with a back-up of auxiliary forts where needed.

Whether or not the Corieltauvian settlement survived the arrival of the Roman army cannot be known. Nor do we know how large the settlement was, but the large number of Iron-Age and Bronze-Age objects found in the River Witham to the east of Lincoln, including the superb 'Witham Shield', suggest that the area had long been of considerable ritual importance to the Celts. The evidence discovered so far suggests only a small community, but the Celtic settlement at Lincoln may have consisted of a number of small communities scattered over a wide area. By this time the eastern boundary of such an area may have been marked by the rather mysterious double- and triple-ditch system of the late Bronze Age or Iron Age that has been discovered running northwards from the Greetwell area, and for some miles beyond to the west of Nettleham.

THE ROMAN FORTRESS

It was probably during the reign of Nero (A.D. 54-65) that it was decided to build a major, permanent fortress on the level ground on top of the steep hill to the north of the river, capable of housing the whole of the XIVth Legion. The precise date for the establishment of this uphill fortress cannot be known. Pottery and coin finds have suggested to some experts that it was no later than the mid-'60s, and probably in A.D. 61, following the suppression of the rebellion led by Boudicca, the Queen of the Iceni tribe, the Corieltauvians' neighbour to the east. During the first stages of the rebellion at least part of the IXth Legion was rushed from Lincoln in a vain attempt to defeat

3   *Tombstone of a Roman soldier of the IXth Legion.*

Boudicca's army following the sack of Colchester, and suffered very heavy losses. After the eventual suppression of the revolt it would have been necessary to rebuild the legion. Of the forces that fought against the Iceni only the cavalry escaped the slaughter. Other authorities, however, have suggested that the fortress was probably begun in A.D. 66, when military reorganisation was necessitated by the withdrawal of the XIVth Legion from Britain, and the evidence of fine imported pottery from Gaul (known as Samian pottery) has caused at least one expert to suggest a date in the early '70s.

The strategic advantages of the hilltop site are fairly obvious, and it is possible that an earlier fortress, south of the river, would have been subject to flooding. The new fortress enclosed an area of 41 acres and was a timber and earth rectangular structure. Although not large by the standards of Roman fortresses, this would have been a remarkable and potent symbol of Roman military might for the local people, whose own settlement may well have been cleared to make way for the fortress. The ditch was six feet deep and 15 feet wide, and there may have been a series of such ditches, although only a small section of the course of a second ditch has been located. The earth from the innermost ditch would have been used to construct the rampart, which was reinforced with timber posts and carried a walkway for the patrolling guards. There was probably a gate in each of the four walls, although the remains of only the East Gate have yet been found, beneath the later stone gate. The defences were strengthened by the addition of wooden towers either side of the gates, probably when the IXth Legion left Lincoln to be replaced by the IInd Legion in A.D. 71.

The fortress housed up to 5,000 soldiers. Much of the space behind the walls would have been taken up by the rows of wooden barracks, separated only by narrow lanes, and each housing at least 80 combatant troops. Space would also have to be found for workshops, granaries, stores and latrines. At the centre of the fortress, however, was the imposing headquarters building, the *principia*, found during excavations in 1978-9. Here the two main streets of the fortress intersected and the *principia* faced eastwards, towards the main gate. This consisted of a large aisled hall, the *basilica*, used for administrative purposes, the dispensing of justice and for assembling the troops when their commander, the *legatus legionis*, wished to address them. In front of the hall, immediately to the east, was a large courtyard, surrounded on three sides by colonnades. Here, in store rooms surrounding the courtyard, would be kept the legion's standards, armaments and equipment, and the pay chest would also be kept nearby, probably in the legion's chapel, adjoining the main hall. The courtyard floor would seem to have been kept fairly clean, for few artefacts were discovered here. In the north-east corner, however, a well was sunk, and water from it seems to have been stored in large bowls or tanks in the courtyard, probably partly for religious ceremonies.

Not far away would be the commander's palace and the houses of his six tribunes, his seconds-in-command, although these have not yet been located. A large bath house may also have been built inside the walls, although this was often found just outside, as was the amphitheatre, where the new recruits would receive their arms drill, possibly on a stretch of level ground just outside the West Gate. This would have been a wooden building, as would be most of the buildings at this stage, but the bath house had to be built at least partly of stone, to accommodate the furnaces needed to heat the bath buildings.

The fortress would have had an enormous impact on the economic life of the surrounding area. Farmland up to 12 miles from Lincoln probably become part of the fortress's *territorium,* providing at least some of the grain and other food requirements for the soldiers, and pottery kilns and iron mines were also pressed into service over a similarly wide area to meet the fortress's demands. Timber from surrounding woods was used to build the barrack blocks and other buildings and to provide the revetments for the fortress wall, and much iron would be needed for tools and weapons and to make the vast numbers of iron nails needed in the construction of the fortress.

FROM FORTRESS TO CITY

The evidence of military tombstones has led archaeologists to believe that it was probably early in the last decade of the first century that Lincoln was chosen to be a *colonia*, a town for the settlement of retired soldiers and their families. It has been suggested that Lincoln may have been chosen owing to the need to keep a close eye on the area to the west and north, the former territory of the Brigantes. Wherever they were established, however, the *coloniae* were a means by which Roman culture and ideas could be spread among the native people. As the only large Roman town between Leicester and York, Lincoln quickly became the principal centre of Roman civilisation for a wide area, where prosperous, ambitious Celts might learn and adopt the ways of Rome. The process of

4   *The discovery of the Bailgate colonnade in 1878.*

Romanisation would also have radiated, to some extent, to the surrounding rural areas, advanced by former legionaries who were given farms in the *territorium*.

It was probably not long after the settlement had been given this new status that a start was made replacing the wooden walls and towers with stone. The boundaries of the *colonia* were established identically to those of the former fortress, although the IInd Legion may have left the fortress some years before. This would seem to have become Roman policy, probably as a means of reducing local resistance and resentment. The new walls were therefore built immediately outside the existing wooden walls. The ditch that had been dug surrounding the former fortress walls was filled in and the new walls erected on the infill. The existing bank of the former defences now became the core of the rampart behind the new walls.

Four gates were also built, one in the centre of each of the four walls, and one – Newport Arch – in the north wall, survives to this day. The main arch of Newport Arch is 16 feet wide, and a smaller arch to the east, for pedestrians, is six feet six inches wide. Originally there had been a second pedestrian arch on the other side of the road as well, and archaeologists have found the remains of towers flanking the gateway.

The principal gateway, however, remained the East Gate. Archaeological research here has found that in the early years of the *colonia* the wooden towers were probably retained and simply clad in stone on the outer face, and the massive stone gate that replaced this was not built before the third century. This was a double-arch gateway, allowing two roadways to pass beneath.

Similarities in design and building construction suggest that the Newport Arch was probably also built at this time, and most likely replaced an earlier, smaller stone-clad gateway. The West Gate was buried in the mound erected in the 11th century for the north-west corner of the Norman castle, but a drawing made in 1836, when it was briefly revealed, shows that it had a single arch and no flanking smaller arches for pedestrians. Less is known about the South Gate, although part of it still stood in the 18th century. Recent work, however, suggests that it had a double carriageway with smaller side portals for pedestrian use. The road pattern largely followed the grid-like layout of the former fortress, with some existing roads being simply resurfaced.

The new city clearly grew rapidly and quickly outgrew the confines of its walls. Indeed, so rapid was the city's growth down the hill, south of the walled area, that by about A.D. 200 it was also felt necessary to extend the walls southwards, down to the banks of the River Witham, although the scale and cost of the work was such that it may have taken many decades to complete. Evidence from the east wall suggests that it was not completed until about A.D. 250. Today, the medieval Stonebow occupies the site of the south entrance to the Roman Lower City and Saltergate and Newland follow a line just to the south of the southern wall. The line of the east wall is just behind the frontages of the properties on the western side of Broadgate, and the road itself has been built over the infill of the Roman ditch. The remains of the Roman wharf, beside the riverbank, have yet to be revealed, but the shelving beaches along the Roman riverfront have been located, about 164 feet north of the present line.

5   *Newport Arch as it appears today.*

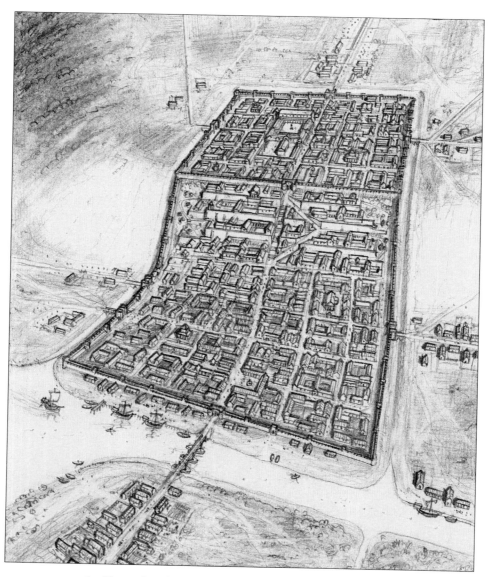

6 *The city from the south in the early fourth century (reconstruction).*

Numerous archaeological finds leave little doubt that in the second century A.D.
Roman Lincoln was already a fine example of a wealthy and successful Roman city,
which must have proved quite awe-inspiring for the local people coming into the town
from the surrounding countryside. At the centre of the Upper City was the forum, the
city's civic centre. A large paved area was laid out in the last years of the first century,
or early in the second century, with bases for statues, but at some time between the
late second century and the early third century the area was redeveloped, to reflect the
city's growing size and importance, and to meet the demands of administrators and
merchants. Colonnades were built to mark the eastern side of a new forum-*basilica*
complex and to line the western side of the main north-south road, now followed fairly

closely by Bailgate. Immediately to the west of the colonnade a double set of rooms were built facing into the forum courtyard. On the north side of the forum stood the *basilica*. This was the town hall and the seat of the law courts, and a fragment of its north wall can still be seen, known popularly as the 'Mint Wall', standing about twenty-three feet high. This would have been a most impressive building; about forty-two feet wide with a portico to the south, facing onto the forum, and at least 30 feet high. It would have dominated the forum and was the largest and tallest building in the city. It also stood at the highest point of the city, adding to its grandeur. The forum was also a trading centre and excavations of the east range of the forum have revealed evidence of copper and silver working, shops or possibly a refreshment area.

A large public bath house – covering an area of at least 195 feet by 147 feet – was also erected in the first years of the *colonia* in the north-eastern corner of the town, possibly on the site of the earlier fortress baths. Floors of stone flags, hypocausts and tessellated pavements have been found. This would have been one of the most important buildings in the town; the Roman bath house was the principal social centre for many townspeople, where citizens could meet, exercise, relax and gossip. The excavations of the Lincoln bath house do not, unfortunately, allow us to reconstruct the layout of the various different rooms that comprised the bath complex, but we might still imagine the daily bathing rituals of the truly Romanised citizen of Lincoln. He would begin by plunging into a cold bath. This would be followed by a visit to the tepid room, then on to a hot room and possibly also to a sweating-hot room, before scraping himself down with a hook-shaped 'strigil' and enjoying a massage with oil and perfumes from the bath attendants. But this was not quite the end of the process. The routine was only complete once there had been a final plunge into an ice-cold bath.

Such was the popularity of the bath house in Roman Britain that many towns had more than one. Lincoln was no exception. As the Lower City developed in the second and third centuries it was clearly felt appropriate to the city's dignity to erect a number of public buildings and monuments along the main north-south street, and among them was a substantial bath house. A heated room about twenty feet square belonging to the baths complex was discovered in 1782, in the yard of the *King's Arms* public house adjacent to the Theatre Royal, and nearby, under the corner of Clasketgate and the High Street, the flue arches for the hypocaust under-floor heating system were discovered in 1925 during building work.

Both bath houses were probably provided with water carried in pipes by an aqueduct from the Roaring Meg spring almost two miles away, to the north-east of the town. As the spring lay more than 65 feet below the level of the town the water had to be pumped up to large collecting tanks just inside the wall. The water was also used to feed a public drinking fountain in the lower town, on the main north-south roadway (now the High Street), to meet the demands of numerous wealthy private consumers and to flush the town's sewers. This last feature was unusual even in Roman towns in Britain, and probably indicates the importance of the *colonia* to the Roman administration. It would certainly have made a considerable difference to the standard of hygiene and the consequent mortality levels. The main sewer ran under the main north-south roadway in the Upper City, but branches also ran east and west from this, under other streets, and manholes were inserted at intervals to make cleaning possible. The discovery of hypocaust under-floor heating systems, numerous fragments of mosaic floors and plastered walls, painted in blue and red, in both the Upper and Lower City, are all evidence of Roman housing, sometimes of particularly high status. Excavations in 1946-7 on the east side of Flaxengate, in the south-east corner of the lower town, revealed a particularly fine colonnaded building, embellished with imported Mediterranean marble veneers.

Fragments of numerous extensive houses have been found in the lower half of the city in the last 40 years, and by the early fourth century there were clearly many wealthy people living in Lincoln. The city prospered in the third and early fourth centuries, partly because no rival trading centres were established nearby and partly because of the good communications that the city enjoyed (although the Foss Dyke, linking Lincoln to the River Trent at Torksey, may not have been a Roman achievement, the first reference to it coming only in the 12th century when Simeon of Durham claims that it was built by Henry I, in about 1121). The city's growth and prosperity can also only have been assisted by its new status, from the end of the third century, as capital of the new province of *Flavia Caesariensis*. As a consequence of this the city walls and gates were strengthened, and the city received a major boost to its status as an administrative and taxation centre.

From the middle of the second century the low-lying land to the south of the city had been drained, and lines of traders' and craftsmen's houses and shops were by this time beginning to appear along Ermine Street, and would soon extend for about 0.6 miles south of the lower town. An industrial quarter also seems to have developed to the east of the lower town, in the Monks Road area. Coin casters seem to have been at work in this area in the second and third centuries, and a pottery kiln was discovered in 1936 at the Technical College in Cathedral Street. Just a mile south-west of the city, at Swanpool, large-scale Roman pottery works have been discovered, producing pottery for more than a local market, and in a wide range of forms, including colour-coated fine wares and mortaria. Moreover, by the fourth century the city had become a major centre for the processing and storage of agricultural produce. Large quantities of animal bone and spoilt grain have been found in deposits next to the Brayford Pool. Excavations on the waterfront have revealed a modest inland harbour, with a number of artificial piers jutting out into the Witham on the north side, just to the east of the bridge crossing. By the fourth century sufficient reclamation had taken place to establish the riverfront about sixty-five feet south of the city wall, and the process of reclamation seems to have continued into the third quarter of the century.

The discovery of a small stone-relief carving of a boy charioteer might suggest – if the limestone is of local origin – that very highly skilled craftsmen were at work in the city, for the relief is of the highest quality of artistry. This little carving might also be evidence of the entertainments of the town's inhabitants. It has been suggested that the carving of the young charioteer is evidence that the sons of the local aristocracy organised chariot races and other games outside the city walls. Unfortunately, no archaeological evidence of a Roman theatre or amphitheatre at Lincoln has yet been found. The most commonly suggested location was just outside the West Gate, probably just to the north of the road leading out of the gate, on the site of the earlier fortress training ground. It would have been a timber and earth structure, so subsequent building works would have probably completely destroyed any evidence of its existence. Roman amphitheatres were often reused in later years as public meeting places, and a large number of eighth- and ninth-century pottery finds from the nearby Lawn area suggests that this might have been the case at Lincoln.

The discovery in the town of a bronze foreleg of a horse, either at the end of the 18th or the beginning of the 19th century, also throws some light on the grandeur and spaciousness of the town at the height of Roman power. The foreleg is part of a life-size equestrian statue that probably stood in the forum, although just whereabouts in the city it was found is not known. The stance of the leg has been compared with the equestrian Capitoline statue of the emperor Marcus Aurelius in Rome and such statues were common in the *coloniae* and larger towns of Italy. It is therefore quite probable that this, too, was part of a bronze statue cast in honour of one of the emperors, possibly as part of the imperial cult.

It has been suggested that the statue may have stood at the southern end of the Bailgate colonnade, where the discovery of the remains of a six-columned portico might indicate the site of a temple dedicated to the worship of the emperor. We can be absolutely certain that such a temple stood somewhere in the town in the third century, because an inscription found at Bordeaux in 1921 records how an official of the imperial cult at both Lincoln and York, one Marcus Aurelius Lunaris, had, in the year A.D. 237, set up an altar in honour of the Celtic goddess Tutela Budega, in fulfilment of a vow made when he started on a journey from York.

Another temple, dedicated to the god Mercury, probably stood in the lower town beside the main north-south road, close to the public baths and the public fountain. Stones and pillar bases of the temple were found in 1845 at the site now occupied by J.W. Ruddock & Son. An inscription on one of the stones – now unfortunately lost – described the temple as being established by the guild of the worshippers of Mercury. Another inscription, of a guild of the worshippers of Apollo, had been recorded as having been found in 1785 'on the east side of the old Roman wall below the hill at Lincoln on making the new road'. This inscription is also now lost, but the description given of it suggests that it was from part of a portico, and the size of the letters and the description of other moulded stones found near it suggests that it, too, may have been a temple, or perhaps the guild room of the worshippers, where they would meet regularly for dinner parties and to discuss the guild's business.

7   *Roman boy charioteer.*

Altars dedicated to various Roman gods, and sometimes also associated with the imperial cult, have also been found in the city. An altar found in 1885, in the south-east corner of the Lower City, during the building of the tower of St Swithin's Church, was dedicated by the guild of the worshippers of 'the Goddesses, the Fates, and the Deities of the Emperors'. This would have been very close to the city wall and it has been suggested that this is evidence of another guild room, probably that of a burial club, that stood beside the wall. Burial clubs, guaranteeing a decent funeral for the members and their families, were common across the Roman Empire, as was the worship of the Fates, whose powers over life and death were well known and enormously respected.

Nearby, and probably built into the east wall of the Lower City, was an altar dedicated to Mars, the god of war, found in 1932, right on the line of the east wall, during the digging of foundations for the *Duke of Wellington Hotel* on Broadgate. A few years earlier, in 1924, another altar had been found a little way to the east of the Upper City, just to the south of the Wragby Road, dedicated 'to the Genius of the place'. In both these cases the inscriptions are incomplete and it is not clear whether the altars were for the private use of a family or for public worship. Finally, a sculpture of the three mother goddesses, found in Lincoln, may reflect the presence in the town of veteran soldiers. The mother goddesses were a very popular deity in Britain, particularly among soldiers, and many sculptures and inscriptions have been found across the country dedicated to them.

The end of Roman Lincoln

It has been estimated that by about A.D. 300 there were probably between 5,000 and 10,000 people living in Lincoln. It was a relatively large and prosperous community, numbering many wealthy and sophisticated citizens, fine public buildings, equally luxurious private housing and excellent communications by road, river and possibly canal.

The size and economic success of Lincoln, together with its geographical position, probably explains why it was chosen to be one of four provincial capitals at the end of the third century, when Britain was divided into four. This new status brought even further wealth and more public building works. The provincial governor and his staff required comfortable residences, good communications and strong defences. During the first half of the fourth century the walls of the city were thickened and raised to a height of 23 to 26 feet, and the surrounding ditch was considerably widened, to about eighty-two feet.

The city would also have benefited from its position as a tax-collecting centre and, from A.D. 313, from a new role as a metropolitan bishopric. In that year the emperor Constantine declared toleration of Christianity and established bishops in each of the four provinces of Britain. In A.D. 314 Bishop Adelphius of Lincoln attended the Christian Council at Arles, in southern Gaul, and the foundations of a church, possibly dating from the late fourth century, were discovered on the forum during excavations on the site of the medieval church of St Paul in the Bail in 1978. Precise dating is not possible, but a rectangular wooden structure found beneath the foundations of an apsidal church was probably also a church, constructed in the middle of the fourth century. The apsidal church was larger, follows the same alignment as the earlier structure, and was probably constructed towards the end of the fourth century. A coin

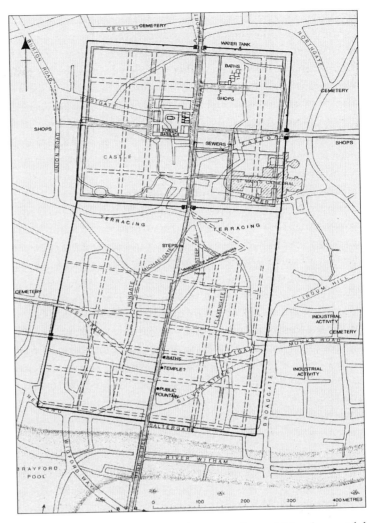

8   *Map of Roman
      Lincoln.*

of Arcadius (A.D. 388-92) was found on the latest forum surface within the apsidal structure, and this may indicate that the church was in use in about A.D. 390. A grave, lying north-south beside the chancel screen, which may have been a foundation relic, has also been tentatively and approximately dated by radiocarbon analysis to the late fourth century.

The location of the governor's residence is not known, but Greetwell Villa, just over a mile east of the walls, is a likely candidate. This was a very high status residence indeed, built on a grand scale with the finest quality mosaic floors and painted wall plaster. Coin finds show that it remained occupied into the late Roman era. Mining operations in the 19th century destroyed the remains of the villa, but paintings made at the time of the villa's discovery have preserved a record of its palatial magnificence. During the early years of the fourth century the rich lavished money on their townhouses, but there seems to have been less willingness to invest in public buildings, other than in the improvements to the city's defences.

A long, slow process of decline may be discernible as early as the middle decades of the fourth century. The improvements to the city walls were completed by about A.D. 350 and little other public building seems to have occurred after this date. Dateable evidence from the public baths suggests that they were being used less and less from this time and there is much evidence that the population was in decline in the second half of the century. The last evidence of upkeep of the urban infrastructure seems to date from the end of the fourth century or very early in the fifth. Excavations in the park in 1970-1 found a very late Roman road surface leading out of the lower West Gate, and a similar date has been given to road works found on Ermine Street, just to the north of the river crossing.

It has been estimated that by about A.D. 370 around half the sites known to have been occupied at the beginning of the century were no longer in use, and many are known to have been already demolished. Where new building work took place it was invariably of a lower quality. Timber structures are found on the sites of earlier stone buildings, and in both the southern suburbs along Ermine Street and in the Lower City deposits of earth over the foundations of former buildings can be taken as evidence of a city that was gradually shrinking and decaying. In some areas, notably Hungate, Flaxengate, Grantham Street and St Mark's Station in Wigford, thick layers of soil appear to have been deliberately deposited on demolished buildings during the second half of the fourth century, suggesting that parts of the city were reverting to agricultural use. In other areas this 'dark earth' has been found to be much more thinly spread, suggesting that it was wind- or rain-blown, and simply represents the city's slow decay as abandoned buildings fell down and were covered over by natural accretions of soil. A good example is a house in Silver Street, where a thin layer of soil was found overlying a level of stone rubble, which in turn overlay fragments of plaster and mortar that still lay on the house floor. There is also some evidence that by the middle of the fourth century industrial activities, such as lead-smelting and iron-working, were moving from the suburbs and into the city, behind the protection of the city walls.

Internal revolts against the emperors in the second half of the fourth century, foreign invasions and the need to reduce the number of soldiers kept in Britain all damaged trade and made life more difficult for the city's craftsmen and merchants. Moreover, from A.D. 326 there had been no mint in Britain and all coins needed to pay troops and officials had to be imported. The decline in urban life at Lincoln and elsewhere probably accelerated after the ending of the shipment of coins in the first decade of the fifth century. The economy stagnated as trade came to depend on barter, and was further damaged by the flight of rich families and the removal of the last Roman troops in A.D. 407. By this time the appearance of the city had changed considerably. It was now a much smaller community than it had been 50 years earlier, and almost all would have lived in houses made of wood, not stone. Most Roman buildings had already been robbed and demolished, surviving only as earthworks or ruins. The community that survived was becoming increasingly self-sufficient, with agriculture and animal husbandry already established within the city walls. Roman civic life could not be maintained, but as we will see in the next chapter, it is unlikely that the site was completely abandoned in the succeeding decades and some continuity with its Roman past may have been preserved.

Two

Britons, Anglo-Saxons and Danes

Capital of a British Kingdom

When, in the fifth and sixth centuries, succeeding waves of invaders from North-Western Germany – known to us today as the Anglo-Saxons – conquered and settled the eastern shores of Britain, Lincoln seems to have remained, for perhaps at least most of the fifth century, independent and unconquered. It may even have continued to exert some authority over the area to the east being settled by the newcomers. Following the departure of the Roman governor it is probable that powerful local figures attempted to fill the vacuum left by the former rulers. The entire Roman province of *Flavia Caesariensis* could not have remained long under the control of the authorities in Lincoln, but from the former Roman province a smaller kingdom, ruled by a king in Lincoln, may have emerged soon after the legions left. This in turn was probably transformed – by marriage or conquest – into the Anglo-Saxon kingdom of Lindsey that is known to have been in existence early in the seventh century.

The principal evidence suggesting that the former Roman city remained an important and influential British centre is the absence of fifth- and sixth-century Anglo-Saxon cremation cemeteries from the area surrounding Lincoln. A map of early pagan cemeteries shows them forming a half-circle to the north, east and south of the city, but the nearest are at Loveden, 17 miles to the south-west, and at Cleatham, 19 miles to the north. In this respect Lincoln was unusual. The other, smaller, walled towns of the region were apparently unsuccessful in resisting Anglo-Saxon incursions in the fifth century. The former Roman town of Caistor is less than two miles from the Anglo-Saxon cremation and internment cemetery at Fonaby, there is a cemetery immediately outside the walls of Ancaster, and Horncastle is only seven miles from the pagan cemetery at West Keal. Moreover, cremation cemeteries have also been found very close to both York and Leicester. The British monk, Gildas, writing in about A.D. 550, tells us that local 'tyrants' had assumed control of former Roman cities following the departure of the Roman armies and administrators. It is possible that this is what happened at Lincoln. A local military ruler, perhaps assisted by a bishop, and protected by the formidable Roman defences, may well have attempted to maintain some semblance of the authority once enjoyed by the Roman governor, at least over a small part of the former Roman province. It would seem that he was able to ensure that the earliest Anglo-Saxon settlements, and their cremation cemeteries, were kept well away from his capital. Indeed, when they were created it may only have been with his agreement.

A genealogy of Aldfrið, one of the later kings of the Anglo-Saxon kingdom of Lindsey, drawn up in the eighth century, includes the British name 'Caedbaed' among the earlier kings, suggesting some co-existence between the incoming Anglo-Saxons and the local British population. It is also likely, however, that on a number of occasions conflict would have arisen between a Christian British kingdom centred on Lincoln and the pagan invaders, even if the latter initially accepted some degree of overlordship and authority from the British king. It is tempting to speculate whether a British king, ruling from Lincoln, may have inspired some of the stories later associated with King Arthur. A popular story told in the county in the Middle Ages associated King Arthur with a great battle near Lincoln in the first half of the sixth century in which 6,000

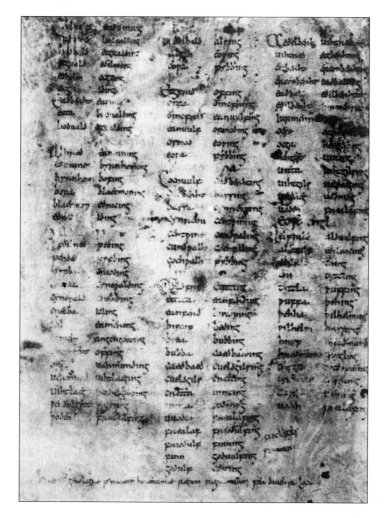

9 *The eighth-century genealogy of King Aldfrið of Lindsey.*

Saxons were killed. A battle list of Arthur's victories compiled in the ninth century by the Welsh writer Nennius claimed that four of his battles had been fought beside a 'river that is called Dubglas and is in the district Linnuis'. There is no river Dubglas in Lindsey, but Linnuis is almost certainly Lindsey. Kevin Leahy has suggested that the River Ancholme could well have been the Dubglas (dark water) of Nennius's account, and its crossing at Brigg a likely site for repeated conflicts. Any discussion of this subject must be mainly speculation but, as Leahy comments, 'Lindsey looks a much better setting for the Arthurian legends than Wales and the west, where Arthur might have struggled even to find Anglo-Saxons to fight.'

Continuity between a British and Anglo-Saxon kingdom centred on Lincoln is suggested by the survival of the late British name for the city, *Lindgolun*, both in the Anglo-Saxon name *Lindcolun* and in the name given to the seventh-century Anglo-Saxon kingdom of *Lindissi*, later Lindsey. When the kingdom first enters the historical record, early in the seventh century, it had probably long since passed to Anglo-Saxon control. Apart from Caedbaed, all the names given in the genealogy of Aldfrið suggest Germanic origins of the rulers. It is likely that at some time in the mid-sixth century the former British kingdom, centred on Lincoln, became absorbed into the Anglo-Saxon kingdom of Lindsey. The archaeological record suggests very heavy Anglo-Saxon migration into Lincolnshire from the early sixth century. Substantial pottery finds from Cherry Willingham and Middle Carlton show that the immigrants were beginning to settle within four miles of Lincoln by the early years of the sixth century. Some shards of Anglo-Saxon pottery have also been found within the area of the city walls. Moreover, although no fifth-century Anglo-Saxon cremation cemeteries were established close to Lincoln, later Anglo-Saxon inhumation cemeteries have been found only a few miles to the north of the city at Welton-by-Lincoln and Ingham. It has also been suggested that a reference to 'men of Lindsey' fighting in the North of England, at the Battle of Catraeth in about A.D. 570, in the poem 'Y Gododdin', were British warriors who had joined the war-band, having lost their homeland to the Anglo-Saxons.

One building that archaeologists have found, which may have still been in use at least in the first few years after the Roman withdrawal was the Bishop's Church. We have seen that the foundations of possibly two successive wooden churches have been excavated on the site of the Roman forum. The foundations of the first structure were cut through the courtyard paving and this probably formed the floor. It was rectangular, about forty-nine feet long, and would only have held about fifty people. If it was a church, which seems very likely, the nearby Roman well would have provided a baptistery. At some later stage, however, this little building was replaced on the same site – later the site of the medieval church of St Paul in the Bail – by a rather larger structure, though still a wooden one. The shape of this later building leaves no doubt that this was a church. Its nave was about eighty-two feet long and about twenty-six feet wide, and it had an apsidal chancel. The western entrance was reached by a flight of stairs from the west porticus of the forum. It has been estimated that it could have held about a hundred people.

Radiocarbon dating of the bones found in graves around the site are consistent with the church having been demolished by A.D. 550, but Christianity would appear to have survived in the city as the area was then being used instead as a high-status

10 (Left) The early
Christian church in
the Forum courtyard
(reconstruction).

11   (Below) The
apsidal eastern end
of the fourth/fifth-
century church
on the site of
St Paul in the Bail.

Christian cemetery. The graves are also evidence that a community of British Christians was still to be found in Lincoln in the first two decades of the seventh century, although Bede's description of the mission of Paulinus, the Bishop of York, to Lincoln in about A.D. 627-8, suggests that no church was then standing. We are told that Paulinus was obliged to build a new church, after baptising the pagan Anglo-Saxon ruler, Blæcca, together with his family and household.

AN ANGLO-SAXON ECCLESIASTICAL CENTRE

Bede tells us that Paulinus had been sent to Lincoln by King Edwin of Northumbria, who by this time had acquired Lindsey as a client kingdom and no doubt saw this as an opportunity to assert his authority over both Lincoln and Lindsey. Blæcca was probably the King of Lindsey. His name does not appear on the genealogy of Aldfrið, but this was not a king list and Blæcca may have belonged to another branch of the royal house. Bede describes Blæcca as the *praefectus*, a term which can have a number of meanings but usually implies a man of highly exalted status, and is probably used by Bede in this context to describe a client king of Edwin's. Blæcca was certainly the figure with the most authority in Lincoln under King Edwin. It is not known when the small kingdom of Lindsey had first come under the control of more powerful neighbours, but we can probably assume that at least a few of Blæcca's predecessors had enjoyed rather more independence than he appeared to have.

During the next 50 years the kingdom of Lindsey would change hands on numerous occasions, as the kings of Northumbria and Mercia struggled against one another for pre-eminence. Shortly after the conversion of Blæcca, Paulinus baptised a great many people in the River Trent, just to the north of Lincoln, probably near the village of Littleborough, and in A.D. 631 the Archbishop of Canterbury, Honorius, was consecrated by Paulinus in the new church he had built in Lincoln. But only two years later, in A.D. 633, King Edwin lost his life and kingdoms in battle against the pagan Mercians, led by the formidable King Penda, and Paulinus's church was probably destroyed by the invading Mercian army.

The archaeological record for Lincoln in the seventh century is extremely meagre and it is quite possible that for some years the city was deserted. When Bede completed his *Ecclesiastical History* in A.D. 731 the walls of Paulinus's church still stood but the church was in ruins. He tells us that it was 'a stone church of remarkable workmanship' and had become a centre of pilgrimage much revered by Christians. Paulinus himself had been declared a saint, but his church lay unrepaired: 'its roof has now fallen either through long neglect or by the hand of the enemy, but its walls are still standing and every year miracles of healing are performed in this place.'

Just where Paulinus built his church in Lincoln is not yet known. When it was discovered, in 1978, the apsidal church on the site of St Paul in the Bail was at first thought to have been Paulinus's church, but the carbon-dating of the graves inserted over the site of the church make this unlikely. Moreover, Bede appears quite certain that Paulinus had built a stone church, and there is no evidence that the apsidal church was a stone building. It seems unlikely that either Bede or his probable informant, the Bishop of Lindsey, Bishop Cyneberht, would have made a mistake about whether the church was built in stone or wood, especially as the church was still standing in his day, albeit in a ruinous state, and was regularly visited by pilgrims. A better candidate for Paulinus's church might prove to be the Saxon church found in 2013 by archaeologists carrying out excavations in the grounds of Lincoln Castle. This *is* a stone church and the excavation has revealed a complete stone coffin, as well as many skeletons, but at the time of writing it has not yet proved possible to carbon date the skeletons or to remove the coffin to allow it to be opened and thoroughly examined. This promises to be a most exciting discovery. The stone coffin indicates that this was the grave of a high-status and wealthy person, perhaps Blæcca himself or a member of his family.

In the eighth century an important new church seems to have been built in the Lower City, just to the north of the Roman southern gate. In the medieval period this was the site of the church of St Peter at Pleas, also known as St Peter at Mootstone. A case can be made for arguing that this church may have been the site of the first cathedral for the Bishopric of Lindsey. The bishopric had been created in 677 and the first cathedral was built by Bishop Cyneberht, the fourth bishop of Lindsey, probably in Lincoln. Bede wrote an epigraph to be placed in the apse of the cathedral and refers to it as being dedicated to one of the apostles. Of the few medieval churches in the city thought to have been founded before the 10th century, only St Peter's bears a dedication to an apostle. Moreover, when William the Conqueror later granted Bishop Remigius of Lincoln the church of Wellingore, Domesday Book tells us that he was probably restoring to the bishop what his predecessors had held nearly four hundred years earlier. Wellingore church is described as having once 'belonged to the church of St Peter in Lincoln'.

In the early medieval period this was an important ecclesiastical site. Immediately to the south of St Peter's, and standing parallel to it, was another St Peter's Church, St Peter at Arches. It has been suggested by Michael Jones, the Director of the Lincoln Archaeology Unit, that the two churches may have originated from the ruins of the aisles of one great early church. Could this have been Bishop Cynebeht's cathedral? There is as yet no archaeological evidence to support this theory, except for the discovery of an early cemetery located nearby. But other evidence is also supportive. The Roman fountain beside the High Street stood only a few feet away, immediately to the north of St Peter at Pleas. As with the earlier churches on the forum courtyard, the presence of a fountain or well close by, to provide water for the baptistery, would have been of crucial importance in choosing the site for a church, whether by Paulinus in the seventh century or Cynebeht in the eighth.

Sir Francis Hill drew attention to the wealth and importance of St Peter at Pleas at the time of Domesday Book's compilation, noting that as there were a number of churches dedicated to St Peter in Lincoln by this time, the reference to this church as simply 'the church of St Peter at Lincoln' implies some precedence. It was richly endowed and had probably once been the property of Earl Morcar, the brother of King Harold, and probably inherited by him from Earl Leofric of Mercia. Moreover, as Sir Francis also noted, the fact that the church was built next to the mootstone, the site of the early Anglo-Saxon moot court, also implies an early and important foundation.

Caistor, Horncastle, Louth and Stow have all been put forward as possible alternative locations for Cynebeht's cathedral. None, however, seem to be very strong candidates. Bede described the new cathedral in his epigraph for it as being located *in urbe,* a term he used for important Roman cities, such as Lincoln. There is no compelling evidence that either Louth or Stow had Roman origins, and although Caistor and Horncastle could claim to have been Roman walled towns, neither was ever a major Roman centre. The only document in which a Bishop of Lindsey refers to the location of his cathedral appears in a record of a church council held in 803, attended by Bishop Eadwulf. He subscribed as *Syddensis civitatis episcopus,* an apparent misrendering of 'Bishop of the Southern City'. The reasons for this mysteriously vague phrase cannot be known. Could 'southern' refer to the 'Lower City' of Lincoln, in which St Peter's was located, or perhaps there is a reference here to York as the northern city and to Lincoln as its southern neighbour? The vagueness of the term is not helpful but it does not suggest an obvious alternative site outside Lincoln. Significantly, of the eight bishops attending the council of 803 who were described as *civitatis episcopus,* the dioceses of six can be identified and all, like Lincoln, were former Roman cities: Canterbury, Leicester, Worcester, Winchester, London and Rochester.

In the seventh or eighth century an important grave was dug on the site of Lincoln's earliest Christian church, on the Roman forum, and enclosed in a single-cell stone mausoleum. When discovered in 1978 the grave was empty except for a beautiful seventh-century bronze hanging bowl. The bowl is now in the Cathedral Treasury and is a fine example of Celtic craftsmanship. It would seem to have been left inadvertently, in a corner of the grave, when the human remains were removed. This must have been a very high-status burial; possibly the first burial place of either a king or bishop of Lindsey, whose remains were then transferred to a more suitable resting place, perhaps to Cynebeht's new cathedral after its completion, or perhaps later, in anticipation of a Viking raid.

12 *The seventh-century hanging bowl from St Paul in the Bail.*

13 *A silver penny of King Alfred, c.875, found during the excavation at St Paul in the Bail.*

Under Mercian rule, Lincoln was an important ecclesiastical centre in the eighth and ninth centuries. Those Roman buildings still standing would have been in ruins, and the former city must have resembled a collection of farmsteads. Much of the land that had once been occupied in the Roman era by shops and houses, both within and outside the walls, was wasteland. Unlike some other former Roman cities, Lincoln did not develop into a riverside trading settlement in these years. The greatest concentration of eighth- and ninth-century pottery has come from the grounds of the Lawn, just outside the walls of the Upper City. This may have been a farmstead or an Anglo-Saxon meeting place, using the remains of the former Roman amphitheatre that may have stood here, beside the Roman road.

At the time of the Viking invasions the Roman walls and gates seem to have been still largely intact, but a sufficient number of Roman buildings had either fallen down or had been pulled down to allow for new lanes to develop, cutting through the grounds of former Roman properties. Some were short-cuts, cutting diagonally across the settlement from one Roman gate to another. Thus Chapel Lane developed in the Upper City, linking the North and West Gates and, in the Lower City, Silver Street, ran from the East Gate to the South Gate. The archaeological record suggests that economic activity and population both increased in the ninth century, and the number of coin finds from the latter half of the century suggests growing wealth. By this time, however, a new threat to both wealth and peace had appeared in the region: Viking raiders in search of plunder.

A Prosperous Danish Town

Very little is known about the Viking conquest of Lincolnshire in the 860s and 870s, but it is very likely that they passed through the region on a number of occasions in these years. Their ships sailed up the Humber and Trent and in A.D. 872 the 'great army' wintered at Torksey, beside the River Trent, only 12 miles west of Lincoln. The conquest initially brought only terror, murder and mayhem, but the subsequent settlement of Lincoln by the Vikings in the last decades of the ninth century was to make possible a remarkable period of sustained growth, and to restore Lincoln once more to something like the size and relative importance it had once enjoyed in the days of the Romans. It became one of the 'Five Boroughs' of the 'Danelaw', together with Derby, Nottingham, Stamford and Leicester, a centre for administration by the Viking army, and later also for a 'shire'. Lincoln would be the largest and fastest growing of the five towns, with its shire also incorporating Stamford.

Numerous archaeological excavations have revealed a marked increase in economic activity from the end of the ninth century and there can be little doubt that the population also grew steadily from this time. The settlement in the city of wealthy Viking leaders with money to spend soon attracted highly skilled craftsmen to meet the new demands. Silver Street, the Anglo-Saxon footpath between two Roman gates, very quickly became an important industrial centre, boasting a complex of pottery kilns and potters skilled in the more advanced continental styles favoured by the city's new ruling class. This south-eastern corner of the Lower City may have been the first part of the city to grow rapidly. Two churches, St Swithin and St Edmund the King, were established here in about A.D. 900, and Flaxengate and Grantham Street were new developments, probably begun before this and settled by tradesmen and craftsmen. Pottery containing fragments of shell was a particular speciality of the Silver Street potters from the end of the ninth century.

The next area to spring back into life was Wigford. This important Roman suburb appears to have remained completely unoccupied since the beginning of the fifth century, but early in the 10th century new development can once more be detected, with many tradesmen's and craftsmen's houses dotted at intervals along either side of Ermine Street,

14   *A reconstruction of the waterside area in the Viking era, looking west towards the Brayford. The area between the wall and the river is now being developed and land reclamation has begun to narrow the width of the river.*

and the development of trade beside the river probably stimulated some growth here as well. Moreover, it was also probably about this time that the Sincil Dyke was cut to the east of Ermine Street to improve drainage for the properties now beginning to line the Roman road once more. When St Mark's Church – a little wooden structure – was built in about A.D. 950 it was not the first church in the suburb and seems to have been built in a gap between earlier developments. An indication of the area's continuing growth came a century later when St Mark's graveyard had to be enlarged.

Further evidence of the development of this area from about A.D. 890 was the construction of a new street about six-hundred-and-fifty feet to the west of Ermine Street and parallel to it. Subsequently, a link road was also built linking the two. Both streets were soon lined with craftsmen's workshops. The excavation of rubbish pits has shown that bone and ivory combs and pins were probably being made in the area; crucible and mould fragments are evidence of metal-working trades, and glass, jet, silver and copper alloy were being made into personal ornaments and jewellery, including rings.

Little is yet known about the Upper City in the 10th century, but the discovery of a scattering of coins from the late ninth century during the excavations of St Paul in the Bail suggests that a market was held here from that time. Similarly, little is known about the south-western part of the Lower City save that a mint was established here by about A.D. 920, for pennies of St Martin appear from about this time. The first St Martin's Church, just to the west of the High Street, was probably built at about the same time. The suburb of Butwerk, which means 'outside the fortification', may also have been first occupied before the end of the 10th century.

During the 10th century Lincoln was rapidly becoming not only an important regional manufacturing centre but also an important market, serving a wide area. Goods made in Lincoln, agricultural produce from the surrounding area, and exotic goods from far beyond these shores could all be found for sale. A silk scarf of Byzantine origin was found during the excavation of the Waterside North area in 1987-90. The merchant who brought the roll of silk from which it had been made clearly also visited York: a scarf from the same roll was also found. Lincoln's importance as a trading centre was made possible by good road and water communications and local trade must have been assisted by the building of a new timber waterfront on the north side of the river in the 10th century. Wooden and leather goods, including shoes, were found preserved in the mud during the 1987-90 excavations, together with seeds and other microscopic evidence of the diets of Lincoln's 10th- and 11th-century inhabitants.

The city's growth also owed much to its role as the main centre of royal government in the region. It was the location for the king's shire court, from which the king's representative, the sheriff, administered the king's business. By the middle of the 11th century the court was meeting twice a year, drawing to the city many of the region's great landowners. It was also the location for one of the king's largest and most productive mints. It has been estimated that between the years A.D. 1000 and 1066 Lincoln produced more than a tenth of all the coins minted in England, probably twice as many as were produced in Stamford. Between them, the two centres were probably producing more coins than even London in the last 20 years before the Norman Conquest. There were 55 moneyers at work in Lincoln in the last two decades of the 10th century, under

King Æthelred, and between A.D. 979 and 1066 there were 95, compared with 91 in York. In these years Lincoln was second only to London in this respect. A great deal of silver was clearly in circulation in the area, generated by considerable trade and wealth, and reflecting the relative prosperity of the region. Of the 'Five Boroughs' of the area known as the Danelaw, none grew faster than Lincoln in the century before 1066.

Little is known about the trade of the region in the 10th and 11th centuries, but it seems very likely that a very substantial trade in raw wool already existed long before the Norman Conquest and that Lincoln was at the heart of it. Evidence of sheep bones found at Flaxengate suggests that the numbers of sheep in the county rose significantly from the end of the 10th century, and that the great majority of sheep were bred primarily for their wool rather than for meat, as most of the bones were from animals that were three years old or more. In the 11th century the sheep flocks of Lincolnshire may not have been much smaller than they were in the 1280s, when Boston exported an annual average of about ten thousand sacks, or about three million fleeces. Trading contacts would seem to have been especially well established with Scandinavia and north-western Europe in the 10th century, as well as with other parts of England.

It is also likely that Lincoln was already a centre of high-quality cloth-making before the Norman Conquest. There is evidence that wool was dyed in Wigford in the 10th century and it seems probable that simple fabrics called *haberget*, made both in Lincoln and Stamford, were exported from the city. There is no evidence, however, that the 'scarlet' cloth for which Lincoln would later become famous, was being made before the conquest. By A.D. 1000, imports from Scandinavia probably included falcons, hawks, stockfish (dried cod) and furs, all of which were recorded as imports in the 12th and 13th centuries. Walrus ivory was also being imported into Lincoln in the 10th century to be made into combs by the highly skilled, specialist craftsmen to be found in the Flaxengate area.

Estimates of the size of the population of Lincoln on the eve of the conquest vary. Domesday Book suggests a population of between 6,000 and 8,000, if we assume that there were about five people per household and that there was only one household on

15 *A selection of Lincoln mint coins from the 10th century.*

each tenement. In *Anglo-Saxon Lincolnshire*, Professor Sawyer has argued, however, that rapidly growing towns such as Lincoln tended to have rather larger households and that more than one household would often be found squeezed on to one tenement. Excavations at Flaxengate, he notes, have shown at least three buildings occupying a single tenement.

The Flaxengate excavation has also thrown some light on the type of housing to be found in Lincoln during the 10th and 11th centuries, and on some aspects of domestic life. Most houses were roughly 16 feet wide and between 32 and 52 feet long. One was built on stone footings but most had only wooden walls, made of horizontally laid planks set directly in the ground, with roofs of thatch. The houses appeared to have a lifespan of about twenty-five to thirty years, after which they were demolished and replaced with new buildings. Some had rush and sand floors and many combined living quarters with a workshop, in which a wide variety of raw materials were found, including glass, iron, silver, brass, copper, bone and antler. Meals were probably taken on low seats around the hearth, eaten straight from the cooking pot. No pottery tableware for individual servings of food was found, but wooden plates and bowls may have been used. Water or ale was served from pitchers or spouted pots and various types of small pottery lamps provided lighting. Animal bones found at the site suggest that about four-fifths of the meat consumed was from cattle and that relatively small quantities of sheep and pig meat were consumed. Both freshwater fish, presumably caught locally, and fish from the North Sea – mainly haddock, cod and flat fish – were also important. The quantities of cereals eaten cannot be deduced, but for many they would have provided the staple diet.

One of the more striking aspects of the growth and prosperity of the city in the 10th and 11th centuries was the number of new churches that were built. By 1100 at least 32 churches were in existence. Scandinavian lords would seem to have found it in their interest – financially as well as spiritually – to found churches for use by their tenants. The initial Viking raids of the ninth century had prompted the removal of the see to Dorchester on Thames, at the southern end of the huge diocese, but the settlement of the Danes was soon followed by conversion, and church building and the creation of parishes became an integral part of the city's expansion in the 10th and 11th centuries. By 1100 there were 14 churches in the Lower City, three in the Upper City, and 11 in the southern suburb of Wigford, all lining the Roman road. Four new churches also stood just to the east of the Lower City, in the new suburb of Butwerk. Sir Francis Hill argued that all four were post-conquest foundations, but a strong case can be made for arguing that two, St Bavo and St Rumbold, may have been founded before 1066. The other two, St Peter at Well and St Augustine's, on the eastern edge of the suburb, are described by Domesday Book as very recent additions. They had been built by Colsuen – the only great English landowner then living in the city – on wasteland that the Conqueror had given him 'that was never built upon before'. Among other new churches built since the Danish Conquest there was possibly an early minster, St Mary's, built in the south-east corner of the Upper City. Those historians who believe that there was such a church usually place it on or near the site later chosen by Bishop Remigius for his first cathedral, work on which began within 10 years of the Norman Conquest. A little to the west, however, on the site of the earliest known Christian church in the city, St Paul in the Bail remained a simple parish church.

THREE

The City in the High Medieval Era, 1066-c.1300

PROSPERITY FROM WOOL

The initial impact of the Norman victory at Hastings in 1066 was disastrous for the people of Lincoln. Well-established trading links were disrupted, many of the city's wealthiest inhabitants were dispossessed, and at the time of the Domesday Survey in 1086, seventy-four houses are described as having been laid waste on account of 'poverty or fire'. Significantly, the Domesday clerks, or jurors, add the reassurance that these 74 houses had not been destroyed 'on account of the oppression of the sheriffs', as they clearly thought might have been expected. A significant proportion of the town's population may have lost their homes, and to add insult to injury the people of Lincoln were forced, by their new overlords, to give their labour freely to build a new castle. They also had to pay the king a much heavier 'farm' than had been the case before. In Edward the Confessor's reign the city had paid an annual tax of £30. By 1086 this had been raised to £100 (equal to that of York and second only to the taxation paid by London), and a further £75 had to be rendered annually by the Lincoln mint, whose payments previously seem to have been included in the £30. Moreover, as the whole of the Upper City had been taken over as the bail of the new castle, equal in taxation value to 166 houses, virtually the whole of the burden had to be now borne by the inhabitants of the Lower City. The Upper City would remain outside the jurisdiction of the city council until the 19th century.

The city's early decline, however, was short-lived and the prosperity of the mid-11th century was soon re-established. Much of the city was burnt down in 1123, but it was resilient enough to survive the catastrophe and, in spite of further fires, and the depredations wrought by the civil wars of Stephen's reign (1135-54) in which the city was heavily involved, Lincoln had become one of the wealthiest and most important cities in England by 1150, with its importance proclaimed by its royal castle and a magnificent cathedral. The Danes had been able to restore the prosperity of the city, build new churches, and make it once more a bustling mercantile community, but it was still a settlement of wooden houses and workshops lacking the splendid public buildings of its Roman predecessor, save for the Roman walls and gates that still stood

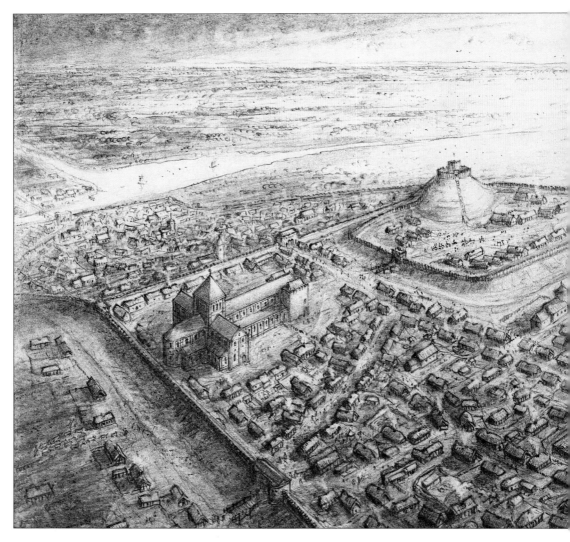

16   *An artist's impression of Lincoln at the end of the 11th century. At this time the castle still only had one motte, but an inner bailey wall may have recently been constructed. The cathedral has been completed but the west end of the building is shown as a fortified tower built primarily for defence.*

largely intact. During the first two centuries after the Norman Conquest, however, it would once again become a city of fine public and private buildings of stone, a few of which still survive to this day.

The city's prosperity in the 12th and 13th centuries relied largely on the growth in the trade in raw wool and on the manufacture of cloth. The city's links to the Midlands' wool-producing areas were much improved by the building of the Foss Dyke, linking the city to the River Trent at Torksey, in about 1121. This was a considerable achievement. The popular belief that the canal had been built by the Romans is probably mistaken, but even if it had it would probably have been difficult to find, let alone to use, after more than 700 years of neglect.

The town's commerce had also received a significant boost when Bishop Remigius transferred his episcopal see from Dorchester to Lincoln in 1072, before beginning the building of his new cathedral. Most important, however, in explaining Lincoln's success in these years was the quality of the local wool. Lindsey's long-wool sheep were recognised as producing some of the finest wool in the country. Such was their reputation that at the beginning of the 13th century Lindsey rams were being exported to other parts of England for breeding purposes. The international trade was largely in the hands of foreigners, especially Flemings and Italians, but they had to pay for the right to operate in the city, and be members of the Merchant Guild, as did all other merchants who came from outside the city. Exports of raw wool, principally to France and Flanders, were mainly through the ports of Boston and Torksey, both of which also prospered as Lincoln's trade grew, but all foreign trade in the county had to be conducted in Lincoln, even by merchants from other Lincolnshire towns.

This valuable monopoly may have dated from the reign of Henry I (1100-35), but it was confirmed by the granting of a royal charter by Henry II when he visited the city in 1156. St Mary's Guildhall, which still stands today in Wigford, was probably built especially for this occasion. It provided an appropriately grand residence for the monarch. By the 1150s a small number of local landowners and merchants were also able to afford to build fine stone houses for themselves, and by the 13th century stone houses were ceasing to be exceptional. One of the first stone houses in the city, and one of the most famous Norman houses in the country today, is the so-called Jew's House at the bottom of Steep Hill. It was built in about 1150 and is known to have been first occupied by a Jewish merchant.

17   *A late 18th-century drawing of St Mary's Guildhall by Hieronymous Grimm.*

18   (Left) The Jew's House as it appeared in the late 18th century, drawn by Hieronymous Grimm. Some of the features that are shown here have now disappeared.

19   (Below) The Jew's House as it appears today.

The other Norman house to survive today was also once associated (wrongly) with the city's medieval Jewish population: 'Aaron's House', at the top of Steep Hill, named after one of the city's wealthiest Jewish inhabitants of the second half of the 12th century. Jewish immigrants had arrived in the city in the middle of the 12th century and were soon providing a useful money-lending service for the city's merchants. By the end of the century they constituted one of the wealthiest and largest Jewish communities in the country. Aaron had a house in the Bail, in the upper part of the city, and most likely it was a stone one, but not the house that today still bears his name, and dates from about 1180. At his death, in about 1189, Aaron's debtors included the King of Scotland and numerous earls, bishops and abbots. Moreover, nine Cistercian abbeys, including Kirkstead, Louth Park and Revesby, had borrowed from him to finance their building programmes in the middle of the century. At the end of the 12th century Jewish money lenders were almost certainly helping finance residential building in the city as well as trade. In 1202 merchants from Lincoln and Boston together were paying more tax than those of London, and many could well afford a fine new stone house, complete with a tiled roof, clay or mortar floors and a rudimentary toilet. Their wool warehouses lined the north side of the Witham, to the east of the city wall.

Until the last quarter of the 13th century, however, much mercantile wealth came not from the sale of raw wool but rather from the cloth trade, in which each of the manufacturing processes added significant value, and therefore profit, both for the craftsmen and for the merchant entrepreneurs controlling the enterprise. The weaving of cloth became an important industry in the city in the 12th century. The weavers of the city set up their own guild in 1130, and in 1157 received a charter from the king recognising their guild's right to control the industry both in Lincoln and in the surrounding countryside, up to a radius of 12 miles from the city. In return they agreed to pay the king a farm of £6 per year. The fine-quality dyed 'Lincoln' cloth had a widespread reputation, still known today through the stories of Robin Hood and his 'merrie men', invariably attired in 'Lincoln green'. Most prized of all was 'scarlet' cloth, which was sold throughout England and abroad. When a group of the city's wealthiest merchants formed the Guild of St Mary in 1251, both the wool and cloth trades were at their peak, and the guild was able to take over and use as their guildhall the palace built in Wigford about a hundred years earlier for Henry II's visit. The city's principal export was a fine woollen cloth, known as 'says', which gave its name to a popular type of woollen cloak.

Cloth was produced in small workshops and back rooms all over the city, but the south-western corner of the Lower City developed into a distinctive cloth weavers' quarter and the street of the dyers and fullers (Walkergate) was in the centre of it, lying alongside the line of the southern city wall, west of the High Street. At its height, in the early 13th century, the cloth trade probably employed about two thousand workers, or about forty per cent of the city's total population. Most of the cloth was sold not in the city but rather at the great fairs of Stamford, Boston, St Ives, St Giles Winchester and Northampton. The small quantity intended for local purchase was sold at the cloth market (outside the South Gate of the Upper City), at the thread market in Clasketgate and at the fair in Newport, held in the last two weeks of June. There are no population figures for this period, but it is likely that the city's population grew rapidly in these years, and many of those who now settled in the city would have been drawn to Lincoln by the prospect of employment in the cloth trade.

20 *Aaron the Jew's House as it appears today.*

One particularly successful wool and cloth merchant of the late 13th century was William Cause. He was one of the city bailiffs in 1263, represented the city in the Parliament of 1295 and served as mayor in 1298. He regularly traded at the fair of St Ives and in 1273 obtained a special licence to export raw wool during the war with Flanders. In the early 14th century the city's wealthiest merchant was probably Stephen of Stanham. He was able to keep a shop in London and gained the right to supply cloth, wax, fish and sugar and spices to the Royal Household. He also traded at the St Ives and Boston fairs and kept a ship at Boston that sailed regularly to Flanders to carry wool and other goods. Altogether at least 20 Lincoln merchants are known to have traded regularly at the great fair of St Ives between 1270 and 1324, six of whom also served either as mayor or bailiff for the city, and a similar number were also to be found at the Winchester fairs. Indeed, so regular was their attendance that it paid some of the city's merchants to keep permanent shops at both places.

Excavations have helped build up a picture of the wide range of crafts to be found in and around the city in the 12th and 13th centuries. Important stone quarries, supplying stone for churches throughout the county, seem to have been in existence at this time just to the east of the Upper City. Pottery had been produced in Lincoln from the end of the ninth century and excavations in Wigford show that production probably began in this area in the 12th century, and there were at least two kilns in the area dating from the 13th and 14th centuries, manufacturing rather sandy, low-quality pottery for local use. A kiln has also been found dating from the early 13th century on the steep hillside at Gibraltar Hill, producing glazed jugs. Tile production seems

21 *An 18th-century drawing of St Andrew's Hall in Wigford, drawn by Moses Griffith. Like St Mary's Guildhall, this long-vanished building was probably built in the late 12th century as a meeting place and headquarters for a trade or religious guild.*

to have been largely confined to the very southern tip of the Wigford suburb, in a triangular plot of land between the Great and Little Bar Gates, occupied by tilers from the end of the 12th century.

Documentary evidence shows a wide variety of metalworking trades at the end of the 13th century. In 1293 and 1297 there are records of smiths, shearmen, shear-grinders, plumbers, locksmiths, lead-beaters, farriers and goldsmiths. Metalworkers' shops – and particularly goldsmiths' – seem to have been concentrated in the part of the High Street known at this time as Mikelgate, just to the north of Stonebow, in the parishes of St Peter at Pleas and St Peter at Arches. It has been estimated that there were probably at least 17 goldsmiths in the city during the 13th century. Also nearby, in the area later known as Mint Street, the moneyers of the Lincoln mint appear to have been concentrated in the 13th century, although the precise location of the mint is not known.

Documentary sources also indicate the existence of a number of tanneries in this period concentrated in the Wigford area, and particularly to the west of the High Street in St Margaret's parish, and the skin (or parchment) market was located in the Lower City, at the junction of Hungate and Michaelgate.

The Lincoln Warden's Accounts for 1293 and 1297 give some indication of the considerable range of activities and crafts that were to be found in the city, and the contrast between Lincoln and smaller centres is quite striking. By far the largest number were employed in the various victualling trades (288 in 1293 and 227 in 1297) and numerous craftsmen were also employed in the clothing trades (hatters, girdlers, glovers and tailors) and the metalworking trades. However, the complete collapse of cloth production in the last two or three decades of the 13th century is indicated by the small numbers of cloth workers listed: just eight in 1293 (only one weaver, three fullers, a lacemaker, a teaser, a woadseller and a yarnmonger) and four years later there were even fewer (just two woad sellers and a fuller).

Some indication of the wide area from which the population of the city had been drawn during the previous 200 years is provided by the taxation returns of 1332. For all classes, from the wealthy merchant to the skilled craftsman and the landless labourer, the city offered opportunities and employment not to be found in the countryside. In 1332 at least a third of Lincoln's wealthier inhabitants, and possibly half, had been born outside the city. Most originated from villages and small towns within 30 miles, but some came from much further, especially merchants and craftsmen involved in the wool trade. There were men and women from York, Beverley, King's Lynn, Thetford and Norwich, all important centres of the wool trade. Two people had even originated from Winchcomb in the Cotswolds.

As the population of the city grew in the 12th and 13th centuries it became ever more over-crowded, smelly and unhygienic, particularly in the poorer areas of the town, the rapidly expanding suburbs at the margins of the city, where poor immigrants built their flimsy hovels close to the yards and workshops of the leatherworkers, fell mongers and potters. The suburbs that already existed at the time of the conquest, Wigford to the south of the Roman walls and Butwerk to the east, both continued to expand and some of the town's richest inhabitants, as well as the poorest, were to be found in both. Both were already rich in churches by 1100, but during the next 200 years there was

22 *St Mary le Wigford.*

also much rebuilding and enlargement. Here and throughout the city wood was replaced by stone, naves were widened, west towers added to carry a peal of bells and chancels were extended. Today, few of the city's medieval churches have survived, but the two best surviving examples of the Romanesque style are both to be found in the towers of two churches in Wigford: St Mary and St Peter at Gowts.

New suburbs also appeared at this time. The first reference to the suburb of Newland, just to the north of the Brayford Pool, appears in the 12th century. This was the product of a long process of reclamation that culminated in the 14th century, when the extension of the city walls southwards to the river was completed by the erection of a new south-western tower at the edge of the Brayford Pool (named, inappropriately, the Lucy Tower). Reclamation of the low-lying land immediately south of the river also made possible the creation of another suburb, Thorngate, which by the 14th century extended half a mile eastwards

23 *St Peter at Gowts and St Mary's Hall, from a drawing by Hieronymous Grimm.*

24   *The High Bridge, as seen from the west.*

from the High Street. The Norman bridge, which today still carries the High Street over the Witham, was erected in about 1160 as part of the reclamation and improvement of this area. The earliest of the post-conquest suburbs to be developed was probably Newport, immediately to the north of the Bail. The name means 'new town' and it was probably created to house those who had been made homeless by the building of the castle in 1068. It had its own market, adjacent to one of its two churches, and by the end of the 13th century extended more than a quarter of a mile northwards either side of the Roman Road, protected by a defensive ditch. Some early maps also show that it was provided with a wall and towers, but evidence of these is yet to be found.

By the early years of the 13th century a wall and two gates – the Bargates – also protected the southern limit of the Wigford suburb, and immediately to the south of the wall there already existed two hospitals and a priory, founded in the previous 100 years. The Hospital of the Holy Innocents, which was also known as the Malandry, had probably been built in about 1100, on the east side of the High Street, and the Hospital of the Holy Sepulchre was founded shortly afterwards, just across the road. St Katherine's Priory, a Gilbertine house, had been founded in the mid-12th century, immediately adjacent to the Hospital of the Holy Sepulchre, and had quickly gained numerous endowments and

become an important wool producer. Today almost nothing
survives of any of these institutions; a coin hoard has been
found at the site of the Malandry and building work has
revealed fragments of the priory.

Four friaries were also founded in the city during the
13th century, the Franciscans in the south-east corner
of the walled city, the Dominicans to the east of
the Lower City, the Carmelites in Wigford
and the Austin Friars in Newport. The
building known today as the Greyfriars'
was once the infirmary of the Franciscans
and may at first have been the order's
church. It survived the Dissolution
by being converted into a grammar
school, in which guise it remained for
more than 300 years, before becoming
the City and County Museum for much
of the last century. But the rest of that
order's properties have long disappeared,
and nothing whatsoever remains of the other
three. The first of the friaries, the Franciscans,
were welcomed to Lincoln and encouraged to
settle in the city by Bishop Grosseteste, who

25   *The seal of the Malandry.*

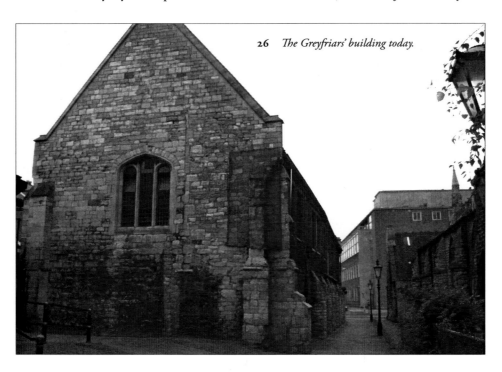

26   *The Greyfriars' building today.*

admired their preaching skills and dedication, but their presence was not appreciated by the parish priests, who tended to see them as dangerous rivals. The friars reached out to the poor and illiterate masses, to the sick and the dying. Only five years after the death of St Francis of Assisi, in 1226, Franciscan friars were established in Lincoln, and they were popular with the growing population of poor townspeople because they preached to them, lived among them, and shared whatever they had with them. The success and growing number of friaries in the 13th century reflected, and was made possible by, the growth of the city in these years.

Bishop Grosseteste adopted a less welcoming attitude, however, towards the Jews of the city. Richard the Lionheart's preparations for the Crusades had led to very heavy taxation of the Jews throughout the country and prompted violent attacks on the community in Lincoln. Although those responsible were fined, further attacks on Jewish houses in 1219 and 1220 led to the murder of two Jews. In the 1190s Bishop Hugh of Lincoln had sought to protect the Jews, but the official position of the Church under Archbishop Stephen Langton was extremely hostile, and Bishop Grosseteste followed the Archbishop's lead when he urged all members of his diocese to have nothing to do with any Jews. Such a stance could only encourage the vicious anti-Semitism that appeared to grip elements of the city in 1255, two years after Grosseteste's death. In the summer of 1255 a vile, trumped-up story circulated in the city, claiming that local Jews had conspired with other Jews from all over the country to carry out a sacrificial murder of a young boy. The only evidence was the confession of a Jew named Copin who, under torture and hoping to save his life, claimed that the eight-year-old boy, Hugh, had been abducted and imprisoned in his house before being crucified, disembowelled, and thrown down a well. Rioting broke out, according to one account, and Jewish houses were attacked. Copin himself was tied to the tail of a horse, dragged to the gallows and hanged on Colbeck Hill. Scores of other Jews in the city were arrested and despatched to London to be imprisoned in the Tower of London. Eighteen were subsequently hanged when they refused to plead before a jury that had no Jews on it, and although most of the others seem to have been eventually released, their properties were confiscated and sold off by the Crown. The body of a child was taken to the cathedral to be added to the collection of relics, and for many years his tomb was among those visited by pilgrims, to which offerings were made, and the story was sufficiently famous a hundred years later for Geoffrey Chaucer to make reference to it in the *Prioresses' Tale*. A few impoverished Jews continued to live in Lincoln, but in 1290 all Jews were expelled from the country by Edward I. The popularity of 'Little St Hugh' declined in the 15th century as the Jews were by then but a distant memory, and before the end of the century, when the citizens were appealing to Richard III for relief from the burdens of taxation, they recalled that the Jews had once brought much trade and wealth to the city.

THE GOVERNMENT OF THE CITY

The Danes had given the city a system of local government. The city's freemen were required to attend meetings of the borough court, or 'burwarmot', at the mootstone on Mikelgate, by St Peter's Church. By the time of the Norman invasion, however, most day-to-day decisions seem to have been taken by a committee composed of 12 freemen, known as the 'Lawmen', probably drawn from the wealthier inhabitants. At the time of the Domesday Survey their responsibilities included the collection of the annual tax paid to the king, interpreting the laws and customs of the city and acting as judges over the people. Anglo-Saxon kings had allowed the cities of the former Danelaw considerable independence, provided taxes were collected and paid regularly to the king's sheriff, and the Lawmen and burwarmot had therefore enjoyed little interference in their administration of local affairs.

Later, charters granted by successive monarchs to the city make it clear that one could become a freeman if one's father was free, if one lived in the city for a year and a day, and if one paid a land tax known as 'land-gable' to the bailiff, who was a freeman appointed to serve as the king's representative. Following the Norman Conquest freemen also had to pay towards the cost of maintaining knights at the castle and for the repairs of the city walls. In return most freemen would be given a plot of land in the city that he could sell or pass to his children at his death, plus a few strips of land in the open fields that surrounded the city, each about a furlong long and four rods wide (22 yards), and rights to keep animals on the city's pastures. Although civic responsibilities for freemen could prove onerous and expensive, the rights of freemen were highly prized. At the end of the 13th century the usual fee was half a mark (6s. 8d.) but some people are recorded as paying twice as much.

In 1194 the freemen of the city bought a charter from King Richard I for 500 marks (about £333) that confirmed their ancient right to hold a weekly burwarmot and gave them the right to choose their own bailiff to work with the bailiff appointed by the king. A second charter, obtained from King John five years later for 300 marks, gave

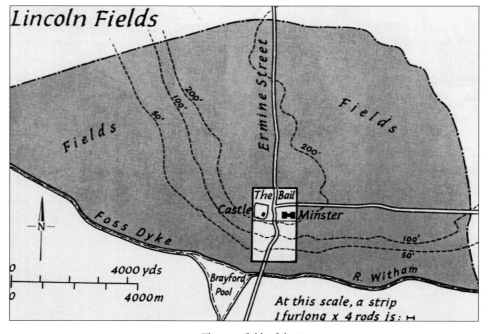

27   *The open fields of the city.*

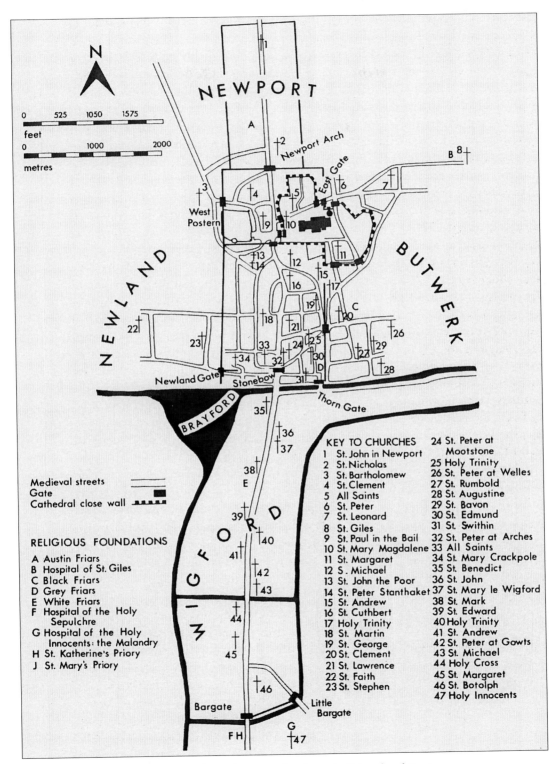

28   *Medieval Lincoln: streets, churches and religious foundations.*

KEY TO CHURCHES
1 St. John in Newport
2 St. Nicholas
3 St. Bartholomew
4 St. Clement
5 All Saints
6 St. Peter
7 St. Leonard
8 St. Giles
9 St. Paul in the Bail
10 St. Mary Magdalene
11 St. Margaret
12 S. Michael
13 St. John the Poor
14 St. Peter Stanthaket
15 St. Andrew
16 St. Cuthbert
17 Holy Trinity
18 St. Martin
19 St. George
20 St. Clement
21 St. Lawrence
22 St. Faith
23 St. Stephen
24 St. Peter at Mootstone
25 Holy Trinity
26 St. Peter at Welles
27 St. Rumbold
28 St. Augustine
29 St. Bavon
30 St. Edmund
31 St. Swithin
32 St. Peter at Arches
33 All Saints
34 St. Mary Crackpole
35 St. Benedict
36 St. John
37 St. Mary le Wigford
38 St. Mark
39 St. Edward
40 Holy Trinity
41 St. Andrew
42 St. Peter at Gowts
43 St. Michael
44 Holy Cross
45 St. Margaret
46 St. Botolph
47 Holy Innocents

Medieval streets
Gate
Cathedral close wall

RELIGIOUS FOUNDATIONS

A Austin Friars
B Hospital of St. Giles
C Black Friars
D Grey Friars
E White Friars
F Hospital of the Holy Sepulchre
G Hospital of the Holy Innocents: the Malandry
H St. Katherine's Priory
J St. Mary's Priory

the freemen the right to choose both bailiffs and set up 10 new civic officials. Four of the 'more lawful and discreet citizens' were to be chosen as coroners. They had to ensure that legal cases that the king claimed should be heard only by his judges were reserved for the royal justices and that the city's bailiffs should treat both rich and poor fairly and according to the law. There would also be four 'bedells' appointed as officers of the burwarmot, with special responsibility to keep the peace, and two clerks who would attend all meetings of the weekly court to keep the court records and conduct all official correspondence. To obtain these privileges the city had to increase its annual payment to the Crown from £100 to £180. The chief responsibility of the bailiffs themselves was the collection of this tax. For this they were personally liable and hence only the wealthiest of the city's merchants could aspire to this office. This charter also stipulated that men who were members of a craft guild could not become freemen unless they renounced their craft and got rid of their tools. Two hundred years later, when the city was in decline and the council keen to attract freemen, this ruling would be dropped.

The bailiffs also had to ensure the smooth running of markets and fairs and to oversee the collection of all tolls, the testing of weights and measures, and the supervision of the quality of bread and ale. In 1206 there appears the earliest reference to a Mayor of Lincoln, an exceptionally wealthy guild merchant known as Adam of Lincoln, who had previously been referred to as an alderman. From 1206 it would seem that the council was effectively run by an inner council of the mayor and two bailiffs, elected not by the whole 'commonalty' of freemen but by a self-electing body of the 24 wealthiest merchants, known as the Common Council. Adam would seem to have held the position for most of the next 10 years, until he was deprived of it by King John, who had been incensed by his participation in the baronial party that had forced the king to sign the Magna Carta at Runnymede the year before (a copy of which is still preserved in the castle today).

Complaints about corrupt practices, misgovernment and particularly excessive taxation of the poor were frequent, and on three occasions during the 13th century the king temporarily withdrew the city's rights of self-government and re-installed his own appointee, the county sheriff. On the last occasion, in 1290, the suspension of local rule lasted for 10 years. In 1290, when King Edward I ordered the expulsion of all Jews from the country and the forfeiture of their property to the Crown, he was extremely angry to learn that in Lincoln the mayor and bailiffs, with the agreement of the Common Council, had kept back some of the property and wealth of former Jews of Lincoln for themselves, and promptly levied a fine of 200 marks on the city. His patience with the city's authorities expired

29   *The Mayoral Seal.*

30 *Packhorses carrying woolpacks.*

completely, however, when he subsequently found that the fine had not been promptly paid. This had instead led to a major tax revolt in the city as the mayor and his friends attempted to raise the 200 marks from the city's population as a whole, and many local people were refusing to pay, even on pain of losing their property.

There was never any question of genuine democratic reform, but resentment of the power of the wealthy merchant and landowner classes who monopolised the mayoralty was never far below the surface. Any suggestion of unfair taxation or unjust use of power would be certain to prompt bitter complaints from the poorer classes, and particularly from the city's craftsmen, many of whom, by 1300, had organised themselves in craft guilds. The chief object of all craft guilds was to maintain high standards of workmanship through a system of careful inspections. No one could become a journeyman craftsman without serving his apprenticeship to a master, and the terms of his apprenticeship were governed by a contract known as his 'indentures'. But each guild was also a friendly society, dedicated to protect the interests of its members. In return for a small subscription the member would enjoy an annual dinner, help with money if he was too sick to work, and a fine funeral attended by all his former fellow members.

In 1325 King Edward II received a series of complaints from the 'commonalty' of the city against the unfair practices of the mayor, bailiffs and common council. The 'great lords', it was said, contributed nothing at all to the city's annual farm but the 'mean people' were taxed at will and without their consent. They alone were forced to keep the nightly watches, an often dangerous and thankless task, and it was claimed that the taxes they paid for the maintenance of the city walls were pocketed by the members of the council, the walls were left to decay, and no accounts of how the money was spent were ever produced. This, and later similar complaints, prompted no response from the monarch and Lincoln would never again be taken under the king's direct rule, but this did nothing to lessen the frustration and sense of grievance of the population at large. In about 1350 a guild of the 'common and middling folk' was established, which specifically sought to exclude from membership anyone who had ever served as mayor or bailiff. One rule stated that if any such person should insist on joining the guild they were to be excluded from ever holding any office.

In the 12th century the city's governing body had met in the hall of the Merchants' Guild (rather than outdoors, by the mootstone), but from the first half of the 13th century an upstairs room was provided instead over the arch of the gatehouse that stood on the site of the present Stonebow. This became, and would remain for many hundreds of years, the centre both for local government and local justice, and at least once a year also a place for much feasting and merriment, when the full council met to celebrate the mayor-making.

31   (Left) 'Spinsters' at work: spinning, carding, drawing out and twisting the yarn.

32   (Opposite) Dyers at work.

THREE EXCEPTIONS:
BAIL, CLOSE AND BEAUMONT FEE

The full powers of the mayor and his fellow officials did not extend to the whole of the city. The area known today as Beaumont Fee enjoyed a considerable degree of independence from the city authorities. In the 11th century this area was known as Hungate and at the time of the Domesday Survey was under the authority of the manor court of Alfred of Lincoln. All other independent manor courts from the pre-conquest era disappeared during the 11th and 12th centuries, but the wealth and status of Alfred and his successors ensured that his family were able to maintain the independent authority of their court, and to insist, on pain of a fine, on the attendance of their tenants.

Another, more powerful and separate authority was that exercised by the constable of the castle. The constable was a royal appointee enjoying the power to hold a court for all those who happened to live in the area of the old Roman Upper City, which had become the outer bailey of the castle, or the Bail. He also claimed the right to test the quality of bread and ale and to test weights and measures, to take any fines levied on those found in breach of the recognised standards, to collect tolls for market stalls and to hold hiring fairs. These rights were a constant source of grievance and annoyance for the mayor and aldermen and, as we will see in Chapter Five, on at least one occasion late in the 14th century, the mayor and bailiffs were accused of leading a riotous mob in an attack on the constable's market. Relations between the two authorities were always strained during the Middle Ages, but they would become particularly bitter when Lincoln slipped into economic decline in the 14th century and the income from market tolls began to decrease. Complaints and disputes about the rival claims of authority of the two jurisdictions would continue for many hundreds of years, until the Bail was finally united with the rest of the city in the mid-19th century.

A cause of perhaps even more bitter disputes, however, was the independence enjoyed by the Close; the community of clergy headed by the dean and chapter that was housed mainly in the eastern half of the Upper City, surrounding the cathedral. The inhabitants of this area contributed nothing to the city's farm, held their own court, and could not be summoned to appear in the borough court held by the mayor. Moreover, disputes also arose as to the rights of the dean and chapter of the cathedral to hold markets and collect tolls. There were even allegations that the independence of the church court meant that the cathedral authorities were protecting fugitives from justice. The dean and chapter made their independence very clear in 1285 by gaining permission from the monarch to build a 12-foot-high wall surrounding the Close. To justify the building of such a wall they claimed that so lawless was the city that it was not safe to even walk from their lodgings in the Close to the cathedral.

This independent, self-contained community of churchmen had been set up by the first bishop, Remigius, when he created an establishment of 21 canons, in line with continental practice, together with a treasurer, a chancellor and a dean. This number quickly increased. There were soon 42 canons and Bishop Alexander added two more. Before the end of the 12th century it had also been found necessary to employ numerous vicars, to help the canons share the burden of cathedral services and to act as substitutes for them, as many were only rarely resident. By this time there were also many chantry priests living in the Close, serving numerous minor altars in the cathedral and acting as assistants to the vicars. The bishops did not at first live in the Close, but Bishop Alexander's successor, Robert de Chesney, gained the king's permission to build the first palace immediately to the south of the cathedral. His work was continued by his successor, the saintly Bishop Hugh, and, as we shall see in the next chapter, by the end of the century the bishops of this vast diocese would possess a palace worthy of their august station, and far grander than any house that even the richest of Lincoln's merchants could afford.

FOUR

Castle, Cathedral and Close

THE CASTLE

When William the Conqueror arrived in Lincoln in 1068 he knew that any hope he might have once had of ruling his newly won kingdom by consent had vanished. He had already faced, and crushed, rebellions in Kent, the South-West and in Yorkshire and a programme of castle building was already underway. The new castle he ordered to be built at Lincoln was designed to control not only the city but also a wide area surrounding it. The East Coast was particularly vulnerable to Scandinavian invasion and any invasion fleet in the Humber could expect a friendly welcome from the Anglo-Danish populations of Yorkshire and Lincolnshire.

After London and York, Lincoln was one of the largest cities of the kingdom and an obvious choice for the site of a royal castle. Much of the Roman walls still stood and the steep hill above the Lower City was an obvious site on which to build a castle, just as it had been a thousand years before, when the Roman legionaries had built their

33 *An extract from the Bayeux Tapestry showing men building a castle for William shortly before the Battle of Hastings.*

fortress. Indeed, it is now believed that, on William's orders, the whole of the Roman Upper City was at first adopted as the new Norman castle. No doubt the walls and gates would have required repairs but the principal addition would have been to erect a motte, surmounted by a wooden tower. The motte can be still seen today, although the stone 'Lucy Tower' was erected much later, in the 12th century. Excavations at the Norman West Gate suggest that the castle we see today, occupying only the south-west corner of the Roman Upper City, was probably erected about thirty years later.

The building of the castle did nothing to endear the Normans to the people of Lincoln. The use of local forced labour, at first to raise the steep sloping motte, would have been bitterly resented. And then, about a generation later, the local populace were pressed into service again to erect a great earthen bank, 29 feet high and 82 feet wide, to protect the new, smaller bailey. The Roman walls on the south and west sides of the Upper City, together with the remains of the Roman West Gate, disappeared under the great earth bank.

At first the new castle walls and gates were probably wooden structures, but during the first half of the 12th century they were replaced by stone, up to 19 feet thick and 30-40 feet high. When the wooden tower on the motte was replaced by a stone keep (named after the Countess Lucy de Taillebois, wife of the Sheriff of Lincoln) it was originally 26 feet high and nine feet 10 inches thick. Today it is only half as high. In about 1149 a second motte was added in the south-east corner of the castle, on what is now the site of the observatory tower, and a square tower was erected on top of it.

34   *The first Norman motte with its wooden tower about 1080. A drawing by Tig Sutton.*

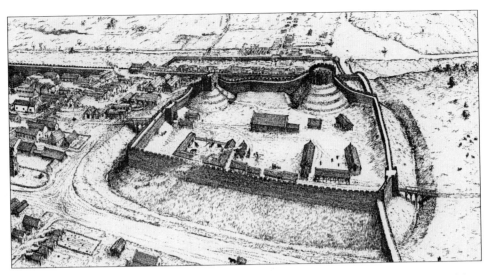

35 *The castle in about 1190. By now a second motte has been erected in the south-east corner of the castle and the wooden fencing has been replaced with stone. A drawing by Tig Sutton.*

The remaining two-thirds of the Upper City not occupied by the castle became the outer Bail, and was placed under the authority of the constable of the castle. The castle and the Bail, together with the Cathedral Close, were to remain independent of the rest of the city until the 19th century. William appointed an Englishman, Colsuen, to the Constableship, and he would be one of only two great English landowners in the whole country holding land directly from the king at the time of the Domesday Survey in 1086. The many manors William gave to Colsuen are an indication of the loyal service he gave his royal master, and of his usefulness to him. It can be assumed that for most of Lincoln's inhabitants he was a figure despised and hated as a traitor, just as much as he was feared.

For a number of generations the Constableship would be held by Colsuen's descendents; first by his son, Picot, and then by his son-in-law, the Norman Robert de la Haye, in whose family it would remain throughout the 12th century. One particularly notable holder of the office would be Robert de la Haye's granddaughter, a remarkable woman, Nicolaa de la Haye, who was also appointed Sheriff in 1216. Although the constable was expected to provide some of the knights for castle-guarding duties, the majority, about sixty, were provided by the bishop, as part of the 'knight's fee' he owed to the king for the estates granted to him.

The de la Hayes proved to be loyal subjects but they were unable to prevent Ranulf, the Earl of Chester, from seizing the castle in 1140, cynically championing the cause of the Empress Matilda against the claims of King Stephen in an attempt to boost his already considerable power. The king himself led the attempt to retake the castle and placed his siege weapons, as well as his archers, on the west front of the cathedral. His army was defeated, however, outside the castle gates, by the forces of Ranulf's ally, the Duke of Gloucester, and by Ranulf's own forces arriving from Wales. Stephen was taken prisoner but managed to keep his throne and eventually, in 1146, regained his castle. However, in 1149 he was obliged again to allow Ranulf to have the use of it as the price

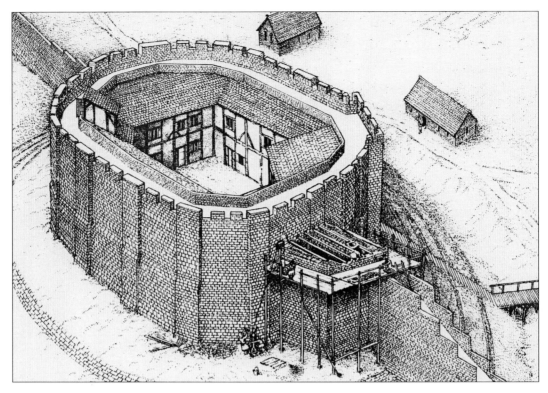

36 *The Lucy Tower in about 1185. A drawing by Tig Sutton.*

for his support against Matilda's son, Henry of Anjou, and it was probably at this time that the second motte and tower were erected. With the Earl of Chester now an ally the

castle remained in Stephen's hands until his death in 1154, when it was surrendered to Matilda's son, the new king, Henry II.

The castle would never again be the focus for so prolonged a conflict, but the attempt by disgruntled barons to drive King John from the throne and replace him with the French dauphin, Louis of France, in 1216, involved both city and castle in a further brief episode of bloody conflict. Louis's support in

37 *The second, 12th-century motte today, with part of the original square tower surviving, surmounted by the 19th-century 'observatory' tower.*

England quickly diminished following the sudden death of John at Newark Abbey on 18 October 1216, and when Louis and his allies attempted to storm Lincoln castle in the following spring they soon found themselves confronted with a powerful relieving force led by the 75-year-old William Marshal, Earl of Pembroke, the newly appointed Regent for John's nine-year-old son, King Henry III. Nicolaa de la Haye, the constable, managed to admit part of the Earl's forces by the postern gate in the Lucy Tower to reinforce her small garrison, while the remainder of the Regent's forces fought their way into the town through the Newport Arch. The battle for Lincoln, on 20 May 1217, proved decisive. The aged Regent was a wily and effective campaigner. Louis's forces found themselves attacked both from the north and the west as the reinforced garrison now sallied forth to engage the enemy in the streets of the Upper City and to join up with the forces coming in from Newport. Bitter hand-to-hand fighting raged through the Bail and down the High Street. As one browses in a second-hand bookshop today on Steep Hill, or sips a cup of coffee in one of the many cafés that now line the High Street, one might reflect on how these streets once rang with the clash of steel and the screams and moans of the dying as a bloody battle was fought upon them. The battle quickly became a rout and then a massacre as many of Louis's soldiers were driven down the hill and into the Witham and drowned. Their swords and chain-mail would be discovered six hundred years later when the river was deepened. Louis himself escaped and after this crushing blow soon gave up his hopes of becoming King of England and returned instead to France to succeed his father to a more secure throne. But the people of Lincoln were less fortunate. It was felt by the Regent and his men that too many had shown rather too much support for Louis, even though almost every baron in England had supported his right to depose and replace the hated John when Louis had landed in England only a year before. The Regent's victorious forces celebrated their success by pillaging the city and the cathedral, burning houses and putting many innocent

townspeople to the sword. With a sense of ironic humour, the whole horrible episode would later become known in the city as the 'Fair of Lincoln'.

Neither castle nor city would be the scene of further conflict for more than 400 years, until the civil wars of the 17th century. However, during the first few years after the Battle of Lincoln, strenuous efforts were made to repair the damage of Prince Louis's siege and to bring

38 *The East Gate today.*

39 *The castle as it probably appeared in the 14th century. The East Gate is shown now defended by a barbican and Cobb Hall tower has been built to strengthen the north-east corner of the inner bailey wall. The buildings shown in the inner bailey are partly conjectural but the large building shown is suggested by John Speed's map of 1611.*

40 *The vaulted 13th-century Cobb Hall, as it appears today. The steps down to the dungeon below can be seen in the foreground.*

the defences up to date. When Nicolaa de la Haye finally retired as Constable in 1226, almost 40 years after she had succeeded her father to the position, the castle was far stronger than it had ever been before. The Lucy Tower had been repaired, a barbican had been erected to defend the eastern gate, complete with two new towers, battlemented side walls and a portcullis, and the D-shaped Cobb Hall tower had been erected in the north-east corner of the walls. The design of the tower reflected the latest military styles and was one storey higher than it is today. A catapult was built on a firing platform on the roof and its ammunition was the small round stones, or 'cobbs', that give the tower its name, 200 of which were found in a recess in the tower in 1831.

Just a hundred years after so much expensive improvement, however, the castle was in such a poor state of repair owing to prolonged neglect that a survey in 1327 deemed it incapable of defence and too ruinous to justify the huge expense required to complete repairs. The walls, towers and great hall were all said to be in a most dilapidated condition.

THE CATHEDRAL

In 1067 William appointed Remigius, the almoner of the abbey of Fécamp in Normandy, to the bishopric of Dorchester, a huge diocese stretching from the Thames to the Humber. It was said that Remigius had asked for a bishopric as the price of his support for the conquest, and William was also keen to replace the English bishops with men such as Remigius whom he felt he could trust to do his bidding. Then, five years later, in 1072, at a council held at Windsor, William decided that bishops' sees should be in walled towns rather than in villages. Within a year Remigius had gained the permission of both king and pope to transfer his see to Lincoln, and by 1075 land was being cleared in the south-east corner of the Roman Upper City, opposite the recently built castle motte, and building work had begun.

Remigius would not live to see the completion of his cathedral and died just days before its consecration, in 1092. Much of his cathedral was destroyed by a fire in 1141 and only the west front survives today. We cannot be sure, therefore, about the appearance of this first cathedral, but there is good reason to believe that the west end of the building was fortified, and had as much the appearance of a castle as a cathedral. It is now believed that it might even have been at first a separate tower with niches that could be used by bowmen, exceptionally thick walls, and machicolations, through which a variety of projectiles might be aimed at an assaulting army. Evidence for this can still be found in the earliest surviving sections of the west front of the cathedral. Remigius would have felt, quite rightly, that he was entering hostile territory when he moved his see to Lincoln and neither he nor William could be sure, in 1075, that there would be no more major rebellions in this area. The cathedral was probably seen at the time as being not only a place of worship but also part of the defences of the outer bailey of the castle.

The fire of 1141 was only the first of a series of disasters that would befall the cathedral. In 1185 an earth tremor destroyed the recently rebuilt cathedral – one contemporary said that it was split asunder 'from top to bottom'. In 1217 the cathedral was pillaged by royal forces following the Battle of Lincoln, in 1237 the central tower collapsed, and in 1547 the central spire blew down in a gale.

The catastrophic earth tremor of 1185 may have been partly owing to defects in the design of the new stone vault that had been erected shortly after the fire on the orders of Bishop Alexander. He was an extremely powerful and wealthy politician-prelate, with castles at Newark, Banbury and Sleaford. He was known later as 'the Magnificent', and with his uncle, Bishop Roger of Salisbury, played a major role in the baronial wars of Stephen's troubled reign. It would seem that he and his architect were determined that their rebuilding would both beautify Remigius's rather austere exterior and also reflect the very latest ideas in continental cathedral architecture. The decision to vault the nave

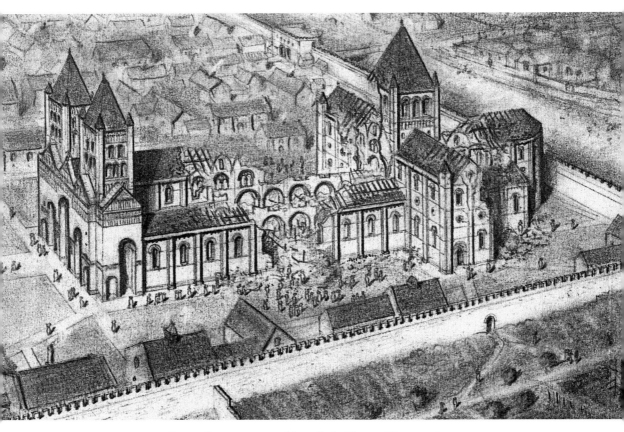

41   *An artist's reconstruction of the cathedral damaged by an earth tremor in 1185.*

42   *A contemporary illustration of stonemasons and carpenters at work in the 13th century.*

43 *The west front of the cathedral today.*

was perhaps the most ambitious aspect of the work, for this was still very rare in England in the mid-12th century. The design of much of the west front, which Alexander had decorated with the frieze of sculptured Biblical scenes that we see today, and the new west doorways, sumptuously decorated with birds, beasts, grotesques and geometrical ornamentation, were probably inspired by the work only just completed at Saint-Denis Cathedral in Paris in 1140. The west towers were probably begun at this time, and like the west front they, too, were richly decorated by an arcade of arches.

Following the collapse of the roof in 1185, the cathedral lay in ruins for seven years before sufficient funds could be raised to begin another rebuilding. By now Lincoln had a very different bishop, the saintly, unworldly, former Carthusian monk Hugh of Avalon. It would be the work begun during his time at Lincoln that would give us the magnificent Early English Gothic cathedral that survives today, widely regarded as the most beautiful example of this style of architecture in the country.

Alexander's and Remigius's architects remain anonymous, but we are given the names of the two men who seem to have been responsible for the work begun under Bishop Hugh. Geoffrey de Noiers has usually been credited as the designer as he is described as the 'nobilis fabriciae constructor', but his role is not entirely clear because a contemporary, Richard the Mason, is described at the end of the 12th century as 'magister', suggesting that he, too, may have been the designer.

44 *Detail of mid-12th-century relief, showing sinners entering the jaws of Hell, west front of the cathedral.*

These men, like Alexander's architect, were experimenting at the limits of their technology. The collapse of Bishop Alexander's nave was probably owing as much to the daring experimental nature of the design as to any earth tremor, and the collapse of St Hugh's main crossing tower in 1237 may also have been due to the same reason. St Hugh's architects, and their immediate successors, were just as keen as Alexander's had been to adopt the very latest design ideas from the continent. The extreme steepness of the roof of St Hugh's choir is an example of this. Completed just a few years after

45 *St Hugh's Choir, with the Angel Choir and great east window in the background.*

St Hugh's death in 1200, the roof is thought to have been one of the earliest examples in England of the steep Gothic roof found on the continent. A variety of novel strengthening devices had to be adopted as the architects experimented with different ways to try to ensure that the roof stayed up. Similarly, the adoption of flying buttresses to hold up the high clerestory walls and windows of St Hugh's choir was also quite a new idea, little known yet even on the continent and only recently introduced into England, having been first used at Canterbury in the 1170s. The vaulting of St Hugh's choir was also daringly imaginative. It is the first example of rib-vaulting designed purely for decorative reasons and set the pattern for cathedral rib-vaulting throughout England.

It is not clear just how much of the cathedral had been rebuilt at the time of Bishop Hugh's death, but it is probable that he lived to see only the choir and part of the east transepts completed. Progress was slowed by the difficulty of raising the huge sums of money required. The wealthy merchant members of St Mary's Guild, which Bishop Hugh is said to have founded, pledged to contribute the considerable sum of 1,000 marks a year to help meet the expenses and Hugh also offered generous pardons for sins to all who contributed. The poor as well as the rich were expected to pay. The poor swineherd of Stow, who is said to have given his lifesavings of 16 silver pennies, could be celebrated as an example to all, and as such his statue was later placed high on the north pinnacle of the west front of the cathedral, to partner that of St Hugh himself, whose statue was placed on the south pinnacle.

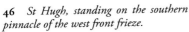

46   *St Hugh, standing on the southern pinnacle of the west front frieze.*

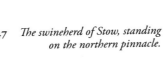

47   *The swineherd of Stow, standing on the northern pinnacle.*

48 *The east end of the Angel Choir. The much decorated plinth for St Hugh's head shrine can be seen in the background, in front of the great east window.*

49 *The Lincoln Imp, the Angel Choir's most famous 'inhabitant'.*

To extend the new choir further east, and to give the apse a series of radiating chapels, Hugh's architect was obliged to take down part of the Roman wall. Less than 60 years later, however, this new apse would also be demolished to make way for a new retro-choir, better known today as the Angel Choir, to make room for a grand shrine for the mortal remains of St Hugh, who was canonised in 1220. The work on the Angel Choir was completed by 1280, when it was consecrated, and the remains of the saint were transferred to their new resting place in the presence of King Edward I and Queen Eleanor, the Archbishop of Canterbury and eight bishops. During the intervening years the saint's head had unfortunately become detached from the rest of the corpse and two shrines were therefore required, both rich in gold, silver and precious stones. Both disappeared in the despoliation of Henry VIII's reformation, but the arcaded pedestal of the head shrine survives today in the easternmost bay of the Angel Choir and an open table tomb in black marble behind the high altar marks the site of the main shrine.

Work on the cathedral seems to have proceeded steadily in the first few decades after St Hugh's death and both the nave and main transepts may have already been completed when disaster struck again in 1237, with the collapse of the central tower during a sermon. Shortly before this, in about 1235, the chapter house had been completed. It had been begun before 1220, and once again Lincoln's architect was attempting something quite new: a centrally planned 10-sided structure, the ribs of the roof vaulting spiralling from the central pillar. It would again set the pattern for others to follow and the centrally planned chapter house would become an English speciality. Again, the names of the architects

50 (Left) The Chapter House.

51 (Below) The nave, looking east.

of this period are known. In about 1230 the 'magister operis' was called Michael, and five years later his name is given as Alexander. Michael would have overseen the completion of the main transepts and probably also the vaulting and roofing of the nave, which is thought to have been completed in about 1233. Alexander would have had to cope with the rebuilding of the central tower and would also have finished the west front, considerably widening the façade.

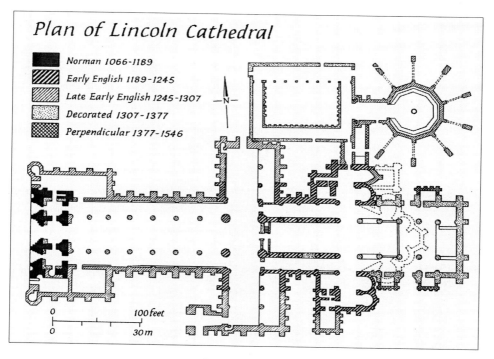

Plan of Lincoln Cathedral

- ■ Norman 1066-1189
- ▨ Early English 1189-1245
- ▨ Late Early English 1245-1307
- ▨ Decorated 1307-1377
- ▨ Perpendicular 1377-1546

—N—

0 _____ 100 feet
0 _____ 30 m

52   *Plan of Lincoln Cathedral.*

The Angel Choir was begun in about 1255, when the cathedral authorities petitioned Henry III to allow further sections of the town wall to be taken down to extend the cathedral again. This most beautiful part of the cathedral would complete the work begun in St Hugh's time with a wonderful flourish, but perhaps its crowning glory was the great east window, completed in about 1275. It is the earliest eight-light window preserved anywhere. It is over 59 feet high, beautifully and logically proportioned, and on a sunny morning it allows the whole vast area of the Angel Choir to be filled with glorious light.

With the consecration of the Angel Choir the cathedral was almost complete. The cloisters were added by Bishop Sutton in the last decade of the 13th century and are mentioned in a letter of the Bishop in 1296, and his successor, John of Dalderby, had the central tower raised and the great spire added. The master mason for this brave work was Richard of Stow, and he completed it in four years, between 1307 and 1311. When finished, the spire stood 482 feet high and the cathedral was the tallest building in the world. Today, standing on its hill above the city, the cathedral is a most beautiful sight; but with so great a spire completing the work the cathedral must have appeared truly breath-taking: the greatest triumph of the technology of its day.

After this final and most audacious success there could be little left to do except embellish, replace and improve. In the 1330s the great circular window of the main south transept was replaced by the very beautiful flowing tracery of the window we see today, the Bishop's Eye, providing a fine contrast to the less elaborate 'plate' tracery of the older Dean's Eye window of the main north transept, that also happily still survives today, and was completed about a hundred years earlier. Late in the 14th century the great 13th-century west window was replaced by an equally enormous window, but with the latest perpendicular tracery, and a gallery of seated kings was inserted immediately beneath it, cutting into the top of Bishop Alexander's central portal. The two west towers were also raised at about this time to take their place beside the great central tower, and topped off with recessed spires.

THE CLOSE

We have seen already, in the previous chapter, that with the building of the castle and the decision to make the rest of the Upper City the castle's outer bailey, much of the Upper City came under the jurisdiction of the castle constable. The Bail was legally not part of the rest of the city, and this would remain the case for almost 800 years. Within the eastern half of the Upper City, however, and spilling over into the suburbs to the east of the town wall, a second separate jurisdiction also developed in the 13th century, that of the Cathedral Close. At first there was no physical barrier separating the lands and properties belonging to the cathedral and its canons, but in 1285 King Edward I gave permission to Bishop Sutton to have a wall erected to protect the cathedral and its properties from robbers and burglars. Work on building the walls and gates of the Close followed soon afterwards, but as the cathedral's precincts expanded further eastwards in the next few decades, permission from the king for further walls and gates had to be sought again in 1316. This was granted and by 1327 the Close walls were complete.

The Close occupied more than forty acres of the upper town and six gates and numerous towers punctuated a crenellated wall that ran for more than 3,300 feet. Today, only one of the 14th-century gates survives: Exchequergate, due west of the cathedral's west front.

53   *Exchequergate today, from the east.*

Standing three storeys high, and consisting of three arches, it was always the largest of the gates. An outer gate on the west side was taken down in 1816 and blocked openings show where there were once shops inside the gate. The only other 14th-century gate, Pottergate, at the southern end of the street bearing the same name, was completely rebuilt in the 1880s. None of the other gates survive at all. Priory Gate, standing at the northern end of Minster Yard, was erected in 1816, a year after the original medieval North Gate was taken down, and is an insubstantial shadow of the former gatehouse that once stood here.

The area occupied by the cathedral's clerical community was already densely populated, long before the walls and gatehouses had been erected. Close to the cathedral's massive walls were housed its

54   *North Gate of the Close, as it appeared at the beginning of the 19th century.*

canons and their deputies, the vicars, together with the 'young vicars' or lesser clerks, who were still pupils in the chancellor's grammar school, choristers and chantry priests, clerks, copyists and accountants, school masters, organists, bell ringers and vergers. Most of the masons who were at work on the cathedral lived outside the Close, but some workmen were permanently employed about the building, including carpenters, sweepers and a glazier. Tailors, seamstresses, laundresses, messengers and general servants were also essential elements of the community, together with those employed as searchers and watchers of the shrines, the candle-lighter, the night watchman who blew a flute to mark the hours, and the constable of the Close.

Today, the area once occupied by the Close is still full of buildings of interest, many containing fragments dating from the 12th, 13th and 14th centuries. The most important survival of all is the bishop's palace, standing to the south of the cathedral and dating from the mid-12th century. Enough of the building survives for the visitor to be able to picture in his mind something of the splendour once enjoyed by the medieval bishops, especially if equipped with an audio-guide. The great west hall, begun by Bishop Hugh at the end of the 12th century, and completed by Hugh of Wells (1209-35), has been described as one of the most impressive of its date in England. The Purbeck marble pillars have gone, and the rich tapestries that once hung on the walls have to be imagined, but the scale of the hall – approximately eighty-two feet long and sixty-five feet wide – is very striking. The numbers to be catered for when the bishop and his household were in residence is indicated by the size of the adjoining buttery, pantry, cellars and, above all, the kitchen with its five huge fireplaces. An upper chamber at the southern end of the hall, above the buttery and pantry, was the bishop's private quarters to which he could retire at night while most of his household slept on the floor of the hall.

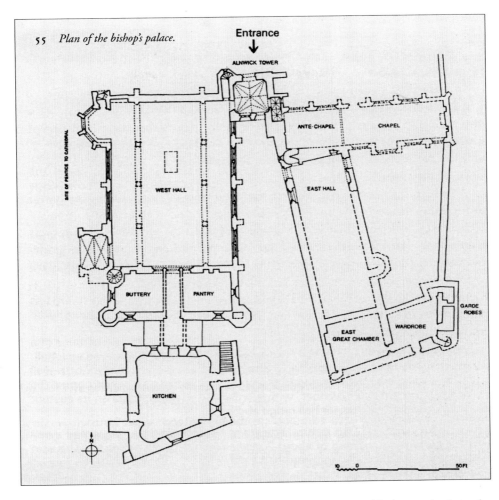

55 *Plan of the bishop's palace.*

Immediately to the east of the bishop's palace the two-storied lodgings, built at the beginning of the 14th century by Bishop Sutton and known as Vicars' Court, still survive, although much altered and added to. The southern range, containing six lodgings, is the earliest and most complete. The kitchen and adjoining hall have long gone, but an original spiral staircase survives, together with wooden floors, windows and roof trusses all dating from the 14th century. Bishop Sutton built the court to house the 25 senior vicars-choral who sang the daily offices in the cathedral in place of the non-resident canons. This picturesque, peaceful and secluded corner of the city is one of Lincoln's best-kept secrets.

Further east, where Minster Yard and Pottergate meet, a fine late 15th-century house, The Chancery, faces the street, and hides within it and behind it much earlier buildings. In the north gable two reset windows reveal the earlier existence of a substantial 13th-century house, and the long range that runs west to east behind consists of two late 13th- or 14th-century upper living rooms, or solars, and a 14th-century chapel. The only trace to survive of the great hall to which they would have been once attached, however, are three doorways, now on the outside of the building but once part of the hall, and the staircase from the central door to the chapel above. The first chancellor to live here was the formidable Antony Bek, who would later become Bishop of Norwich. He was given the property because he wanted a larger house, more in keeping with his station. Before that the rentals had been used to help finance the completion of St Hugh's Shrine.

In 1390 the Chancery acquired its most famous tenant, Katherine Swynford, the mistress of the king's uncle, John of Gaunt, the Duke of Lancaster and also the richest man in England. The great hall was pulled down in 1714. It was a large and impressive structure, probably half-timbered, about forty feet long and about thirty feet wide, sufficient for successive chancellors and for Katherine and the Duke to hold court and entertain their guests in style.

A little to the north, along Minster Yard, and close to Priory Gate, a twin-gabled 17th-century house (2, Minster Yard) also hides a much earlier medieval house: a 13th-century hall house that all but disappeared when the present house was created from it in the late 1660s. The external east wall and a medieval doorway at its southern end are almost all that survives of the original hall, although a slightly later 14th-century tower, complete with spiral staircase, can still be seen at the north end of the house. It is a reminder of the fears of robbery and violence that the Close's wealthy inhabitants were well justified to harbour in the 14th and 15th centuries, and the consequent need they felt for strong, secure lodgings.

The earliest surviving building of the Close is Deloraine Court, on James Street, to the north of the cathedral. It appears to date mainly from the 17th and 18th centuries, but in fact hides much earlier origins and a long, thick-walled, 12th-century vaulted undercroft still survives. It is about ninety-eight feet long and nineteen feet wide. Evidence of the original hall also survives; it would have been about forty-five feet long and thirty-two feet wide. In the room above the undercroft a stone Tudor fireplace is located in a Norman chimneybreast, dated to about 1180. The roof of the hall, typically

56 Vicar's Court.

57 *The Chancery.*

at right angles to the undercroft, dates from about 1300. The first occupants of this fine house are not known, but it would seem to have become the property of the dean and chapter about a century after it was built, in three separate portions

Other houses in this area are of a slightly later date. A little further down James Street the Cathedral School Boarding House hides the remains of a pair of 13th-century lodging houses in its east-west wall. To the south of the boarding house, and facing on to Eastgate, Atherstone Place is a medieval hall house refurbished in the early 16th century but still betraying a little of its origins, including a reset Norman doorway and a pair of 13th-century windows. Immediately to the north of the boarding house, on James Street, is the mostly mid-18th-century Burghersh Chantry, but it also contains fragmentary evidence of its 14th-century origins. The Chantry was founded in 1345 for five priests and six boys. Chantry priests were maintained out of the large chantry and obit funds accumulated by the dean and chapter. A second house for chantry priests, the Cantilupe Chantry, still stands close to Vicars' Court, immediately to the south of the Angel Choir. This was founded in 1355, by Sir Nicholas Cantilupe, in the earnest expectation that the prayers of the chantry priests would speed the passage of his soul through the pains of purgatory. Among the survivals from the original building is an oriel window and a number of blocked windows, and a crownpost roof of the northern part of the building also dates from the late 14th century.

These two chantries were founded just before and just after the Close was devastated by the 'great pestilence', or Black Death, of 1349. More than half the inhabitants of the Close were wiped out in two terrible months in the early summer of that year. This small, claustrophobic community, living literally on top of one another, in their little rooms huddled together around courts and greens, would be especially susceptible to a

58   *Deloraine Court.*

disease that proved so infectious that a mere cough from a dying man could cause the death of half a dozen more. Across the country about a third of the population would be killed by the disease, but the death rate in cathedral closes and monasteries was almost always much higher.

The impact of the Black Death on the city as a whole will be a topic for the next chapter, but we might note now that the days of the city's growth and prosperity were already coming to an end even before the plague struck. The history of the castle and the cathedral can also be seen to reflect this end of an era in the first half of the 14th century. The cathedral was complete and the heroic years of brave and glorious experimentation were over, while the castle had been allowed to deteriorate so woefully that it was already judged to be beyond repair and of no military value. For the Close, the city's decline in the 14th century brought the most bitter disputes yet between the city authorities, desperate to raise whatever income they could from market tolls and fairs, and the dean and chapter of the Close, determined to protect their traditional rights and freedoms.

FIVE

The Late Medieval City

LINCOLN IN THE EARLY FOURTEENTH CENTURY

When Edward I chose to hold a Parliament in Lincoln in January 1301 the city was still one of the most important in the country. The population was probably in excess of 7,000 and among its inhabitants were many rich merchants. A charter granted in 1327, on the accession of Edward III, confirmed the city's rights to hold markets three days a week and a fair once a year in June. The mayor and bailiffs were finding it increasingly difficult to enforce the city's right to a monopoly of foreign trade in the county, but in 1326 the city gained an equally valuable privilege: the right to be one of only eight staple towns of the country for the trade in wool, hides, skins and tin. For the time being it seemed that the city's position as a prosperous trading centre was guaranteed.

The city's weekly markets were held on Mondays, Wednesdays and Fridays. The corn market was held on Steep Hill, close to the Jew's House, and at this time a market cross stood nearby. The meat market was on the Upper High Street and cloth was sold between Steep Hill and Mikelgate, an area which was still known as 'The Drapery' in the 1930s. Skins were sold further down Mikelgate, just to the north of the site now occupied by the Stonebow and the butter market, complete with butter cross, was to be found a little to the west, in Newland.

On market days the streets would be thronged with farmers, craftsmen and country traders, but on the days of the annual fair Lincoln became an international commercial centre, visited by merchants from many different countries. The fair of St Botolph was held in Newport for 12 days, from the feast day of St Botolph, 17 June, to the feast of St Peter and St Paul, 29 June. The tolls paid by the merchants were an important contribution to the city's income and it was because of this that in 1327 the city authorities gained permission from the king to extend the fair of St Botolph by a further 13 days.

The Staple Place, and therefore also the wool market, was established on the north bank of the Witham, beside Thorn Bridge and the wool warehouses that had lined the north bank for over a century. Here, wool and other staple goods had to be inspected, weighed and packaged. The staple both reflected and symbolised the city's importance as a centre for international trade.

59 *Edward II's charter of 1326 granting Lincoln the right to be a staple town for the sale of wool and other goods.*

The city was not, however, as prosperous as it had once been, for its once proud cloth trade was now a shadow of its former self. It had declined sharply in the last quarter of the 13th century, unable to compete with Flemish competition, unable to adapt to changing markets and less well-placed than English rural competitors to exploit the savings offered by the new fulling mills. Consequently, it had rapidly lost both its foreign and domestic markets. Since the time of Henry II, when there were said to be over 200 spinners in the city, the Weavers' Guild had enjoyed the right to demand that all weavers in the city and in the surrounding countryside, up to 12 miles from Lincoln, must be members of the guild. In return the weavers had paid £6 every year to the king as their contribution to the city's farm. By the 1320s, however, the number of guild members had fallen dramatically and the annual payments could no longer be afforded. Between 1321 and 1331 there were no weavers at all in the city and between 1331 and 1345 only a few spinners. By 1348 the guild was in substantial arrears and was appealing to the king to be relieved of the burden. It claimed that the guild had long lost all control over the industry in the region.

The collapse of the cloth trade had a very damaging effect on the city for it had once generated large profits, especially for the finishing trades, and many other trades were closely linked to it. It is quite likely that the city's population was consequently already declining before the Black Death struck in 1349. In 1332 there were only 433 taxpayers in the city. Other factors, however, were also responsible. In the first two decades of the 14th century the city was badly affected by widespread famine in the region, brought about by a series of very poor harvests and severe flooding. Moreover, by the 1330s the city's export trade was also being severely damaged by its failure to maintain the Foss Dyke properly. By 1334 it had slipped to sixth place in the country, in terms of export values, and it had been overtaken by its rival, Boston, in fourth place. From 1335 there are repeated complaints that the ancient Navigation was blocked and impassable. This would have a lasting impact and make it impossible for the city to ever regain its status as a major port.

THE BLACK DEATH

During 1349 the Black Death probably wiped out about half the population of the city. The county as a whole probably lost about forty-five per cent of its population, but it is almost certain that the death rate in Lincoln was even higher. Records kept by the Bishop of Lincoln suggest that about sixty per cent of the clergy in the city died. Those who were living in close proximity to one another in lodgings in the Close were particularly vulnerable, and many of the clergy would have contracted the disease when, in fulfilment of their duties, they entered the houses of the dying to hear confessions and grant forgiveness of sins. Some of the wealthier inhabitants might have been able to escape the plague by leaving the city and the evidence of wills shows that the mortality rate was probably rather lower among the wealthier classes than among the population as a whole.

The great majority of victims died in just two months, in May and June. A year later, in March 1350, the city's common clerk recorded that:

> ... in 1349 there was that great pestilence in Lincoln which spread over all parts of the world beginning on Palm Sunday in the year aforesaid until the Feast of the Nativity of St John the Baptist (24 June) next following, when it ceased, God be praised who reigns for ever and ever, Amen.

The swiftness with which the plague devastated the city might suggest that many of the victims died from a particularly virulent and vicious form of the disease: pneumonic plague. Unlike bubonic plague, this did not leave a rash of black spots on the victim's body. Instead it attacked the lungs and the victim died very quickly, coughing up blood, and thus transmitting the infection and innocently causing yet more deaths. It was said that those who contracted this form of the plague could feel perfectly well in the morning but be dead before sunset. And although a few might survive the better known bubonic plague, death was virtually certain for victims of pneumonic plague.

It is likely, however, that among the many victims of pneumonic plague there were also those who succumbed to bubonic plague, and died a lingering and painful death, their skin covered in the ghastly black buboes. Many would also have been victims of a third variant, septicaemic plague. The bubonic form was carried mainly in the fur of rodents, but particularly by the black rat, while septicaemic plague was carried by insects, and particularly by human fleas. The filthy conditions of Lincoln's streets and houses meant that rats were teeming in all parts of the city and the human flea was ubiquitous. Modern concepts of hygiene and cleanliness were utterly unknown and, in the absence of sewers and any adequate system of waste disposal, quite impossible to achieve.

It is very difficult to comprehend the psychological, social or economic impact of such a devastating blow to any community. And Lincoln was hit harder than most cities, not only in terms of the level of mortality, but because plague was now established as a recurrent feature of the city's life. There would be periods of recovery but they would be only temporary.

For those at the bottom of the social scale, however, one of the long-term consequences of the plague was probably an improvement in living standards. Although there would have been many grievous personal losses and much heartbreak caused by the death of so many loved ones, for those peasant farmers in the Lincoln area who survived the Black Death there was at least now the prospect of being able to demand from their lords reductions in rent and feudal dues, and for labourers the chance of higher wages. The impact was almost immediate. As early as March 1350 the surviving canons of the cathedral were complaining that neither they nor their parishioners could find enough labourers to till their farms, and the few labourers there were demanded excessive wages. Their lands were consequently lying fallow and rents could not be collected. In December the canons bowed to the inevitable and agreed that the rents of several of the chapter's manors had to be reduced, including those of Newport, Nettleham and Glentham. Through the notorious Statute of Labourers Parliament would soon also attempt to ban any attempts by labourers to increase the wages they demanded, but to little avail while labour remained at such a premium.

Neglect, Decay and Increasing Social Tension

It seems likely that due either to incompetence or corruption, or possibly because of the evident economic problems facing the city, the mayor and bailiffs were already neglecting to ensure even the most rudimentary street-cleaning measures before the Black Death struck. It is possible that Lincoln was consequently even dirtier by this time than many other cities. In the years following the Black Death the signs of neglect and decay are very evident. Indeed, so appalling was the state of the city's streets in the 1360s that many merchants, compelled to come to Lincoln to trade due to its status as a staple town, complained bitterly of the dangerous and filthy conditions in the city. By 1365 their complaints had reached the king. In that year he issued a clear warning to the city authorities declaring that:

> It has lately come to the king's ears that by default of good rule in their city, to which merchants, alien and denizen, and others of the vicinage are wont to come at this time with merchandise, such merchants on account of the deep mud and the dung and filth thrown in the streets and lanes, and other loathsome things lying about and heaped up there, come but seldom, and thereby the evil name of them and their city grows worse and worse.

The king then went on to make it very clear to the mayor and bailiffs just what he expected them to do about it:

> He therefore enjoins on them to have the streets and lanes cleansed at once and kept clean, and everyone having dwellings or domiciles in the city charged, and, if need be, compelled by grievous methods to pave before their dwellings, under a heavy penalty to be paid to the king and to the city, sparing neither poor nor rich, that within a year

the city may be completely paved and brought into a state of cleanliness and the king be not by their default troubled further in the matter, whereby he would have to lay his hand more heavily upon them.

Had the city not already been suffering a decline in the numbers of merchants who came to trade and the collapse of its cloth-making industry, it might have been able to recover from the blow dealt by the Black Death. As it was, by wiping out so many townsmen the plague had made the city's economic recovery even more unlikely. The king may have been right to say that the falling number of visiting merchants was due in part to the city's failure to pave and cleanse its streets, but the mayor and his colleagues could reply that their city's inhabitants could not easily afford to undertake so costly a scheme, and that their attempts to raise the necessary taxation could only cause conflict and bitterness between themselves and the city's tax payers. This would certainly seem to be implied by the sad picture of neglect and decline that characterises much of the next 150 years.

It is clear that the city authorities failed to respond adequately to the king's demands, and this might have led to another mighty blow just four years later: the loss of the staple to its younger and now more successful rival, Boston, whose merchants had long sought this privilege. As access to Lincoln became more difficult with the gradual deterioration of the Foss Dyke, so the advantages of Boston's position as a port became more apparent. We might also speculate whether some of the complaints

60 *Memorial brass of a wool merchant from Stamford, made around 1400. He has a money purse on his belt and his feet rest on two wool sacks. There were probably a number of similar memorials to Lincoln's merchants in the cathedral until the Civil War.*

61 *An artist's impression of the city in the mid-14th century. The spire has been built on the central tower of the cathedral and, in the foreground, standing on the High Bridge, is the 13th-century chapel of St Thomas à Becket. On the site of the present Stonebow stands the old Roman South Gate. By this time it was in a sad state of disrepair and would be pulled down in 1390.*

that reached the king concerning the state of Lincoln's streets might have come from Boston merchants.

As the century progressed, signs of neglect and decay were everywhere. It wasn't just the streets that were in a poor state. The dilapidated condition of the castle's defences had been noted as early as 1327 and the city's walls and towers would seem to have been in a similarly woeful state by the 1370s. Successive monarchs made it clear that they expected the mayor and his council to ensure the city's defences were repaired regularly, and gave them the right to tax the local people specifically to raise funds for this purpose (the 'murage') so that 'the king's city' might be protected. A similar right to raise taxes to pay for the paving of the streets (the 'pavage') was also frequently granted. Very little, however, seems to have been done. The city authorities complained that they found it very difficult to collect the taxes, owing to the poor state of the city's economy and the resistance of the city's increasingly discontented population, but many citizens alleged that the taxes were collected but misappropriated by corrupt officials. The growing poverty of the city was clearly driving a wedge between the unelected city oligarchs and the population as a whole. Resentment of wealth and privilege had never been so apparent.

When, in 1371, instructions were sent to the city to repair the walls, towers and streets, the mayor was told that any who resisted paying the necessary taxation must be arrested and imprisoned. It would seem that some taxation was collected (on goods coming into the city) but it was alleged that little work had been done because the tax collectors had used much of the money for their own purposes. Another grant of 'pavage' was made in 1377, but this time commissioners were also sent to the city to enquire into what had happened to the previous money that had been raised. More grants were made in 1381, 1384 and 1387, and more commissioners were sent out to check up on the city's officials. Little seems to have come of their enquiries, and the work was apparently not completed because more grants were made again in 1397 and 1401.

Although the inhabitants of the city did not join in the Peasants' Revolt in 1381, there was little doubt where their sympathies lay. The revolt was triggered by a poll tax imposed on the country to meet the costs of the wars against France. John of Gaunt, the Duke of Lancaster, was the constable of Lincoln castle and the king's chief minister, and was held mainly responsible for the wars. He and his mistress, Katharine Swynford, kept a house in the city. Dislike of the duke was widespread among all classes, and was particularly shared by the mayor of Lincoln and his bailiffs, who especially resented the independent rights of the constable to hold a market in the Bail and collect the tolls, and thereby deprive the city of much-needed income. In 1384 a mob attacked his mistress's house and her servants and overturned market stalls in the Bail. Katharine accused the mayor, Robert de Saltby, and the city bailiffs of leading and organising the attack. Three years earlier the peasants of Kent, marching through London behind Wat Tyler, had burnt down the duke's palace, the Savoy, and made it clear that they would have killed him, along with the Archbishop of Canterbury, had they been able to catch him. If Katharine Swynford's accusation was correct then Robert de Saltby and his bailiffs appear to have been attempting to exploit this popular dislike of the duke for their own ends, and were perhaps hoping also to divert some of the local resentment away from themselves.

Another sign of the town's decline was the dilapidated state of the guildhall. By 1390 it had had to be taken down, but progress in building a new hall, on the same site, was extremely slow. In that year the king wrote to the mayor to demand that the new hall be built quickly. It is clear from the letter that the mayor's problem was yet again the unwillingness of the city's taxpayers to meet the expense. The king ordered him to compel the citizens to do their duty, and to allow no exceptions. He knew, he said, that certain citizens:

Reckoning naught of honesty and advantage to the city, but with evil mind cleaving rather to their own will are refusing to contribute to the building thereof.

The mayor was once again in a difficult position; caught between the demands of his monarch and the seething resentment of his fellow townsmen. The latter, however, were much closer at hand and he would seem to have once again decided to exert rather less forceful persuasion in raising the necessary sums than the king's letter called for. Three years later the king was again demanding to know why more progress had not been made, but to no better effect, and the new guildhall – today known as the Stonebow – would not be completed until the early years of the 16th century.

The decline in the city's trade inevitably meant a fall in the annual revenues of the city, but the taxation owing to the king, the city's farm, still had to be paid, and the city's bailiffs were personally liable for the payment. To help spread the burden it was agreed in 1378 that the number of bailiffs should be increased from two to three, and in 1401 it was felt necessary to increase the number to four. As the financial burdens of office increased it is hardly surprising to find allegations of corruption, particularly that officials were pocketing funds that were supposed to be spent on repairing the city

walls, paving the streets or building a new guildhall. Other prominent citizens sought to escape office either by buying from the mayor a right of permanent exemption from office, a practice that a number of mayors in the 1370s and 1380s found most lucrative, or by leaving the area of the city under the mayor's jurisdiction and moving instead into the Close, a practice calculated to inflame relations between the city authorities and the dean and chapter.

Relations between the city authorities and the Close reached their lowest point in the last years of the 14th century. Resentments that had long simmered now boiled over. The chief complaint was that the inhabitants of the Close refused to pay anything towards the city's taxes and yet the dean and chapter allowed rival markets to be set up in the Close and took for themselves the tolls chargeable on the stalls. Numerous violent attacks on the clergy, and on merchants setting up stalls in the Close, prompted the dean to seek redress in the royal courts, claiming that it was impossible for the cathedral authorities to have justice in the borough courts as citizens would not bear witness against one another. On one occasion, in 1382, the dean complained that he and his canons had been personally threatened and that damage done to goods in his market was valued at over £100. Attacks continued, however, even after the king had threatened to fine the city £1,000 if the assaults did not cease. In January 1394, for instance, it was alleged that:

> Evildoers lately leagued together and came to the cathedral church of St Mary of Lincoln, assaulted and maimed several clerks and ministers of the church, besides servants of the canons and other lieges, in the church and its cemetery ... and so polluted both church and cemetery that divine service that Christmas ceased, and still continued unperformed.

It was during this long and unpleasant dispute that King Richard II visited the city with his queen and presented the mayor, John Sutton, with a splendid sword to be carried in procession on ceremonial occasions. The sword can still be seen today in the Stonebow and is still used for ceremonial occasions. The arms of Richard's grandfather, Edward III, are engraved on the pommel. In modern parlance, it would seem that Richard had embarked upon a charm offensive in an effort to win the support of a number of cities as he was already engaged in a struggle with the Lancastrian faction. Before arriving in Lincoln he had recently presented similar swords to the cities of Chester and York. Richard was well aware of the disputes in the city and was careful to give offence to no one. Therefore, he graciously allowed himself and Queen Anne to be admitted by the bishop and chapter, in a ceremony in the chapter house, as 'brother and sister' of the cathedral.

62   *The Stonebow as it appears today. The lower sections were completed in about 1400, but the upper storey was not built until the early 16th century.*

The Fifteenth Century

By 1400 Lincoln was in a sorry state and a mere shadow of its former self. Many houses stood empty and abandoned, some parishes were completely deserted, and the city had shrunk almost to a one-street town of perhaps no more than 3,000 people. Recurrent outbreaks of the plague prevented any recovery of population and, hardly surprisingly, by the 1390s the city authorities were trying hard to persuade Parliament and the king that the city could no longer afford its annual farm. Petitions were presented to Parliament in 1396 and again in 1399, but the first success only came in 1409. The farm was not reduced, but the king granted the city a new status – that of a county in its own right – with the power to hold new courts that would meet every six weeks, with jurisdiction over the city, presided over by justices of the peace

63 The royal arms engraved on the pommel of the sword presented by King Richard II in 1387, which is still kept on display in the Stonebow.

elected by the 'commonalty' of twenty-four. This would bring in a little more income as the justices were empowered to keep the profits of justice – the goods of convicted felons and the fines imposed for less serious offences – for the city's coffers. Perhaps more significant for the city's revenues, however, was a second concession: the right to hold a second fair. This would be dedicated to St Hugh and begin on St Hugh's feast day, 17 November, and continue for 15 days.

Such was the continuing sad decline of the city, however, that appeals for reductions or outright exemptions from royal taxes continued and finally, in 1434, the city's plight was recognised. In that year the annual taxation paid to the Exchequer was cut by a half. In 1436 it had to be cut again, also by half, and in 1437 the city was exempted altogether. During the next 15 years the city would be exempted from taxation on six further occasions. It was probably with sincere gratitude, therefore, that it was decided in 1446 that on the occasion of King Henry VI's visit to the city the citizens should meet the king outside the city and, kneeling reverently before him, offer him the surprisingly generous gift of £100 in gold. The procession was led by the 'respectable and better dressed citizens', following the mayor and aldermen, on horseback, while the common folk followed on foot.

The king had also been generous in granting Lincoln's merchants the right to tax exemptions on sales of wool shipped through Boston and Hull, and no doubt the city hoped that its display of humble gratitude would yield similar concessions. This proved to be the case. In the next few years Henry granted exemptions from both the 'tenths' and 'fifteenths' tax, further rights to tax exemptions on wool sales, and lucrative rights to buy property for the city in adjoining manors. Further tax concessions were obtained from Henry's successor, Edward IV, soon after he had deposed Henry in 1461. Five years later a new charter was granted to the city allowing it to incorporate the parishes of Canwick, Bracebridge, Branston and Waddington, and in 1472 the city was once again exempted from paying its annual farm to the Exchequer.

The need for such generous treatment had been clearly demonstrated by a survey of the city conducted in 1428. This had found that four of the city's parishes had no inhabitants at all and 17 others contained no more than 10 persons each. The Wigford area was particularly deserted; three of its parishes were completely devoid of inhabitants. As the century progressed the situation did not improve. Appeals for tax exemptions frequently complain of the 'long-continued pestilence' and the flight of merchants and craftsmen from the city, and they would seem to be quite genuine. In 1457 it was reported that the plague had returned yet again and had pushed mortality rates up to a level not seen since the Black Death. When Edward IV's charter was granted in 1466 it referred to 'the desolation and decay of the city, the ruin of houses, and the poverty and paucity of the inhabitants'. When Richard III made further concessions in 1484 it was, he declared, 'in consideration of the speedy remedy that their city then stood in need of to prevent its utter ruin'. By now there were probably only about two thousand inhabitants.

64 *A much-restored late-medieval house, now the* Green Dragon. *This was originally a wealthy wool merchant's house and is thought to date from the 14th century. It was located conveniently close to Thorn Bridge, the site of the 14th-century wool staple.*

65 *A 15th-century merchant's house, later known as the Cardinal's Hat, in honour of Cardinal Wolsey, who was both Dean and Bishop of Lincoln in the early 16th century. Like the* Green Dragon *(see Fig. 64 above), it is timber-framed and has three-storeys, allowing plenty of room for servants and apprentices.*

As a result of depopulation many parish churches were deserted by this time and falling into decay, and since the late 14th century it had been common for papal indulgences to be offered to penitents giving alms to assist in the maintenance of the churches of the city. By 1500 the city had lost 12 parishes altogether. In such circumstances it is not surprising to find a report stating that in 1475 there was again serious conflict between the city and the Close, but unfortunately no details are given. The 'speedy remedy' for the city's ills, of which King Richard had spoken, would prove most elusive and another 200 years would pass before the city would begin to prosper once again.

SIX

The Early Tudor City

ECONOMIC DECLINE CONTINUES

At the beginning of the Tudor period it would seem that there were only about four hundred houses still standing and occupied in the city and the situation would change little in the succeeding decades. At the time of Elizabeth's accession in 1558 there were still thought to be only about two thousand inhabitants. The city was literally falling down as houses stood empty, decayed and in need of repair. The common council repeatedly attempted to halt citizens pulling down houses and selling off the tiles and timber. Archaeological excavations in the once busy commercial area of Flaxengate and Grantham Street have shown that both streets were largely derelict by the 16th century. One 16th-century observer, William Lambarde, described 'the present estate of Lincolne' in 1584 as 'pietyfull'. His description could be applied just as appropriately to the city in the late 15th or early 16th century. He went on to say:

> For as much as it hath neither the helpe of traffique by water, nor anie handiecraft, or arte by land, the condicion thearof is little better than of a commune market towne: and if a man should judge of the inner wealthe by the outwarde viewe, he might well think that the verie ruine thearof neare at hand, if some politique devise be not ministered in time to staie and uphold it.

The importance of 'traffique by water' was well understood and in 1518 a determined attempt to clean and repair the Foss Dyke was begun. A commission of sewers was appointed to survey the canal and to oversee the appointment of dykers, with both the mayor and bishop active and committed members of it. The common council was persuaded to raise 100 marks from the citizens, Bishop Atwater contributed £100 and by May 1520 men were at work. There was considerable difficulty raising the money from the citizens, however, and additional appeals for funds had to be made in York, Hull, Torksey and other towns. Work stopped in June when the funds ran out and no more could be borrowed, but the appointment of a new mayor, Peter Effard, brought fresh impetus to the scheme. Effard himself laid out £17 and proved very adept in persuading others to contribute too, and the work started again. Both Effard and Bishop Atwater were men of considerable drive and energy, as well as wealth, and for a while there was optimism that the canal might be opened again. But then another blow struck. In February 1521 Atwater died; without his support Effard could not push the enterprise forward and it was soon afterwards abandoned. In 1529 and 1530 landowners along the canal were required to maintain their banks and clear sedge but this was not always done and complaints about the state of the canal continued throughout the century.

A powerful friend to the city at this time was Thomas Wolsey, the Lord Chancellor, who had been appointed Dean of Lincoln in 1509 and served as bishop in 1514-15, before his installation as Archbishop of York. While he was bishop he helped both the city and the guilds obtain new charters and he was probably mainly responsible for the decision at this time to undertake the repair of bridges and roads. He almost certainly leant his support to the attempt to clear the Foss Dyke and he was also probably the impetus behind the effort finally to complete the Stonebow in 1520, an achievement for which Effard was also partly responsible.

Lambarde's reference to the city lacking 'anie handiecraft or arte by land' was also accurate and sorely felt. The city had long lost its manufacturing base with the decline of the cloth trade from the early 14th century. There were still a few weavers in the city, however, and in 1551 the mayor and aldermen agreed to support a scheme to revive the trade and put the poor to work. The promoters were given a disused church to use as a dyehouse and the close at the west end of the church as a tenter ground, where the cloth could be stretched and dried. Housing was also found for the weavers and spinners and a little land set aside for their use as pasture for their animals. Local clothiers were also given help in applying for a royal licence to permit them to buy and sell wool throughout the county, to be shipped at Boston. It was hoped that the enterprise would

66   *The Guildhall over the Stonebow.*

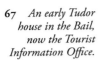

67 *An early Tudor house in the Bail, now the Tourist Information Office.*

be able to produce at least 20 broadcloths a year (high-quality, double-width cloth, dressed and dyed black, mainly for men's clothing) but very little cloth seems to have been produced at all and the scheme quickly died.

Another council initiative to promote local crafts was more successful, however. By the 1550s the council had kept a fund for many years that could be used to make small loans to local young craftsmen of any trade to help them purchase their tools and stock so that they might set up in business once they had served their apprenticeships. In 1557 it was agreed that this fund should be increased, so essential had this help become, and the mayor agreed to forego £10 of his annual salary for this purpose.

The majority of the city's craftsmen served only a local market – the surrounding villages. Although it was a county town with political, ecclesiastical and judicial importance, it was by now no larger than other market towns in the county. Of the 35 crafts listed in the council's apprenticeship records between 1511 and 1541, the most prominent and most successful were the leatherworkers. The cordwainers apprenticed 20 boys; the glovers 20; and the tanners 17, but surprisingly, only one saddler's apprentice is recorded. The leather trades were clearly flourishing in these years and Lincoln enjoyed a good supply of raw material from those areas of the county specialising in livestock farming. The town's glovers may have had a particularly high reputation; the records show that they attracted apprentice boys from an unusually wide area. Eight of the boys came from between 50 and 150 miles. Among other trades that were apparently doing well were those of the metalworkers. During these 30 years the smiths took on 18 apprentices, the braziers 12 and the pewterers nine. Mercers and tailors also benefited from the relatively large numbers of gentry, ecclesiastics and other wealthy people who continued to live either in the city or the surrounding area. Eighteen apprentices were taken on by the mercers and 15 by the tailors. The food trades also seem to have been moderately successful. The bakers enrolled 17 apprentices and the butchers eight.

However, the figures for the cloth-manufacturing industry confirm the sad state of this trade. Only three weavers, three fullers and two dyers were enrolled as apprentices in 30 years. The building trades were in a similarly depressed state. Very few new houses were being built and the demand for apprentices was correspondingly low: just four tilers, four carpenters and one sawyer were taken on. Only repair work and maintenance were needed.

Given the relatively impoverished state of the city throughout this period it is hardly surprising to find that one of the chief concerns for the mayor and his council was always the annual fee or farm tax. The city's annual farm had been fixed at £180 in the 12th century, when the city had been both more populous and more prosperous, and it is an indication of the city's decline that in the 16th century it struggled to make a payment of barely half this amount. The Crown had alienated its right to collect this sum in the 15th century and at the beginning of the Tudor era payment was due instead to the dean and chapter of the cathedral (£80) and to the family of Lord Ros (£100). Recognising the city's problems, Henry VII had obliged the Ros family to accept a substantially reduced payment of 20 marks. The dean and chapter were still paid in full, however, and from the early 1520s the new baron demanded that he, too, should be paid in full. The dispute dragged on for many years with the council constantly protesting its poverty and agreeing only to pay the 20 marks agreed in the 1490s. To mollify the Earl of Rutland (as the 12th Baron Ros became in 1525) and his successors, it was necessary to allow the family influence over council appointments and the election of members of Parliament. Gifts were also made to the family, usually of fish, although in 1553 a huge cask containing over 250 gallons of claret was delivered instead. In 1544 Henry VIII was persuaded to help the city by allowing it to appropriate the benefices

68 *The banner of the Lincolnshire Rising.*

of certain former church properties to make the payments. A settlement was eventually agreed in 1558 by granting the earl the parsonage of Surfleet and a payment of £300, but the 3rd Earl renewed the dispute and a final settlement was only reached in 1574, with another £300 payment.

For many years the city's poverty meant that it was also successful in obtaining exemption from national taxation: the payment of fifteenths and tenths. In 1541, however, Henry VIII's government decided that the city could now afford to pay and demanded taxes in arrears as well. The city was ordered to pay £400 over the next four years. In order to meet this demand it petitioned the king to relieve it of the £80 levy payable every year to the dean and chapter of the cathedral. With support from the Duke of Suffolk, who was himself now a great Lincolnshire landowner, the council managed to obtain Henry's agreement to at least a substantial reduction, just one month before he died, in January 1547.

REFORMATION AND REBELLION

For Lincoln, the Reformation meant chiefly the dissolution of the city's various monastic establishments, a process that began in 1538. Two years earlier, however, the dissolution of a number of minor monastic houses in the county, unpopular taxation demands and a widespread fear that the possessions of the parish churches were threatened had prompted many thousands of Lincolnshire folk to march on Lincoln in protest against the changes. This 'pilgrimage of grace', as the rebels would later style it, had begun with an impassioned sermon in Louth parish church on the evening of Sunday 1 October, by the vicar, Thomas Kendall, denouncing the recent religious changes and voicing his fears of future developments. By the following Friday an 'army' of perhaps 40,000 unarmed or lightly armed men and women had arrived at Lincoln. A few may have found lodgings in the city, among a population sympathetic to their cause, but the great majority camped just outside, at Myle Cross. Local gentry who had joined the rising, often somewhat reluctantly, mainly found lodgings in the Close. Articles of grievances were drawn up by the gentry, including criticism of the king's chief minister, Thomas Cromwell, and sent to the king. The common folk busied themselves making banners and grew increasingly impatient with the gentry, who they correctly believed to be half-hearted at best in their support for the enterprise. A few of the more militant, assisted by a number of local sympathisers, attacked and sacked the bishop's palace. Bishop Longland's support for the recent church reforms had made him a despised enemy in the eyes of the rebels and he was fortunate to be out of the city at this time. A few days earlier the rebels had already drawn their first blood, beating to death Dr Raynes, the bishop's chancellor, just outside Horncastle, as well as hanging his servant. Dr Raynes had gone to Bolingbroke the previous Saturday to inspect the local clergy and address them on the beliefs of the new Church of England and their new responsibilities to preach against the authority of the pope. His servant might have been spared had he not been unfortunate enough to have the same name as the king's former chief minister, Thomas Wolsey.

Many of the common folk were keen to leave Lincoln and march south towards London, especially when they received word early in the next week from Halifax and Beverley that the people of Yorkshire were equally incensed by recent developments and also on the brink of

organising their own rebellion. The gentry, however, were
anxious to avoid an armed conflict and managed
to persuade the commons to wait until they
had received the king's reply to their articles of
grievance. And it came remarkably quickly. At
about three o'clock on the Tuesday, while the
gentry were debating their next steps in the
Chapter House of the cathedral, a servant
burst in with the king's response. It was not
what either the gentry or the commons had
hoped to hear. Henry was clearly furious
and there would be no concessions. He
ordered the rebels to return home, to
deliver up their leaders, and submit to
punishment. He answered each of their
grievances and was particularly incredulous
that they should dare to question his choice
of bishops and ministers:

> How presumptuous, then, are ye, the rude
> commons of one shire, and that one of the
> most brute and beastly of the whole
> realm, and of least experience, to find
> fault with your prince.

69 *Lord Hussey, the only member
of the local aristocracy executed for his
role in the Lincolnshire Rising.*

The 'rude commons' who were gathered
together in the Chapter House with the gentry
to hear this reply reacted with fury, exacerbated by the continuing insistance of the
gentry that they must not march south. A bizarre debate between different groups of the
commons then ensued in the adjoining cloisters of the cathedral while the gentry were
kept in the Chapter House. More moderate elements argued that it would be better to
give the gentry one more day to change their minds, but extremists urged that they had
betrayed them and must be killed immediately. Nothing could be agreed and this group
then made their way to the west entrance, planning to set upon the gentry as they left
the cathedral. However, once again they would be frustrated. Someone tipped the gentry
off and while the commons waited impatiently for their quarry outside the great west
entrance, the gentry made their escape through the south door of the Chapter House and
fled to the Chancery.

The following morning the gentry, fully armed and on horseback, met the commons
and announced their determination to submit to the king's will. Even the most
militant now had to accept that their rebellion had failed, for the great majority of
the common folk were ready to return home and few believed they could continue
without the leadership of the gentry. By the time the king's letter arrived, on the Friday,
accepting their submission, very few of the rebels were still in the city. Henry ordered

that all armour and weapons be surrendered and left in the marketplace in the city. Meanwhile, the Duke of Suffolk made all haste to Lincoln to collect the weapons, round up the ringleaders and begin the interrogations. During the next few weeks more than 140 prisoners were brought to the city and placed in the castle to await their fate. A select few 'notable offenders' were despatched to London for further questioning and punishment, and a few were hanged in Louth and Horncastle as a warning to those towns. Most of those who were condemned, however, were hanged at Lincoln during February and March. The exact number is not known and some may have died in prison. The last victim, Lord Hussey (a major Lincolnshire landowner with estates near Sleaford), was condemned as a traitor for his failure to take firm action against the rebels and was executed in the summer of 1537. According to local tradition he was hanged from a window in St Mary's Guildhall, close to the townhouse of the mayor, Robert Sutton. Henry VIII was keen to make an example of a few of the gentry who he felt had shown insufficient loyalty. Another gentleman-victim was the recorder of Lincoln, Thomas Moigne, a lawyer and an important member of the city council who had also represented the city in Parliament a few years before. At his trial in the castle he argued his defence most eloquently, claiming that he had been forced by the Louth rebels to join the rebellion at Caistor and remained with it only to act as a moderating influence. His prominent role in the rebellion had caused him to become a target for the prosecution, however, and he was condemned to suffer the horrible penalty reserved for traitors; to be hanged, drawn and quartered.

The public execution of Hussey prompted a final, minor disturbance in the city, but the dissolution of the city's own monastic houses, only a year later, passed without any protest. The Gilbertine priory of St Katherine was the first to be surrendered, in July 1538. The prior had been accused of supporting the rebellion but he received a pension of £40, and the 13 canons were also pensioned off. The four friaries were the next to go, but all were reported to be already much dilapidated, and finally the Monks Abbey,

70   *Monks Abbey today.*

a tiny community under the authority of the Benedictine Abbey of St Mary of York. A small fragment of the building survives today just to the north of Monks' Road. The abbot himself had recently complained about the conduct of his brethren at Lincoln – a prior and two monks – but still tried hard to save it, refuting Cromwell's allegations that there was 'no hospitality kept, nor God Almighty served, nor any religious order'. The common council had hoped that it might be granted some of the properties and the city's financial plight was again cited as an argument for such a concession. Its only acquisition, however, was the Greyfriars' water supply, complete with its conduit. A new conduit, which still stands, was then built besides the church of St Mary le Wigford using stone taken from a chantry chapel that was demolished a few years later.

The treasures of the cathedral were the next to go, and the first item on the royal list was the shrine of St Hugh, much coveted by the Crown for its gold and jewels. The cathedral's relic collection was also removed, together with communion plate, a great deal of jewels, gold and silver, copes embroidered with pearls and other rich vestments. The royal orders for this despolation, issued in June 1540, explained that 'divers feigned relics', such as those held by the cathedral, were the cause of 'simple people (being) much deceived and brought into great superstition and idolatry'.

Just a year later the city council received news that King Henry himself was to visit the city and stay at the bishop's palace. The city still lay under the shadow of the rising, and the visit was therefore greeted with great anxiety. However impoverished the city might be, and whatever local feelings might be about the recent plundering of the cathedral, it was recognised that splendid gifts must be made to atone for past sins and to purchase (hopefully) future concessions. Twenty fat oxen and 100 fat muttons would be presented to the king, and a fine collection of fish – pike, bream and tench – would be given to his new young queen, the ill-fated Katherine Howard. The city itself also needed to be cleaned up for the event. Dung hills and other filth had to be removed and the streets swept clean. The royal coat of arms was set up over Bargate and Stonebow to proclaim the city's loyalty and the aldermen purchased scarlet and crimson gowns for themselves.

The royal party was met, as was customary, outside the city by the mayor

71   *The conduit erected outside
St Mary le Wigford.*

and fellow councillors kneeling before the king and queen and humbly presenting to the king the city's mace, the symbol of the mayor's authority, which he immediately returned. The party then proceeded through the city to the palace, led by the mayor on horseback, carrying the mace. To the city's great relief the visit passed without incident, but only a few months later Archbishop Cranmer presented the king with a paper accusing the queen of serious misconduct both before and after her marriage, and her conduct during the royal stay at the bishop's palace – alleged to be flirtatious and grossly inappropriate – was cited in the evidence against her. Many of the gentry who had been pardoned for their role in the rising were present at the royal banquet held in the palace, and at the queen's subsequent trial they were called to give evidence against her.

Shortly before the king's death, plans were drawn up for the dissolution of chantry chapels and for the suppression of religious guilds. Henry's death necessitated the introduction of fresh legislation by the new government, but on this occasion the common council managed to ensure that the city would benefit. In November 1547 it launched a pre-emptive strike. Just a month before the new Act became law the council made arrangements for the properties belonging to the Great Guild of St Mary to be transferred to the city's possession, and ordered the jewels, plate and ornaments belonging to its sister organisation, the guild of St Anne, to be sold off and the proceeds paid to the council. St Mary's guild had been long defunct, but St Anne's guild had until quite recently organised the very popular annual St Anne's procession to the cathedral and the mystery plays outside the west front. It was perhaps sadly fitting that in the same year as the guild's demise a great storm blew down the great spire on the central tower of the cathedral.

The last years of Henry VIII's reign also saw the disappearance of a number of parish churches, victims not of central government reform but of continuing population decline and consequent dereliction. In 1541 the common council ordered that the church of St Peter at Pleas should be taken down and its lead, ornaments and bells sold off. This ancient church stood in the centre of the city, just to the north of the Stonebow, and close to the pre-conquest mootstone, the site of the meetings of the original burwarmot. The parishioners were assigned to other parishes. Other derelict churches

72 *The bishop's palace, as it appears today.*

were soon also being taken down and their stone, timber, tiles, lead and other valuables sold off. The church of St John in Newport was the next to go, followed by St Stephen in Newland, and the chapel on the High Bridge was converted into a house and let. It was realised, however, that a less piecemeal approach was required and in 1549 the council petitioned Parliament for permission to carry out a comprehensive programme of church closures and reassignment of parishioners to enlarged and united parishes. The petition was carefully phrased to win the approval of Edward VI's Protestant government. The livings of many churches, it was reported, had been so reduced that only former monks and friars, keen to supplement their pensions, were willing to take them on:

> Which for the most part are unlearned and very ignorant persons not able to do any part of their duties, whereof the said city is not only replenished with blind guides and pastors, but also the people very much kept in ignorance and blindness as well of their duties towards Almighty God as also the king's majesty their sovereign lord and the commonwealth of this realm and to the great danger of their souls.

The necessary statute was passed in May 1549 and within a year the union of parishes was complete. Every church yielding a living of less than £14 per year was closed down and demolished – all money raised was to be used to enlarge and repair surviving churches, to repair the city's bridges, or for the relief of the poor. Approximately two-thirds of the city's medieval churches had been demolished by the summer of 1550; only 14 still remained.

The dean and chapter also lost numerous properties, as did the diocese, and in the surviving churches the parishioners faced a bewilderingly rapid series of changes. Church walls were whitewashed, their altars and ornaments were removed, services were now to be said in English and the clergy were encouraged to marry. And then, with the death of the young King Edward in 1553 and the accession of his Catholic elder sister, Mary, everything changed again. In Mary's equally short reign (she died of cancer in 1558) England returned to the Catholic fold, the authority of the pope was restored, married clergy were removed, including Bishop Taylor and the dean, Matthew Parker (who would later serve as Archbishop of Canterbury under Elizabeth), altars and ornaments returned, rood lofts were re-erected, and the Catholic mass was again celebrated.

The Guilds

The city's craftsmen all had to be members of the appropriate guild. By the early years of the 16th century, however, the long decline in the city's fortunes necessitated an amalgamation of some guilds as for many crafts the number of masters was now too small to maintain separate organisations. Apart from the weavers and the cordwainers, who held separate charters directly from the Crown, all other crafts came under the control of the common council. Following Henry VIII's confirmation of the city's charter in 1515 the common council invited the guilds to draw up new rules for the council's approval; numerous crafts took this opportunity to amalgamate their guilds. Thus the smiths, ironmongers, armourers, spurriers, cutlers and wire-drawers came together to form one guild, and the glovers, girdlers, skinners, pinners, point-makers, scriveners and parchment makers formed another.

Only those who had served an apprenticeship to a master, and proved his skill in the craft, could become a journeyman, and only after a few more years and the payment of a fee could he then set himself up as a master. Most apprenticeships were for seven, eight or nine years and a master rarely took on more than one apprentice at a time. Apprenticeships were a useful form of cheap labour for the masters, but it was not in their interest to create too many and have a surplus of skilled labour. Rules for the control of journeymen were designed to protect the master from either losing skilled labour or from having to pay excessively to keep it. A master was forbidden to entice a journeyman away from another master, and any journeyman who left his master's employment while the master still wished to employ him would be blacklisted and forbidden to work in the craft again. A master who did employ such a man would be fined heavily. Maximum wages were also fixed and it was forbidden to give work out to a journeyman at home, unless he was sick.

The guilds were closely supervised by the mayor and common council. When a poor tailor set up as a master but could not afford the setting-up fee the head of the guild, the graceman, was told to give him time to pay. Searchers were appointed to report to the mayor and justices any complaints regarding butchers, fishermen, cordwainers and tanners, and the mayor appointed auditors for all the town's guilds. The prices of bread and ale and other essential items were also controlled. This was seen as extremely important if bread riots were to be avoided at a time of violently fluctuating corn prices. The assize of bread varied from year to year. Between 1513 and 1518, for instance, it varied between 5s. and 8s. 6d. per quarter of wheat; in June 1520 it was 12s. 6d. and in 1522 it rose to 24s., but the following year was down to 5s. The price of ale varied rather less, being at different times set at 2d., 2½d. and 3d. a gallon. During the 1550s and 1560s attempts were also made to control the price of other items of particular importance to the poor, including candles, thatch and turf, and firewood.

The guilds were at the heart of much of the social and religious life of the city. As well as craft guilds there were also religious guilds, whose principal function was to organise annual religious processions,

73 *A mason and carpenter making their test pieces, or masterpieces, before the warden of the guild; from a 15th-century Flemish manuscript.*

mystery plays and pageants. In the 1520s there still existed at least three such guilds: those of St Anne, St George, and Corpus Christi. Every craft guild, however, was also expected to play a role in the annual processions through the town, the most important of which was held on St Anne's day. Each guild had to produce a pageant for the procession and each had a special task. The tilers, for instance, had to supply the men who would play the part of the kings and by tradition the cordwainers always contributed the pageant of Bethlehem.

The plays were known as 'mysteries' because it was the crafts (also known as 'mysteries') which performed them, with each craft responsible for a play most appropriate for their skills. During the Corpus Christi plays, for instance, the gardeners might put on the play about the Creation and the Fall of Adam, while the butchers would be responsible for *The Massacre of the Innocents*. A play was always put on to celebrate St Anne's day; in 1521, for instance, the Paternoster Play was performed. Other processions, complete with pageants and plays, were also organised, for the Feast of Corpus Christi, the Feast of St George and Ascension Day. The plays would be performed on a central stage in front of the cathedral, with a number of smaller stages (or scaffolds) at either side.

Every freeman and free woman in the city was expected to play his or her part in both plays and processions. Consequently, as well as their craft members, most of the guilds also had, as part of their membership, 'outbrothers' and 'outsisters' who did not follow the craft but played a full role in the religious life of the guilds. They might be wives, priests or members of the common council. Every alderman, for instance, was expected to supply silk gowns for the kings in the nativity pageant and a servant in clerical vestments carrying a flaming torch to accompany the sacrament. The St Anne's procession was also a civic occasion in which the mayor processed while attended by a sword bearer carrying the sword given by Richard II, and a mace bearer, while the two sheriffs were attended by two axe bearers. Also in the procession were the civic musicians, known as the waits, dressed in the city liveries and chains of office.

Outbrothers and outsisters also took part in the very ancient annual procession at Pentecost, from the chapel of St Thomas on the High Bridge to the cathedral, to make the guild's traditional offerings of a farthing for each member. Each paid a small annual contribution to the guild plus a small additional fee – soulscot – on the death of any fellow members, to help meet the funeral expenses.

With the city's continuing decline the expense of participating in the processions may have dimmed the enthusiasm of many of Lincoln's citizens by the 1520s, for the city council found it necessary to issue various threats of fines on any who failed to fulfil their customary commitments. The guilds were informed, for instance, that any trade that failed to put on a good show risked the very considerable fine of £10. Poverty and population decline meant that the number and size of processions and pageants was probably already rather smaller than it had been in the previous two centuries. One very important guild in earlier times, which had played a major role in the processions, was the Great Guild of St Mary. It had once been the guild of the leading merchants and occupied the guildhall that still stands today near the church of St Peter at Gowts in Wigford, but by the 1520s it was no longer able to meet its expenses and an attempt to revive it does not seem to have been successful. The recurrent threat of the plague also sometimes made it difficult to persuade the gentry of the surrounding countryside to supply the cloaks required. This was certainly the excuse given for their reluctance in both 1515 and 1521 when there were outbreaks of the plague in the city.

The biblical pageants and mystery plays would not survive for many more years. In 1537, the year after the Lincolnshire Rebellion, the bishop banned most annual feasts and holy days throughout his diocese, including patronal festivals such as St Anne's and harvest holidays. Many saw this, no doubt, as the bishop's revenge for the events of 1536, and particularly for the attack on his palace. Following the accession of Mary Tudor the pageants briefly appeared once more, and the Corpus Christi play was also briefly revived, but after the accession of Elizabeth they swiftly died out again. Although the craft guilds would survive, their importance in the life of the city was now substantially diminished and would never recover. Four hundred years later, however, in 1978, Lincoln followed York in reviving a production of the mystery plays, and these have been performed every year ever since.

POVERTY, LAW AND DISORDER

Poor harvests and consequent high prices for beans, oats, barley and rye, the staple foodstuffs of the poor, invariably brought more impoverished and pauperised families into the city, and with them sturdy beggars and vagabonds. Fear of the desperate, rootless and lawless vagabonds would be a constant feature of Tudor England. Vagrancy legislation of the 1530s spoke of violent 'beggars' going about in 'great routs and companies' and threatened them with the stocks and with floggings until their backs be 'bloody'. In June 1512 it was fear of the able-bodied poor that prompted the common council in Lincoln to order that the constables should draw up lists of all the able-bodied men in their parishes. Five years later, acting in compliance with recent vagrancy laws, the council instructed the constables to search out and list any idle men or women in their parishes who would not work and to bring the list to the mayor and his fellow councillors. The following year the unemployed in the city were brought before the mayor by the constables and either put to work or forced to leave the city. Watches were also ordered for vagabonds who might commit robberies and numerous unfortunates from outside the city were arrested for begging and placed in the stocks before being sent on their way.

During the next 30 years the situation for the poor grew worse. During the 1530s and 1540s numerous bad harvests frequently pushed up cereal prices to famine levels and caused much rural unemployment. A pillory was set up in St Benedict's parish as a deterrent to sturdy beggars, but the first record of the council making any distinction between the deserving and the undeserving poor did not come until 1544. In that year the council agreed that the deserving, impotent poor, who had not come recently into the city, could be licensed to beg. The task of granting licenses, in the form of badges which the poor would display, was given to the justices of the peace. Apart from a little financial help to craftsmen to set up in business, however, very little was done to find work for the local unemployed until 1551, when four aldermen attempted to re-establish the cloth trade and employ 'all idle people'. Like many similar schemes elsewhere, however, this was not successful and the attempt was soon abandoned. It is

74   *A sturdy beggar being whipped through the town, a common sight in Lincoln in the 16th century.*

unlikely that many of the paupers had the necessary skills, and competition from well-established centres would also have proved a major obstacle. Meanwhile, the struggle to expel the vagabonds went on. In 1547 the city was divided up into wards and an alderman assigned to each with the task of expelling from the city 'all valiant vagabonds, strong beggars and idle suspicious persons'.

Excessive consumption of alcohol and the playing of unlawful games, such as football, cricket and hockey, had also long been recognised as causes of disorder. In an attempt to enforce the ancient ban on such rowdy and dangerous sports it was announced in 1547 that anyone caught indulging in them would be put in the stocks, and the town crier (known then as the bellman) proclaimed the news throughout the city while every curate was instructed to also read the instructions out in church. Anxiety about the rowdiness in ale houses – usually described as 'tippling houses' – at Christmas time, had meant that brewers were banned from delivering ale to the tipplers at this time of the year, and in 1553 it was decided that there were far too many tippling houses in both the city and the suburbs. In future, no more than 30 would be allowed. They were described by the proclamation of 1553 as causing 'much idleness and evil rule'. Bribery and petty crime were said to thrive in the tippling houses and from this time on the tipplers who ran them would have to convince the justices that they kept 'good order and good rule' and allowed no unlawful games.

SEVEN

The Elizabethan and Jacobean City

CONTINUING ECONOMIC GLOOM

There are some indications that during the second half of the 16th century the gentry of Lincoln enjoyed a modest improvement in their economic position. The evidence for this survives today, partly in the number of attractive and large half-timbered houses dating from this period that can still be seen on the High Bridge, in the High Street, on Castle Hill and in the Strait. Inventories from the late 16th century also indicate the wealth and lifestyle of the more affluent.

There would seem, however, to have been little or no 'trickle down' effect to the poorer classes and certainly no general economic revival. The cloth trade could not be re-established and although Lincoln merchants were active in the growing Yorkshire woollen industry at the end of the century their efforts were considerably hampered by the lack of reliable, cheap water transport. Attempts to scour the Foss Dyke and make it navigable were at best intermittent. In 1571 there were complaints that timber, thatch and turf were too expensive due to the lack of water transport. In 1617 James I leant his support to renewed efforts to clear the waterway but little was achieved and the commissioner for sewers described the canal in 1622 as:

> This Ditch (which) is at this day a current and passage for Boats of small burthen in Winter, but in Summer none at all; though of late great sums hath been expended thereupon.

The Foss Dyke would remain ineffective as a commercial route until the 1670s, but poor communications were not the only impediment to economic growth. The depressed state of its surrounding hinterland also prevented the city's expansion as a trading centre and repeated severe outbreaks of the plague from the 1580s to the 1640s were a recurring cause of poverty and a brake on population growth.

The population may have grown slightly during the century. A survey of the number of families in 10 of Lincoln's parishes, completed in 1567, suggests a population of about 2,300 (about three hundred more than in 1500) and by the beginning of the 17th century it was probably a little higher still. A recent estimate puts the population by 1661 at about three thousand five hundred. But population growth is not necessarily

75   *High Bridge café today; a fine timber-framed house, built for a wealthy family in the 16th century.*

an indication of economic growth and well-being. In Lincoln, as in other towns in the county at this time, it is more probably an indication of the city authorities' failure to either prevent the immigration of impoverished country dwellers into the city or to successfully expel them when they had been detected.

Vagrancy, Poverty and Poor Relief

A determination to seek out and expel any poor people who should be relieved elsewhere was a major concern for the mayor and the common council throughout this period. The first reference in the council records to an overseer of the poor occurs as early as 1560. His duties included, from the outset, ensuring that the Bargates were shut and 'sparred' against beggars, and punishing and expelling vagabonds and 'strange beggars'. A search was made every month for anyone who had not been born in the city or had not lived in it for at least three years and had no apparent means of earning a living. The city had been divided into wards for this purpose in 1547, with each ward under the supervision of an alderman. It was the responsibility of the alderman to determine the punishment of those caught 'according to statute', which would usually mean expulsion preceded by a whipping.

Attempts to set the city's own poor to work also continued to be made. The project of 1551 had been an expensive failure (*see above* p.89) and nothing similar was attempted again until 1578 when the council agreed to set up a 'house of industry' under the supervision of the 'master of the poor', with a stock of hemp and wool provided to employ the poor of all the city's parishes. No more, however, is heard of this and the scheme may also have come to nothing. However, in 1596 yet another attempt was made, and this may have been more successful. William Marrett, from the island of Jersey, offered to set up a spinning and knitting workshop in the city and the council gladly let him have ground-floor rooms in the former Greyfriars' building, while the chapel upstairs was used as a boys' grammar school. Marrett's workshop became known as the 'Jersey school' and similar schemes established later elsewhere in the county would often be given the same name.

To raise the money needed to finance poor relief, the city council was obliged to rely heavily on the income from rents from property left to the council in various charitable bequests. Seven such bequests made between 1566 and 1653 totalled more than £1,140. Some allowed the council complete discretion in how the money was spent, but others were specifically for the relief of the poor of particular parishes, or to maintain a small number of widows, apprentice poor children to a local tradesman or craftsman, or to be used as loans to help young men start up in business, or buy fuel for the poor. Such bequests could not, however, meet the full costs of poor relief. A series of statutes from 1551 gave city authorities the right to collect voluntary contributions from their citizens for this purpose, and urged priests and bishops to use all their persuasive powers on those who refused to give alms to the poor. Systematic parish collections, under the control of the churchwardens, seem to have begun by about 1570, and before the end of the century they operated in all the city's parishes. The names of those who defaulted were collected and presented to the mayor. The introduction of the compulsory parish rate, by the Elizabethan Poor Law of 1601, was therefore only the next logical step.

The distribution of alms was left to the churchwardens of the different parishes, and usually consisted of small sums of money, fuel and clothing, but the common council occasionally made additional gifts, particularly at Christmas and during the winter months, when conditions were most desperate for the poor. One Christmas six poor men were given gowns bearing the city's coat of arms, and on another occasion 20 chalder of coal was brought from Newcastle to be sold at a special rate to the poor. Any freemen who could afford it were encouraged to buy wood, coal, thatch and turf to be sold in winter to the poor to help them cook, keep warm and patch up their hovels.

Widespread concern in the city about the problems of vagrancy and pauperism was mixed with considerable anger about

A Soap-eater, copied from a rare print of the time of Queen Elizabeth

A Tom of Bedlam copied from a old Drawing of the time of Edw: 6 in the possession of Fran: Douce Esq

Copied from a Drawing of the time of Henry VII in the possession of Francis Douce, Esq.

76 *Various types of beggars, copied from 16th-century drawings.*

what many saw as the chief cause of the problems: the enclosure of arable land to create pasture as the local gentry sought to benefit from relatively high wool prices. Lincolnshire and other Midlands counties were especially affected by this development in the last decades of the 16th century. The consequent loss of rural employment and the destruction of the common lands on which the poorest in village society always depended was a tangible and easily understood cause of poverty and vagrancy that all classes in Lincoln, except perhaps the gentry themselves, were quick to blame. When news reached Lincoln in May 1607 that anti-enclosure riots had broken out across the adjoining county of Northamptonshire, the poor artisans of Lincoln were quick to show their support. In the following month a large party of craftsmen and journeymen, very probably with the knowledge and connivance of the city council, marched the two miles north-west of the city to the village of Burton, where Sir Thomas Dallison was known to have enclosed his estates, and demolished his enclosure.

In the next few years the city council redoubled its efforts to both deter and expel the vagrants. In 1615 it was ordered that the 'beadle of the beggars' should patrol the parishes every day, round up any beggars and bring them to the new House of Correction, which occupied the site of Marrett's former 'knitting and spinning school' in the Greyfriars' building. The beadle was expected to use force if necessary and was therefore accompanied by the parish constables who were to be armed with halberds. A further measure, in 1619, reiterated the long-established principle that all 'strange poor' were to be kept out of the city's parishes, and stated that newcomers must prove that they were not likely to become a burden on the parish.

Initiatives designed to set the poor to work continued to enjoy little success. Marrett's scheme had clearly been wound up by 1615 and the new House of Correction seems to have quickly run into difficulties. Those who lent money to the scheme were said to have seen no profit from it and to have lost their money. In 1624 the council agreed to put more of the city's money into the scheme when a local man, Gregory Lawcock, offered to teach the poor the necessary skills of spinning, knitting and weaving woollen goods if the council gave him £20 for the necessary capital expenditure and paid him £10 per annum for his services. Very soon, however, this scheme was also failing. The council urged all inhabitants to buy a suit of clothing and a pair of stockings from Lawcock's workshop but to no effect. By 1629 this latest effort to make poor relief profitable was over, and it ended acrimoniously, with 'general dislike' between all parties. Lawcock was paid off and the council took over his looms and remaining stock. The House of Correction may not have been closed down, however, for 'setting the poor to work' remained one of the responsibilities of the overseer for the poor. Moreover, in 1634, yet another scheme was launched, and this time with the backing of the Bishop of Lincoln and capital of £400 for machinery, tools, and a stock of wool, thread, hemp and flax. Whether the Greyfriars' building was used, however, is not clear, and the scheme may have been abandoned by 1637, when the bishop's enemies alleged that the money raised for the relief of the poor had not been properly used.

A less expensive way for the council to assist the poor was to protect their ancient right to glean in the open fields after the harvest. This was a highly valued right and when farmers complained that the gleaners were damaging the fields the mayor and his council took the side of the poor. It was ordered that no pigs, sheep or cattle should be allowed on the fields after the harvest until they had been gleaned by the poor. Those who broke this rule were threatened with imprisonment and the loss of their animals.

The importance to the council of seeking out and expelling 'poore people from forraigne partes' is never in doubt in these years, but new measures adopted in 1636 suggest that the authorities had been no more successful in this respect than they were in their efforts to make poor relief profitable. This was a problem for most of the county's market towns. When, in 1636, it was heard that the Grantham council had obtained approval from the judges of assize for new rules giving them stricter penalties to deal with this, the common council wrote to Grantham to obtain a copy, and had soon drafted its own very similar measures. The problem was particularly severe during times of the plague, and ever since the 1580s, when the city and the surrounding area had been especially badly affected by it, the council had attempted to ban inhabitants from taking in strangers. The new orders now extended these powers. Some local people had clearly been profiting from the demand for very cheap accommodation. It was now ordered that in future no inhabitant could build cottages or convert barns, stables or outhouses for the use of the poor without prior permission from the mayor. Anyone who had done so in the previous seven years was now ordered to pull down the buildings or convert them back to their former use. Unfortunately, the minutes of the common council stop abruptly in 1638 and, except for a few entries, do not resume again until 1656. Therefore we do not know how effective this latest measure was.

One of the principal causes of the growth of pauperism in the late 16th and early 17th centuries was undoubtedly the continuing rise of basic food prices. In the 1590s the average price of corn was 28s. a quarter; in 1601-10 it was 30s. 5d.; in 1611-20, 36s. 9d.; in 1621-30, 34s. 7d., and in 1632-7, 42s. 10d. These averages indicate the decades of greatest hardship but they conceal individual years of peak prices when the poorest suffered famine conditions. In autumn 1622, for instance, even inferior wheat was 40s. a quarter, the price of malt doubled to 28s. and barley rose from 13s. 4d. to 23s. Prices were again at famine levels in the winter of 1630-1, and the poor were said to be surviving only on oatmeal. Even in May 1631, after farmers' surpluses had been forced on to the market by the justices, wheat was still 56s. a quarter.

THE PLAGUE YEARS

On numerous occasions the misery and distress brought by bad harvests and famine were made even more unbearable by outbreaks of the plague. And it was no coincidence that the common council's concerns over vagrancy were always greatest during years of plague. There was the suspicion that the disease was brought into the city by impoverished outside elements and, more accurately, never any doubt that plague would greatly increase the costs of poor relief.

Although the first year of Elizabeth's reign (1558) was a plague year (the third of that decade) the city thereafter remained relatively free from the disease for nearly 30 years. In 1586, however, it struck again with a vengeance. As in earlier attacks the victims and their whole families were shut up in their houses to prevent the spread of the infection.

This was often a death sentence for the family and many victims therefore tried hard to keep their illness a secret for as long as possible. After the plague had abated the common council agreed that in future it would be necessary to organise much more thorough searches for plague victims, 'there be now great and manifest presumptions of some dregs and offscourings thereof yet remaining'.

The numbers who died of the plague in the summer of 1586 are not known, but in the parish of St Peter at Gowts, where the average number of burials in a year was usually about seven or eight, the total for 1586 jumped to twenty-five. Famine conditions that year would have considerably weakened the resistance of many of the poor to the disease. Overall, 1586 was a terrible year for the county. Flooding had caused considerable devastation, drowning cattle and sheep, destroying crops and driving up food prices. The plague was reported to be raging also in Boston and Grimsby that summer, and in the following year it struck Louth, killing approximately four hundred people, or about a fifth of the population.

Most of the victims in Lincoln were almost certainly the poor, but the more wealthy knew that they, too, were in great danger. Among those who died in 1586 were at least four mayors and when the plague returned again in 1590, the victims included a judge at the Lincoln assize and a justice of the peace. There are occasional references in the minutes of the common council to the use of a pest house, but it is probable that this could accommodate only a very few victims. Although recognised as a cruel and controversial measure, the shutting up of victims with their families in their own homes remained the preferred method of limiting the spread of infection. It was not, however, a cheap solution. In 1610 it was reported that the costs of shutting up, keeping watches, and employing nurses to attend the sick and take them food and drink were such that a special, extra poor rate had to be levied on those assessed as capable of paying. It was also partly for this reason that the government excused the council the normal fifteenth and tenth taxes later that year.

The next mention of the plague occurs in 1624 and it was probably not a coincidence that the council shortly afterwards appointed a parish officer with the duty of preventing large groups of beggars from assembling in the town. The next summer it was back again – although only a dozen deaths were reported it was rumoured that the death rate was actually much higher. In 1630 it was reported that the plague was 'raging' through the city. In the parish of St Peter at Gowts the number of burials was double the average, and the death rate must have been higher still in some of the other parishes. In October Bishop Williams reported that King Charles himself had spoken to him regarding the plague in 'that most commiserable poor city of Lincoln'. Charitable collections for the relief of Lincoln and other stricken cities were begun that winter, but when the warmer weather returned again in 1631 so too did the plague, and in some of the city's parishes the death rate was even higher. In St Margaret's parish the number of burials rose to 45; usually there would be about a dozen. Typically, almost all the victims died between July and October.

Once again we do not know the total number of plague victims but it is likely that the 1630 and 1631 attacks were as deadly as any since the 14th century. The fairs had to be cancelled and all water traffic coming into the city was halted as an additional precaution. Families were again shut in and watchmen placed on the streets to make sure no one escaped. But these were the last two truly dreadful years. The plague returned to some parishes in 1640 and 1642, but the mortality rates do not appear to have been as high as in 1630-1.

CHURCH MATTERS

Elizabeth I and her closest advisors were anxious to find a 'middle-way' religious policy around which the country could unite, rather than be divided, and for many years they broadly succeeded. A clear breach was made once more with Rome when Elizabeth was declared to be the supreme governor of the national church, and many old beliefs were abandoned with the adoption of a new prayer book, satisfying all but the more puritanical Protestants. At the same time, some of the old ceremonial and vestments were kept, in the hope that moderate Catholics would also feel able to continue to worship in the parish church.

Events in Lincoln would broadly reflect the national picture. Across the country the most determined opposition to Elizabeth's changes came from the bishops, with only one bishop, Kitchin of Llandaff, agreeing to take the oath to the royal supremacy. The last Roman Catholic Bishop of Lincoln, Thomas Watson, had no intention of compromising his loyalty to the old faith. He was arrested in London in April 1559 and sent to the Tower of London. He was released after two months and then given 10 days to consider whether or not he would take the new oath. Following his refusal to do so, he was deprived of his bishopric and sent back to the Tower. It was also alleged that he and his predecessor at Lincoln, John White, had attempted to persuade their fellow bishops to excommunicate Elizabeth. He would spend the next 25 years – the rest of his life – in custody, either in the Tower or in various gaols under the authority of the new Protestant bishops. He died in Wisbech Castle Prison in October 1584.

The great majority of the clergy in both the city and the diocese subscribed, as they did in the rest of the country, and this helped ensure that there would be little opposition from the laity as well. Among those clergy who refused to take the oath, however, and who lost their positions, were the archdeacons of Lincoln and Stow, a few of the cathedral prebendaries and the master of Lincoln grammar school. Watson's successor to the see at Lincoln, Nicholas Bullingham, was a former archdeacon who, as a married man, had been deprived of his position on the accession of Mary Tudor. He was a moderate but his successor, Thomas Cooper (appointed 1571) quickly gained a reputation as a zealous persecutor of popish recusants, as did the new archdeacon appointed in 1562, John Aylmer. Like Bullingham, Aylmer had also survived the Marian persecutions by going into exile and during the years abroad had worked with John Foxe in preparing his *Book of Martyrs*.

Aylmer and Bullingham were particularly active in the 1560s in ensuring that the cathedral and all the city's churches were soon free of the 'monuments of superstition'. The churchwardens were required to report on how they had disposed of all items of furniture, vestments and vessels in their church's possession in Mary's reign, which were now regarded as superstitious. Only one return from a city parish has survived, that of St Paul's. Here it was reported that the rood screen had been taken down and burnt within a year of Elizabeth's accession, the priest had removed the

77 *John Aylmer, Archdeacon of Lincoln.*

mass book and various other items had disappeared, presumably hidden away in case the old faith returned.

The Corpus Christi play and the other plays traditionally put on by the guilds also disappeared again after their brief revival in the Marian years, condemned as remnants of a superstitious age. Popular demand, however, prompted the common council to agree to the staging of a play for two days in the summer in 1564. The play chosen, based on the Book of Tobit, from the Old Testament Apocrypha, seems to have been well received because it was staged again in 1566 and 1568. The story may have owed its popularity to its clear and comforting moral message: righteousness is rewarded with prosperity and wickedness in the end with disaster.

As few of the clergy in the parishes were licensed to preach, some being but barely literate, sermons were at first only to be heard at the cathedral. Most of the city's clergy were very poor. In spite of the earlier closure and consolidation of many parishes, some livings were worth little more than £5 a year, and St Martin's only £3 13s. 4d. It was not surprising, therefore, that such parishes failed to attract learned men. The vicar of St Martin's was 78 years old and described in a survey made by the bishop in 1576 as 'little versed in sacred learning'. It was partly to compensate for the poor quality of the city's clergy that the common council agreed in 1578 to pay for a learned preacher to give a sermon every Wednesday in one of the city's churches, as well as acting as reader at the cathedral.

Although the Act of Uniformity of 1559 had declared church attendance to be compulsory, the common council did not take any action to enforce this until 1572. It was agreed that either constables or churchwardens would tour their parishes every Sunday to check attendance at sermons and the aldermen of each ward would fine those individuals failing to attend 2d. for every sermon missed. In 1584 both attendance demands and fines were increased further; now every household had to be represented twice on Sundays and once on Wednesdays or face fines of 20d. (Sundays) and 12d. (Wednesdays) for every sermon missed.

The insistence on church attendance went hand in hand with an increasingly determined concern to enforce Sabbath observance. From the beginning of Elizabeth's reign the common council had approved regulations insisting on the closing of victuallers' shops on Sundays, or other holy days, as soon as the second peal of bells was heard summoning the faithful to morning service. Later regulations then extended the prohibition on Sunday opening. In 1584 it was decided that all shop doors and windows must be kept closed on Sundays unless wares were being brought home from the fairs. No Lincoln folk could be served by any shopkeeper or craftsman, but a passing visitor willing to buy (and heedless of his soul) could be accommodated.

Compulsory sermons and Sunday closing reflected a concern shared by many on the common council, and by some of the clergy, to raise the moral standards of the city. The influence of the archdeacon, John Aylmer, may in particular be detected. He worked closely with the mayor and some of the aldermen in putting the religious settlement into action. This increasingly puritanical attitude was also reflected in the language used and the measures taken to try to reduce drunkenness in the city from the 1560s. In 1566 a meeting of the common council's inner circle declared that:

78 *Musicians playing outside an inn.*

Many great hurts, hindrances and enormities have as late crept into the city, as well by evil rule in alehouses, as also by the continual and daily resort, long continuing, of divers and many workmen, craftsmen and labourers, in the same houses there, loitering and drinking of overstrong and mighty ale, to the increase of idleness and drunkenness.

The council resolved that all aspects of the brewers' and tipplers' trades needed the closest supervision. Only men of good reputation would receive licenses, prices and measures were specified, drinking during working hours was banned, and no brewer would be allowed to sell ale directly. By the 1580s, when questions of religious orthodoxy and allegations of popish sympathies deeply divided the council, it was claimed there had been between 140 and 160 alehouses in Lincoln at the beginning of Elizabeth's reign. By 1585, however, the number had been greatly reduced by refusing licenses to 'unfit persons'. The orthodox, anti-popish faction claimed credit for this. It had closed so many alehouses, it boasted, both 'because of their number' and owing to:

The vile abuses ... on the Sabbath and in sermon time, as in the weekday daily used and practised.

They also claimed that since they had lost control of the council, a few months earlier, the number of alehouses had been allowed to increase again and the 'vile abuses' were, again, much in evidence, which they specified as swearing, gambling with cards and dice, and drunkenness.

In the same document the councillors also took credit for improvements that had recently been made in the provision of education in the city. In 1584 the ancient grammar school of the city had merged with the equally ancient cathedral school to pool resources and ensure that an able master and usher could be afforded. At the beginning of the century the grammar school had been in Skolegate (now Rumbold Street), near St Rumbold's Church, but in 1567 one of the city's MPs, Robert Monson, offered to pay the cost of establishing a new free school in the upstairs chapel of the former Greyfriars' building in Free School Lane. The council agreed to meet the cost of transferring the glass from the old school and demonstrated their commitment further by introducing a compulsory levy to finance an annual salary of £10 for the schoolmaster. The survival of the cathedral school in the Close had been threatened by the dissolution of the chantries, whose funds had supported both this school and a preparatory Song School for the choristers at the cathedral. However, in 1548 it had been agreed by Edward VI's new government (under the Protector, the Duke of Somerset) that the cathedral revenues should be used to pay the schoolmaster 20 marks and his assistant, the usher, 10 marks. Both men would also be housed at the cathedral's expense.

Neither school seems to have flourished in competition. The cathedral schoolmaster from 1563 to 1577, John Maydwell, may have felt undermined by rivalry with the Song School, where the choristers were taught for much of this time by the foremost musician of the age, William Byrd. The school then declined further after Maydwell left because his successor, Christopher Diggles, proved to be negligent and had to be removed and found a living after less than five years. His removal probably helped the negotiations between the dean and the mayor, for the amalgamation of the schools for articles of agreement were drafted the same year. The document made clear the current dissatisfaction with the state of the schools, for it stated:

> ... the scholars that were taught in the said two several schools did not ... so much profit and proceed in learning as it was looked for and wished by their parents and kinsfolk to their no little grief, whereby divers did withdraw their children from the said schools, and others being thereby discouraged did forebear to put their children to school to the hindrance of good knowledge and learning.

The school would remain in the Greyfriars' building, but it was agreed that the dean would appoint the schoolmaster while a committee of councillors headed by the mayor would appoint the usher. Both would be well paid to ensure high-quality applicants. The cathedral would provide accommodation and pay the master £20, but the council would pay him an additional £6.66 and also pay the usher £13.33. Both men would have to be competent to teach Greek as well as Latin and the master had to be a Master of Arts. The bishop undertook to promote no other school in the city, or within three miles.

The councillors and the cathedral authorities could be proud of their joint achievement. The new school would quickly establish a high reputation under able masters. The first was William Temple, a young man fresh from King's College, Cambridge. Unfortunately, he would stay barely a year before becoming secretary to Sir Philip Sydney. He accompanied the gentleman poet to the Netherlands and was with him when he died at the Battle of Zutphen. He later moved to Ireland and became provost of Trinity College, Dublin. Only an admission fee was charged; 6d. for the younger boys to be taught by the usher and 1s. when placed under the master. The boys would have to prove their ability to 'enter into grammar', however,

79 *A 17th-century inn scene.*

and children of poorer families could not afford to forego the earning potential of a teenage son.

A school specifically established for a few poor boys did not come about until 1611, when Christ's Hospital School was opened in St Mary's Guildhall. It would later also become known as the 'Bluecoat School', owing to the boys' distinctive uniforms. The school was funded from money left for the purpose by a local physician, Richard Smith, who had been born nearby at Welton-by-Lincoln and who had prospered in London. The boys stayed at the school until they were 16 and were then apprenticed to local tradesmen and craftsmen. The master was at first paid only £5 per year and allowed a shilling a week to spend on each boy's food. In the next few years the governors of the school would, not surprisingly, find it difficult to attract suitable candidates for the post and it is unlikely that the boys were overfed.

For the orthodox Anglican citizens of Lincoln the principal threat to their church in the new century would come not from Roman Catholicism, in spite of the Gunpowder Plot, but from the puritans. One of the first clashes on the council between an orthodox faction and a puritan faction came in 1600, when the latter managed to introduce new rules concerning the appointment of the city preacher and then chose for the post John Smith, a young man already known for his extreme puritan views. Smith soon proved himself an extremely controversial figure. He strongly criticised local orthodox Anglicans in his preaching, preached without a licence and was removed from his position after only two years in office. But while he made powerful enemies in the city, he also enjoyed considerable support from puritan gentry in the county, including two of the county's MPs, Sir William Wray and his brother-in-law, Sir George St Paul, who had probably helped him secure the position in Lincoln. On leaving the city he went to Gainsborough, where he renounced his Anglican orders. He founded an Anabaptist congregation in Gainsborough, and he may also have established an Anabaptist church in Lincoln before he left, as a church existed in 1626, when it was one of only five in the country.

80   *Bishop John Williams.*

The support of powerful local gentry ensured the protection of numerous puritan clergy in the county, including some of those who followed Smith as city preacher in the first few decades of the new century. In 1615, for instance, the council appointed a puritan minister, Robert Atkinson, to this position. He had been vicar at Blyton and Glentworth, both of which were livings in the gift of Sir William Wray. He had also been briefly excommunicated for his refusal to wear a surplice and for his failure to carry out all the ceremonies prescribed in the prayer book. Atkinson was appointed to preach and give lectures on Wednesdays 'as the mayor should appoint', and still held the post 11 years later when he was joined by another well-known puritan, Edward Reyner, a protégé of Sir George St Paul. He was made the Sunday lecturer and the following year also Rector of St Peter at Arches.

By this time the puritan clergy in the county also enjoyed the support of the Bishop of Lincoln. Bishop John Williams had been appointed in 1621 and soon established a reputation as a friend to both the puritan clergy and gentry of the county. He was a particular admirer of Reyner's preaching and offered him a prebendary position at the cathedral, which Reyner's puritan conscience would not allow him to accept. Reports of such friendships earned him the enmity of Archbishop Laud, who saw Williams as a dangerous opponent whom he had to destroy. In 1628, three years after the accession of Charles I, Laud had Williams arrested and brought before the court of the Star Chamber in Westminster on a false charge of betraying the secrets of the privy council. As nothing could be proved Williams remained at liberty, but as part of his campaign Laud also insisted in 1634 on his right, as archbishop, to carry out a visitation of the diocese of Lincoln. Williams' efforts to prevent this proved unavailing and Laud asked another of Williams' enemies, the chancellor of the diocese, Dr John Farmery, to send him a pre-visitation report. It was predictably strongly critical. Attendance at the services in the cathedral was poor and they were not properly conducted. The visitation itself was carried out by Laud's vicar-general, Sir Nathaniel Brent. His criticisms included the state of the churchyard, where he found dogs, pigs and alehouses, and the failure of the prebends either to preach in the cathedral or to appoint sufficiently suitable deputies.

By 1637 Laud had been able to gather evidence of subornation of perjury against Williams, after he had gone too far in his efforts to defend his registrar against a charge of fathering a bastard child, and he was summoned to the Star Chamber again. He was found guilty, fined £10,000, removed from his bishopric and placed in the Tower, where he was to remain for the next three years. Williams had many friends in the city and Laud's behaviour was widely and deeply resented. This affair, together with three demands for Ship Money levied on the city in as many years (1634-6), may have added to the number of Charles I's enemies in the city when England descended into civil war a few years later.

EIGHT

The Civil War and the Interregnum

LINCOLN ON THE EVE OF THE CIVIL WAR

On 13 July 1642, shortly before the Civil War began, King Charles I came to Lincoln to rally support for his cause. In spite of recurrent outbreaks of the plague, the population – about three thousand – was rather larger than it had been a hundred years earlier, when Henry VIII had visited the city, but there had been no economic revival. Although some of the gentry had prospered towards the end of the 16th century, the economic gloom that had descended on the city in the 14th century had remained for over 300 years and would not begin to lift until the end of the 17th century. The city had described itself, in its new charter of 1628, as 'one of the chiefest seats of our whole kingdom'; but in reality it was far from this.

Some idea of the appearance of the city on the eve of the Civil War can be gained from John Speed's map, published 30 years earlier, in 1610. During the later Middle Ages it had become almost a one-street city, with plenty of open spaces left for gardens, orchards or, as was more often the case, simply waste ground, and the open fields came right up to the city's decaying walls. The fabric of both the cathedral and of most of the surviving churches was in disrepair. Bishop Williams had begun to restore the bishop's palace but had been forced to abandon the project before his arrest and imprisonment in 1637.

The plague, which made one of its last 'visitations' to the city in 1642, was a product of the complete lack of sanitation that still characterised all towns at this time. Alongside the dirt streets ran open sewers; huge pestiferous middens and dunghills were allowed to accumulate on the roads and lanes, and pig sties and cattle sheds stood beside or behind the city's houses. The streets were a muddy swamp whenever there was heavy rain, churned up by the constant passage of animals, and animal excrement added to the general stench. The rats and fleas that carried the plague were ubiquitous, but the least-healthy parishes, where the highest burial rates were recorded in years of plague, were those in the low-lying suburb of Wigford, bounded on one side by the Witham and on the other by the Sincil Dyke. When John Leland visited the city in about 1540 he described this area as 'al marisch and won by policy, and inhabited for the commodity of the water'.

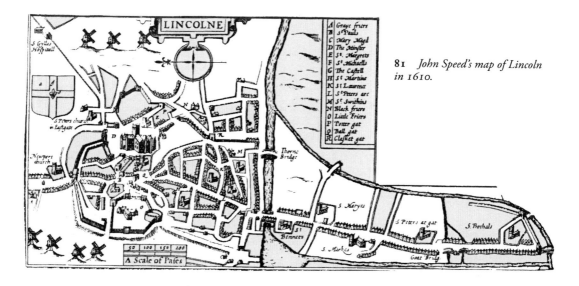

81 *John Speed's map of Lincoln in 1610.*

The Outbreak of Civil War

King Charles was delighted by the reception he was given by the people of Lincoln. Although the city had little notice of the king's arrival a vast crowd, including the city militia and a considerable number of clergy and gentry, assembled to greet him. The official reception party was headed by the mayor and the recorder. The latter, Charles Dalison, was a Roman Catholic who had been particularly active already in the Royalist cause in the city. He had been one of the justices who had heard the bastardy case that had led to Bishop Williams' final arrest and imprisonment. Dalison acted as spokesman for the mayor and corporation, offering the king their complete loyalty, their 'selfe, Estate and Fortune … all that we have to be disposed of by your majesty, for the maintenance … of your just rights'.

The next day, two of the aldermen who had been active in the Parliamentary cause were arrested and, while the king was still in the city, a Royalist petition was drawn up by some of the local gentry and senior clergy to be presented to Parliament. It called on Parliament to order the surrender of the city of Hull to the king and to respect the king's demand for the immediate cancellation of the Militia Ordinance (by which Parliament had recently begun the mustering of local militias in the counties). It also ordered the suppression of 'unparalleled prophanenesses, schisms and disorders that are broken in amongst us', and that Parliament should meet with the king to discuss 'further lawes, as may justly tend to the peace and stability of the Church, … crowne, and state'. The same gentlemen and clergy also took the lead in offering to raise a troop of cavalry for the king. Altogether, a force of 172 cavalry was pledged, although it was hoped to soon increase this to 400 men. Among those subscribing were Dalison, who offered to pay for four horses and was now knighted by Charles for his efforts, Bishop Williams' old adversary, Dr John Farmery, plus the dean, the precentor and the archdeacon, all of whom had sided with Archbishop Laud in the Star Chamber case against Williams. Among the local gentry who also subscribed to this force were Sir Edward Heron, the high sheriff,

Sir William Pelham of Brocklesby, who had charge of the county's military stores and ammunition, and Sir John Monson, whose family had long been closely connected with the government of the city. Like the Pelhams, Monson had often represented the city in Parliament during the previous hundred years.

Many of the gentlemen and clergy who were so prominent in their support for Charles at this time were undoubtedly Royalists. The majority of those who came to cheer the king, however, were less committed and had no wish to choose between king and Parliament; for most, their loyalty was almost certainly to *both* their king and their Parliament. Otherwise it is difficult to explain why, only a month before Charles' arrival, Parliament's appointee as Lord Lieutenant of the County, Lord Willoughby of Parham, had been welcomed to the city by the mayor and had conducted a successful review of the city's trained bands, in spite of the king's declaration that the Militia Ordinance was not legal and that Willoughby acted without his approval. Willoughby also summoned the chief constables of the county to meet him at Lincoln to report on the state of their local militias and military supplies, and, in spite of the king's known opposition, almost all did so. It was said that the royal proclamation was even nailed up on the gates of the inn where Willoughby and his committee were meeting in the city. The only trained bands from the city's area of jurisdiction which did not appear before Willoughby were those from the Bail and the Close. The constable of the Bail reported that fear of the plague prevented this, 'the sickness being below the hill they durst not come down thither', but Willoughby was right to detect the influence of Dalison and his Royalist friends amongst the clergy of the Close. Dalison, Willoughby reported:

> … we may justly suspect, not to be well-affected to the service, and some others of his leaven near the great Cathedral, were so far from sending in their own arms, or giving any countenance to the business, that we rather apprehend they endeavoured to dishearten others therein as much as in them lay.

The dilemma faced by so many at this time was well characterised by the behaviour of the mayor, the merchant John Becke. He was described by Willoughby as 'very forward' in ensuring the arrival of the city's trained bands for the Lord Lieutenant's review on 6 June. At first he complied with Parliament's ruling that the royal proclamation forbidding the muster of the militia should not be published. Under pressure from the king, however, he changed his mind and escaped to York to submit to Charles and ask pardon for his disloyalty.

Many of the gentry hoped that the county could be isolated from any conflict which might erupt. Many of those who subscribed at Lincoln to the raising of a troop of cavalry did so for this reason; they wished to guarantee, in the words of their declaration, 'the peace of the countie'. Charles had called for a commission of array before he came to Lincoln, but no such action was taken in the county and not even the 400-strong cavalry force promised at Lincoln materialised. Moreover, the small force that was raised was not intended by most subscribers 'to be commanded as the king shall direct' as Charles's secretary of state, Sir Edward Nicholas, had contended at the time. A tract published in August stated that the gentry believed the force would be 'disposed of within the countie' to help protect the county from soldiers in adjacent counties, specifically those in Hull who were terrorising the Humber coast. It was also stated that the force would be a means of protecting the county against the riots and insurrections of 'men of desperate fortunes'. This was a reference not to the political situation but rather to the violent attacks of riotous fenmen on those carrying out drainage schemes in the county. In the previous two years violent assaults by the fenmen on the drainage undertakers had become increasingly common. Some of the Royalist gentry, including Sir John Monson and Sir Edward Heron, had invested heavily in fen drainage schemes and were deeply frustrated by Parliament's refusal to take firm action against the rioters.

Although John Becke clearly felt extremely uncomfortable about having to choose between his king and Parliament, his successor as mayor, William Marshall, had fewer doubts. Elected by the common council on 14 September 1642, he was a convinced Parliamentarian. By this time the war had already begun, the king having raised the royal standard at Nottingham on 22 August, and the first battle, at Edgehill, would be fought soon afterwards, on 23 October. The city was deeply divided, but for the time being the Parliamentary faction had the upper hand on the common council. On the same day that Marshall was elected, the Commons ordered the impeachment of Monson, Heron and Dalison. Three weeks later Sir Edward Heron was captured near his house, in Surfleet, and after interrogation committed to the Tower on a charge of high treason. At the same time, the Commons formally removed Dalison from the recordership and ordered the Earl of Lincoln to take control of the castle and ensure the protection of the city against possible Royalist attack. The bishop's palace was made both an ammunition store and a prison for captured Royalists.

The Course of the War

By the beginning of December 1642 most of the county seemed to be under Parliamentary control and it was anticipated that the forces raised by Parliamentarians in the county during the summer might be soon sent to Yorkshire to assist Lord Fairfax. Such hopes were quickly dashed, however, when the Royalist general, the Duke of Newcastle, sent a force under Sir John Henderson to occupy Newark. With a friendly garrison nearby the Royalist gentry in the south-west of the county, who had up to now passively accepted Parliamentary authority, began to raise armies and money for their cause. Parliament's hold on Lincoln, and indeed its control of the county as a whole, now seemed very fragile. In January the Newark Royalists marched on Gainsborough, and the town, although fortified, surrendered without a fight. Shortly afterwards, a raiding party from Newark captured Belvoir Castle. In the same month Grantham also declared its enthusiasm for the Royalist cause when the cavalry from Newark arrived in the town. However, shortly afterwards, when a stronger Parliamentary force arrived and the Royalist cavalry swiftly retreated, the town's authorities had a change of heart, and the mayor was taken back to Lincoln to explain himself.

Parliament's hold on Lincolnshire would clearly remain uncertain while Royalist forces held Newark. Therefore, late in February 1643 a large Parliamentary army, under Lord Willoughby of Parham, entered the county to link up with forces from the garrisons of Lincoln and Grantham in an attempt to recapture the town. The attempt was stymied, however, by the treachery of one of the commanders, and a premature retreat turned into a murderous rout. This failure would prove costly. During March and early April the Newark Royalists took Grantham, Stamford and Peterborough, while Royalist forces from Crowland also raided Spalding and removed any Parliamentary supporters they found there. Royalist cavalry from Newark, led by Sir John Henderson, also rode up to the walls of Lincoln, but made no attempt to attack the city.

A month later, however, an attack did come, but this time from the Royalist garrison at Gainsborough. For much of April, the Lincoln garrison was substantially reinforced by forces under the command of Captain John Hotham, the son of the governor of Hull. This may have been of dubious value, however, for Hotham's forces were notoriously ill-disciplined and Hotham himself would be later found to be a secret Royalist, in touch with the Duke of Newcastle while he was at Lincoln. Briefly, in May, the city also welcomed the rather better-disciplined forces of Cromwell, who had moved up into the county from Huntingdon, and had recaptured Crowland after a three-day bombardment. When Cromwell, Hotham and their forces left the city, however, at the end of the month, the Gainsborough Royalists struck. Some of the Gainsborough forces were said to have broken into the Close, but the depleted Lincoln garrison managed to fight off the attack and then, flushed with success, was able to send a force of 300 cavalry in a rapid overnight dash to the market town of Louth. Here they surprised and defeated a Royalist raiding party that had arrived in the town the day before. Over a hundred

Royalist forces were taken prisoner, but the Royalist leaders, including Lincoln's former recorder, Sir Edward Dalison, managed to escape.

During June the Lincoln garrison was again reinforced by Hotham's forces, although Hotham himself was unmasked and arrested. Shortly before his arrest, Hotham appointed a new governor for the city with secret instructions to assist a Royalist attack by ensuring they could gain access to the city's ammunition and weapons stores. When the planned assault came on 1 July, a joint attack by Royalists from both Newark and Gainsborough, the plot had already been discovered, and

82 *Francis, Lord Willoughby of Parham, the Parliamentary commander in Lincoln, 1643.*

the garrison was forewarned and ready. The Royalists were consequently beaten off, although a few disguised as country folk did manage to get into the Close, expecting to be able to seize the city magazine.

Within a month, however, the city would be in Royalist hands. Perhaps emboldened by success in repelling the assault in July, the Parliamentary commander in Lincoln, Lord Willoughby, attempted to seize Gainsborough just three weeks later and, assisted by treachery in the town, succeeded. But this vital crossing point on the Trent was too important for the Royalists to give up easily, and Willoughby's forces were immediately besieged by both northern Royalists and a force from Newark. Forces under Cromwell and Sir John Meldrum, assisted by cavalry from the Lincoln garrison, moved quickly to relieve Willoughby. The initial siege was lifted, but an enormous Royalist army under Newcastle himself then appeared on the brow of the hill overlooking the town. Cromwell and Meldrum were forced to retreat to Lincoln and, after three days of heavy and continuous bombardment, Willoughby had to negotiate the surrender of the town. Newcastle allowed him to retreat with his surviving forces to Lincoln, but gave him no time to organise his defences there. As Newcastle's army moved towards the city the demoralised garrison, realising it had no hope of successfully resisting the attack, deserted in vast numbers. Willoughby was obliged to swiftly abandon the city and retreat to Boston, leaving behind his heavy guns. Cromwell and his forces had already moved back to Peterborough.

By 5 August 1643 Lincoln was in Royalist hands, having fallen almost without a fight. Newcastle reported that his army had entered the city 'without great difficulty'. The mayor, William Marshall, had fled and Newcastle had the Royalist Richard Somerbie installed in his place. The puritan city preacher, Edward Reyner, was another obvious target. His house was plundered and he only narrowly escaped being shot dead in his church, St Peter at Arches, before also fleeing the city. With so great a force, Newcastle might have followed up this victory by also taking Boston and driving the Parliamentary forces from the county altogether. On 5 August Willoughby wrote to Cromwell in a state of near despair:

> ... I am now at Boston, where we are but very poor in strength; so as without some speedy supply, I fear we shall not hold this long neither.

But Newcastle failed to consolidate his success, choosing to withdraw the bulk of his army to Yorkshire to renew the interminable siege of Hull, and only a small Royalist garrison was left in Lincoln. During late August and September the Parliamentary forces in the south of the county were able to reinforce their positions, while the Earl of Manchester built up a large Parliamentary army in East Anglia. By early October he had also received cavalry reinforcements from Fairfax in Hull, ferried over the Humber, and was ready to move north into Lincolnshire. He chose to march against the recently established Royalist garrison at Bolingbroke, hoping that a siege might draw in other Royalist forces for his new army to confront. His plan succeeded. The day after he reached Bolingbroke to begin the siege, on 9 October, a large Royalist army of dragoons and cavalry, composed of forces from the garrisons of Lincoln, Newark and Gainsborough, arrived near Horncastle and took his forces by surprise. It was already evening and therefore there was insufficient time for more than skirmishing, but the Royalists got the best of it as Manchester pulled his forces back towards a hill overlooking Bolingbroke. Encouraged by their success, the Royalists pushed on towards Bolingbroke the next morning, but only a few miles outside Horncastle, near the hamlet of Winceby, they came up against the Parliamentary cavalry commanded by Cromwell. In the short battle that followed the Royalists were routed, destroyed by well-organised cavalry charges.

The defeat at Winceby left the remnant of the Royalist garrison at Lincoln dangerously exposed, and Newcastle was unable to send help from Yorkshire. On 20 October 1643 it surrendered to Manchester's army and two months later Gainsborough was also taken, leaving Newark as the only Royalist garrison in the region. But this success was short lived. Towards the end of February 1644, the two Eastern Association regiments that had been garrisoning Lincoln left the city to join a diverse mix of other Parliamentary forces in the siege of Newark. Three weeks later, hungry, mutinous and with their commanders divided by jealousies and dissension and barely on speaking terms, the Parliamentary army surrounding Newark was alarmed to find itself being attacked by a relief column led by Prince Rupert. Caught between Rupert's cavalry and the Newark garrison troops, the Parliamentarians suffered heavy losses and were forced to surrender. A shattered band of disarmed and demoralised men was allowed to return to Lincoln under their commander, Sir Miles Hobart, but the men were in no state to organise the defence of the city against Rupert's army, following close behind. On 23 March 1644, just two days after their defeat at Newark, they surrendered Lincoln also.

Once again, the cavaliers over-ran the county. The estates of opponents were seized and cattle and horses rounded up and taken from the fens. But the Royalists' success was extremely short-lived. Just four weeks after the fall of Lincoln the Earl of Manchester was back in the county with the army of the Eastern Association, and on 3 May 1644 his men stormed into the Lower City. The garrison, under Sir Francis Fane, was about two thousand strong and well equipped, but it faced an army of over six thousand. As Manchester's men poured into the Lower City, Cromwell's cavalry was sent to stop a relieving force of Royalists from Newark. The garrison retreated to the Upper City and heavy rain on 4 May prevented the Parliamentarians making much progress. Manchester reported afterwards, 'it being so slippery it was not possible for our Foot to crawl up the hill to come to their works, where the Mount whereon the Castle stood, being near as steep as the eaves of a house'. Under cover of darkness, however, between two and three o'clock in the morning on 6 May, Manchester's foot soldiers reached the castle walls. But the defenders were alert and poured gunfire into the approaching force. In spite of this, Manchester's men pushed on. As scaling ladders were put up against the walls the Royalists desperately resorted to hurling large stones down on the attacking force. Some of the ladders were also too short for the high walls of the castle. Nevertheless, the Parliamentarians' superior numbers, discipline and determination paid off, and the walls were scaled. At this point the nerve of the defenders broke and they turned and fled. Many were cut down. Manchester claimed that only eight of his men were killed,

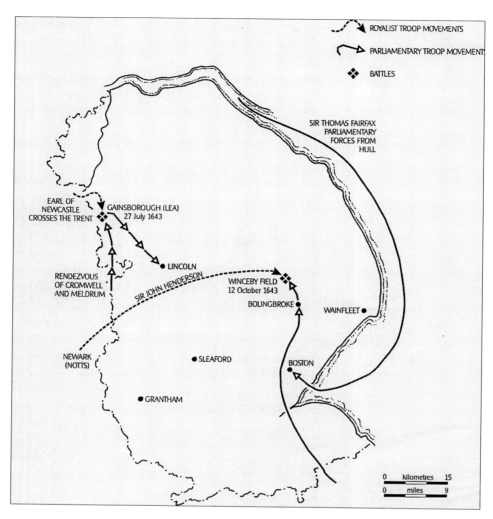

83　Map of Civil War Lincolnshire.

and about forty injured, but about fifty of the Royalists were killed. Among those taken prisoner were Sir Francis Fane and the city's former recorder, Sir Charles Dalison.

The Royalists' resistance was punished severely. The troops were given permission to pillage the upper town and a great deal of damage was done to houses, churches and the cathedral. It is ominous that seven weeks after the city surrendered the Commons sent an order to the earl strictly forbidding the removal of lead or bells from houses and churches. By this time it is likely that much of the damage had already been done. At the time of the Restoration, in 1660, Lincoln's churches were in a pathetic state. Two had been destroyed in 1643, probably on the orders of Lord Willoughby. St Nicholas and St Peter in Eastgate were probably judged to be too close to the city walls and were demolished as part of Willoughby's plans to strengthen the city's defences. Most of the city's other churches, however, suffered damage during and after the assault by Manchester's troops. Two churches, St Swithin and St Bartholomew, were burnt down during 5 May; the day before the castle was taken. St Swithin was blown up when a barrel of gunpowder exploded. Other churches were severely damaged in the first weeks after this. Twenty years later, after the Restoration, it was reported that the churches of St Michael on the Mount, St Mary Magdalene and St Paul had either lost their roofs completely or they were badly in need of repairs. St Michael's Church had been used for target practice by the Parliamentary gunners. Another church, St Botolph, had almost completely collapsed by 1660, the nave and bell tower of St Benedict had fallen down, and St John in Newport was in such a poor state by 1649 that it had been pulled down. Some were in a rather dilapidated state before the Civil War, but there is no doubt that a great deal of damage was done during this period, very often prompted by Parliament's instructions to the troops that church ornaments and furniture should be destroyed.

The houses of known Royalists in the Close and Bail were also particularly targeted by the soldiers. The house of the former chancellor, Dr John Farmery, was said to have been 'utterly demolished or destroyed', and in 1649 his widow sold all that was left: an empty plot of land. 'The Choristers' House' in Minster Yard was also destroyed; what we see today is largely the rebuilding of 1661-2. Similarly, a little further along Minster Yard, the house known today as 'The Priory' dates from the late 1660s, when the earlier, demolished house was finally replaced. The subdeanery was sacked and its hall pulled down and the rest later divided into tenements for the poor. The bishop's palace suffered at least two attacks. In 1644 the lead from the roof was plundered and more extensive damage was done by Royalist soldiers in a later raid, during the so-called Second Civil War of 1648.

Cottesford Place, in James Street, was another target for Parliament's troops, but not because of any Royalist connections. During the first year of the war this had been the home of the Parliamentary commander, Lord Willoughby of Parham. By May 1644, however, he had quarrelled spectacularly with both the Earl of Manchester, who had replaced him as the commander of Parliament's troops in the county, and

84 *St Peter in Eastgate, as it appeared in the late 17th century, having been destroyed during the Civil War.*

with Cromwell, who was extremely critical of what he perceived to be Willoughby's military blunders. The troops who plundered his house were no doubt confident that they would face no censure from their superiors. Utterly disillusioned by the treatment he received, Willoughby had already become a bitter opponent of the radicals in Parliament before the end of 1644, and in early 1648 he left the country and joined the Royalist court in exile.

The cathedral also suffered badly. This was an important symbolic target for an army whose leaders were pledged to end episcopacy, and it was rumoured – probably falsely – that Cromwell even considered blowing the cathedral up completely. The story that he stabled his horses in the cathedral might also be false as it seems to have first appeared as a piece of propaganda in a Royalist pamphlet. The cathedral's windows, however, were smashed, brasses were torn up and statues and monuments destroyed, including the tomb and bronze effigy of Queen Eleanor of Castile.

To what extent the inhabitants of the city in general suffered damage to their property is not known, but the city's trade had already been badly affected by 1644 and the situation would not begin to improve until the conflict finally ceased. Many must have been made homeless, however, and the situation was believed to be sufficiently serious in the summer of 1644 for Manchester to order the distribution of small sums of money among those who had suffered at the hands of his soldiers. By now his heart was no longer in the war and he was reluctant to take part in major engagements. This humane gesture may have been partly prompted by the disillusionment he felt.

While Royalist forces continued to hold Newark and Belvoir, raids on nearby villages would continue, although Lincoln itself was not seriously threatened. The small garrison left behind by Manchester, when he finally quit the city early in September 1644, spent much of its time patrolling the surrounding countryside in the hope of catching and killing Royalist raiders. In the numerous skirmishes both sides had their successes. The Lincoln patrols could not prevent the Newarkers from twice overrunning the little Parliamentary garrison at Torksey, and at the end of September 1644 the Parliamentary committee's treasurer was seized within five miles of Lincoln. However, the arrival of increasing numbers of Parliamentary troops in the county in the winter of 1645-6 meant that the cavaliers' position gradually became ever more hopeless. Belvoir surrendered to besieging forces in February 1646 and the siege of Newark finally ended with the garrison's surrender on 8 May.

For Lincoln and for the county, the first Civil War was over, and there could be hope that normal life could once again be resumed. But the conflict was not quite over yet. Two years later, from his prison on the Isle of Wight, Charles managed to negotiate assistance from the Scottish army, inspiring a brief renewal of hostilities. The prospect of this assistance encouraged some Royalist gentry to take up arms again. On 30 June 1648, the little garrison still remaining at Lincoln received news that a force of 400 horse dragoons and 200 musketeers, led by Sir Philip Monckton, had crossed the Trent at Gainsborough and were marching on the city. There was no time to rally support and the city was taken the same day. The garrison force, a mere 30 men, retreated to the Bishop's Palace, but could put up little resistance and those who survived the cavaliers' assault were soon prisoners. The

85   *Edward Montagu, Earl of Manchester.*

palace was then set on fire and many houses plundered, particularly those belonging to known Parliamentarians. The puritan preacher, Edward Reyner, was unfortunate enough to be a victim once again, having returned to the city three years before to take up his former post as city preacher. Once again, however, he had a narrow escape. As a group of cavaliers came after him he fled into the Minster library but his pursuers followed him, swearing they would take him dead or alive, and he was forced to surrender himself to their mercies. He was then stripped of his coat, robbed of his purse and led away, no doubt fearing that his end had now come. At this moment, however, one of the soldiers recognised Reyner as his former teacher from when he was at school at Market Rasen and, presumably with happy memories of his schooldays, persuaded his fellow soldiers to release him.

Monckton's forces did not stay long in Lincoln for they knew that a large Parliamentary force was swiftly making its way northwards to relieve the city. It moved first to Gainsborough and then was chased towards Nottingham. The Parliamentary forces, under Colonel Rossiter, caught up with Monckton's men near the village of Willoughby-on-the-Wolds and utterly destroyed them. 'The late unhappy broiles' (as Reyner described the wars) were finally over.

THE INTERREGNUM

Reyner would remain in the city until his death, shortly before the Restoration in 1660, assisted in his task by the aged George Scortwreth, who had been licensed to preach in 1605. The challenge facing these earnest puritans was as great as ever. The city and its common council were just as divided on matters of religion and politics as they had been before the wars. During 1647-8 those who had taken an active part in support of the king were removed from the common council, but a minority of the council remained Royalist sympathisers, and the execution of the king in January 1649 did nothing to reduce their number. Colonel Pride's purge of MPs whom the army knew would not have supported the trial and execution of the king was also resented. Only two of the county's members either escaped seclusion or felt themselves able to attend the House of Commons after the army coup. The demands for heavy taxation to finance the war in Ireland and the emergence of radical sects that challenged orthodox religious doctrine reinforced resentment of the new republican government. It also encouraged support in the city for those known to have Royalist sympathies.

When Cromwell dissolved the Rump, as the government had become known, in April 1653, there were few in Lincoln who regretted its passing. The policy of toleration was retained, however, under Cromwell's Protectorate and in Lincoln the Quakers and Baptists particularly flourished, even gaining some support among members of the common council. The Quaker leader, George Fox, preached in the county in 1652 and 1654, and in the latter year the Yorkshire Quaker, John Whitehead, was attacked by a mob for 'bearing testimony' in the cathedral. A fellow Quaker later described how he was:

> Buffetted and most shamefully intreated, being often knocked down by the Rude and Barbarous people, who were encouraged thereunto by Humphrey Walcott who was then in Commission to have kept the peace; but brake it by striking of the said John Whitehead with his owne hands, which so encouraged the Rude People, that so far as could be seene they had slaine the said John, but that God stirred some Souldiers to take him by fforce from amongst them.

The Quakers were particularly unpopular because they interrupted church services, as Whitehead had apparently done on this occasion, and publicly lectured the authorities – both secular and clerical – on the proper performance of their duties. The Presbyterian John Reyner and his fellow city lecturer, George Scortwreth, were both vigorously denounced by the Quaker Martin Mason, a Lincoln scrivener who proved himself to be a gifted and energetic pamphleteer. In one of his pamphlets, published in 1655, he denounced Reyner for addressing the mayor and aldermen as 'right worshipful'. The tone of the pamphlet is evident in its title, the *Proud Pharisee Reproved; or the Lying Orator laid Open*. The Quakers were seen as dangerous because they tended to use such uninhibited language and because they were so scornful of all authority, other than God's. Reyner was attacked both because he represented worldly authority, being the city's paid lecturer, preaching weekly in the cathedral, and because he showed respect for the city authorities. To call the mayor 'right worshipful' was to Mason 'hollow, deceitfull, unwarrantable … Babylonian'.

At a time of social and political upheaval, the Quakers were considered dangerous because they appealed directly to the poor and did not accept that the current social order was God's will; that the poor must accept their lot in life and be grateful for what they had. In the same pamphlet Mason also showed the Quakers' sense of social justice and attacked the conservative message preached by Reyner:

Thou bids them be content with such things as they have, though they have but from hand to mouth; with food and raiment, though they have no more. The poor, it seems, must be preached into patience and contentedness … but the priests and the proud ones, who live in pomp and plenty, may purchase lands and possessions without any check.

The success of the Baptists in gaining recruits and establishing congregations in the county, including Lincoln, was also seen by many as a dangerous development. From 1653, however, much of their energy was spent in bitter squabbles with the Quakers, and nowhere was their rivalry more fierce than in Lincoln. Neither Reyner nor Scortwreth appear to have indulged in pamphlet warfare with Mason, but a Baptist pastor, Jonathan Johnson, who was also attacked by Mason, did not hold back. After an exchange of letters Mason published *The Boasting Baptist Dismounted, and the Beast Disarmed and Sorely Wounded without any Carnal Weapon*, to which Johnson replied with his own well-titled pamphlet, *The Quaker Quashed and his Quarrel Queld*. This was not quite a knock-out blow, but Mason's reply was rather feebly titled *Sion's Enemy Discovered*. Many in Lincoln must have feared that the Quakers were probably right when they boasted that they would 'turn the world upside down'. It is not surprising that alarmed conservatives with Royalist sympathies now prospered on the common council and in 1655 had the temerity to elect both a Royalist mayor and a Royalist town clerk.

Their success, however, was short-lived. In the same year, Cromwell divided the country into military districts, each under a major-general, with extensive authority to police their region and raise a new militia and new taxes to pay for it. The major-general appointed to the Midland counties, Edward Whalley, made the removal of the newly appointed mayor and town clerk one of his first priorities, although he admitted privately to Cromwell that to do so he had to assume 'a little more power then I thinke belonged to mee'. The interference was greatly resented, as the minutes of the common council show. Whalley had acted, they record bluntly, 'by an usurped, illegall, pretended power'. Nevertheless, they grudgingly accepted his nominees, and even felt obliged to admit Whalley and his deputy to the freedom of the city.

Shortly after this, Whalley wrote to Cromwell to report on his triumph and on the challenge that he and his assistant, Berry, now faced in Lincoln:

… the hearts of the enemy are fallen, and a word commands them, and all would be well here, had we a few honest men to bear rule and lead the people. Our ministers are bad, our magistrates idle, and the people all asleep; only these present actings have a little awakened.

Six months later, in January 1656, he was able to report that at least they had not been idle and that the people of Lincoln were truly benefiting from their endeavours:

We are … very busy in casting out scandalous and ignorant ministers, suppressing alehouses, taking order that the poor in all places under our charge may be set a work, and beggars suppressed … You cannot imagine what an awe it hath struck into the spirits of wicked men, what incouragement it is to the godly.

As a much resented outsider, however, Whalley recognised that some of the vices of 'wicked men' might have to be tolerated, at least for the time being, and especially when the wicked were rich and influential. Horse racing, a popular sport in Lincoln for the local gentry since at least Elizabeth's reign, on the heath to the south of the city, was therefore allowed to continue. Although Cromwell himself appears to have enjoyed widespread respect, his appointment of the major-generals, and the powers they assumed for themselves, was extremely unpopular, and this latest experiment in government was swiftly terminated in 1657.

Cromwell would not live much longer, and following his death, on 3 September 1658, there could be no certainty of the direction the nation would take, and many feared a drift into anarchy. One of those who represented the county in the Parliament of 1658-9 was Colonel Edward Rossiter, the Parliamentary commander who had chased Monckton's Royalists from Lincoln 10 years before. He was a moderate whose main concern was the preservation of good order. By this time he had decided, like many other gentlemen of the county with whom he was closely connected, that the best prospect for guaranteeing this was the restoration of the monarchy. By 1659 he was in correspondence with the agents of Charles II and it was planned that in the summer of 1659 he would seize both Boston and Lynn as part of a general Royalist uprising. This did not materialise, but in December he was able to raise forces in the county in support of General Monk, who had also made it clear that he too believed the restoration of Charles II to be the best hope for rescuing the country from possible chaos. Rossiter also presented Monk with the county's petition, in the following February, for the calling of a free Parliament, free from seclusions. Lincolnshire was far from alone in making this request, and when it was granted, in April 1660, the opinion of the city was almost certainly reflected in the election of two Royalists, John Monson and the young lawyer Thomas Meres. Rossiter was also re-elected as one of the county representatives. Towards the end of May, Charles II and his entourage ended their exile in France and returned to England, and Lincoln joined in the national rejoicing.

NINE

Restoration and the 'Glorious Revolution'

THE ROYALISTS' REVENGE

One of Charles II's first concerns on regaining his throne was to punish those who had played a leading role in the previous republican regime, the Commonwealth, and particularly those who had signed his father's death warrant. Oliver Cromwell's rather gentle, ineffectual son, Richard, whom Cromwell had hoped would succeed him, wisely slipped away into early retirement abroad. About eleven other Commonwealth leaders were rounded up, however, and suffered the grisly end still dictated for those found guilty of regicide or treason: hanging, drawing and quartering. Cromwell himself had cheated Charles' hangman but he, too, was exhumed and his corpse hanged before his remains were cut down and his head cut off and stuck on a spike outside Westminster Hall, the scene of Charles I's trial.

The king could also not be expected to look kindly on cities such as Lincoln that had spent much of the civil wars as Parliamentary garrisons, in which the properties of his most loyal supporters had been pillaged and, in many cases, utterly destroyed. The majority of the aldermen still serving on the common council at the time of the Restoration were Parliamentarians, but local Royalists, led by the newly restored recorder, Sir Charles Dalison, would ensure that this did not remain the case for long. One of the first puritans to lose his position was Perkins, the town clerk, who had been imposed on the council by the hated Major-General Whalley. The town clerk whom Whalley had forced out, William South, was reinstated.

A much more thorough purge, however, was soon to follow. In December 1661 Parliament passed an Act for the Well-Governing and Regulating of Corporations. This debarred from municipal office any that refused to take the oaths of allegiance and supremacy, or refused to take communion according to the rites of the Church of England. Moreover, even those who agreed to all these might still be removed from their positions if special commissioners appointed by the Crown should 'deem it expedient for the public safety'. The commissioners appointed for Lincoln were all well-known Royalists. They included Dalison, who had numerous personal scores to settle, and Sir Thomas Meres and Sir John Monson. They acted swiftly. All puritans

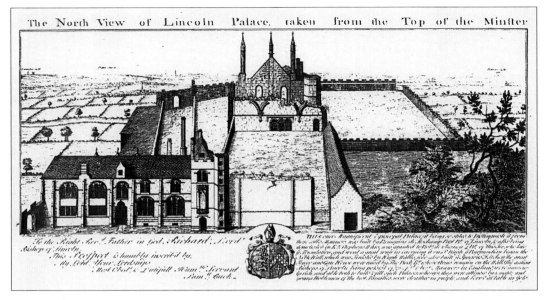

The North View of Lincoln Palace, taken from the Top of the Minster

86 *The bishop's palace in 1726, by Samuel Buck. The palace had been badly damaged during the Civil War and in 1726 it can be seen that only the Alnwick chapel still survived intact. This had been bought in 1652 by one of Cromwell's major generals and turned into a private house.*

were ejected and their places given to Royalists, in particular to those Royalists who had served on the council before but who had lost their positions during the years of puritan ascendency. In August 1662 Dalison and his fellow commissioners expelled seven aldermen, both of the sheriffs, the coroner, one of the chief constables, eight common councilmen, a chamberlain, the sword bearer and mace bearer and William South, the recently reinstated town clerk. From now on, for almost 200 years, only Anglicans would be eligible for service on the common council.

Charles had intended to adopt a rather more liberal approach to his subjects' rights to worship freely, as he had made clear in the Declaration of Breda in April 1660. But the Declaration

87 *Sir John Monson.*

on Ecclesiastical Affairs, issued in October 1660, offered no such guarantee and left local Royalist magistrates free to persecute Baptists, Quakers and Independents, using Elizabethan legislation against recusants and attendance of conventicles. Only Presbyterians would have any protection. Lincoln's Royalist magistrates were not slow to take advantage of this. By March 1661 there were said to be about eighty Quakers in the county and city gaols, and a great many Baptists. The leader of the latter, Thomas Grantham, wrote on behalf of the various Baptist congregations in the county three *Humble Addresses* to the king, protesting that the righteous were being made to suffer with the wicked. Another Baptist prisoner also managed to have his protest published, a dialogue in verse entitled *The Prisoner against the Prelate: or, a Dialogue between the Common Goal and Cathedral of Lincoln.* The irrepressible Martin Mason was again the chief spokesman for the Lincoln Quakers. In March 1661 he wrote to the judges of assize protesting that he had been arrested even before 'that hasty paper called the King's Proclamation' had been published:

> Yea, some of us were haled out of our houses and had to Prison before the Proclamation came amongst us, so mad were the multitude and some of the magistrates that they outpaced the decree of Caesar in showing their teeth against the Innocent.

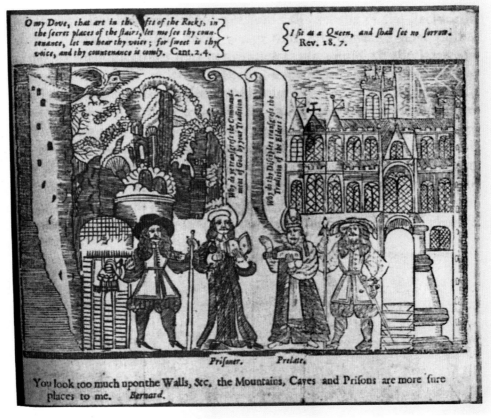

88 *Frontispiece of* The Prisoner against the Prelate.

Most of those arrested served only short spells in prison, but Mason may have been treated more harshly. He was incarcerated again four years later, at which time he published his prison meditations, demonstrating that he had lost none of his talent for spirited invective, in this case against the Bishops' Courts and 'ignorant dreaming priests'.

By the 1670s, however, the magistrates' enthusiasm for the persecution of dissenters seems to have been in decline. This was partly due to the example given by the king, who in 1672 issued a Declaration of Indulgence allowing the licensing of both preachers and private houses as places of worship for dissenters. Before the end of the year there were five houses licensed for the Baptists alone. The Bishop of Lincoln, William Fuller, found this extremely alarming. 'Both Presbyterians and Anabaptists, with the Quakers, are exceedingly increased,' he wrote that year; 'if there be not a sudden stop put to their daring growth, I dread to write the consequences'. But such fears were becoming less common and there was a growing recognition by this time that persecution could be counter productive. Force could too often simply strengthen the conviction and dedication of dissenters. Sir Thomas Meres probably spoke for many of the gentry when he commented in 1673, 'we have seen how little good force will do'.

A survey conducted in 1676 would also suggest that the number of either Roman Catholics or nonconformists was much less than Bishop Fuller feared. The survey covered all 13 of the city's parishes and found over 2,300 conformists, but only 30 Roman Catholics and 122 nonconformists. This may not have been an entirely accurate survey as it included Presbyterians, who sometimes attended the parish church as conformists, but the great majority of the inhabitants of Lincoln were clearly Anglicans.

The purge of puritans among the city's clergy had fewer victims than might have been expected. The city's two official preachers at the cathedral during most of the years of the Commonwealth, Reyner and Scortwreth, both died before they could be purged; Scortwreth shortly before the Restoration and Reyner only a few months afterwards. Scortwreth, however, died in time to have a short-lived successor, James Abdy, who would remain in the city but was deprived of his living. New appointments were also made for the city's churches, but the majority of parishes remained without a resident priest. The man responsible for purging and replacing those ministers who could not accept the demands of the Act of Uniformity, passed in May 1662, was Dr Robert Sanderson. He was the rather saintly and learned minister of Boothby Pagnell before the civil wars, who was appointed Bishop of Lincoln in October 1660, the first bishop for 20 years. Altogether, 26 ministers in the diocese surrendered their livings in August 1662, rather than accept the new Book of Common Prayer or the prescribed rituals and liturgy.

A new dean, precentor, chancellor and subdean also had to be appointed for the cathedral as the previous holders of these offices had all died in the years that had passed since the suppression of the bishopric and chapter. The great task of repairing the damage done to the cathedral during the wars would be in good hands. Sanderson's concern for the undertaking had already been demonstrated. Anticipating the possible consequences of civil war, he had compiled a detailed list in 1641 of the treasures of the cathedral, known today as the *Winchelsea Book of Monuments*. This would prove to

89   *The Wren Library.*

be the only record of many of the tombs and images destroyed in the wars. The main responsibility for initiating repair work and for refurbishing the cathedral, however, fell on the equally learned but self-effacing Michael Honeywood, who was appointed dean. As well as overseeing the restoration of the fabric, however, Honeywood also paid for the building of the library, designed by Sir Christopher Wren, over the ruined north cloister, and endowed it with a great many fine books.

Although the loyalty of the Royalist common council and its mayor could hardly be doubted, it was obliged, along with all other electoral boroughs, to surrender its charter to the king in 1684 and apply, at great expense, for a new one. Fortunately, the council's 'loyal and prudent' behaviour was recognised by the Lord Chief Justice, the infamous Judge Jeffries, to whom the charter was surrendered, and the new charter was quickly granted, in January 1685, with only a few alterations. Most significant was the addition that stated the king's power to remove the mayor or any other official of the council.

The 'Glorious Revolution'

Within a month of the city receiving its new charter Charles II was dead. The accession of his Catholic brother James, was no more popular in Lincoln than elsewhere, and his efforts in the next few years to assert his co-religionists' rights to enjoy complete religious freedom did nothing to endear him to either his Anglican or dissenter subjects. The recent allegations of a Catholic plot invented by Titus Oates had been widely believed by a populace brought up on tales of the Catholic Armada and the Gunpowder Plot, and it was generally accepted that a French Catholic watchmaker had deliberately started the Great Fire of London in 1666.

The little Catholic community in the city had been served by a Jesuit priest since 1680 and now, with royal protection, Catholicism could hope to flourish. A popish bookseller was released from prison on the king's orders, and his stock of books was returned to him. There was also, soon, a small Catholic chapel that held services every Sunday and was said to be well attended. Within a year or so of James's accession it was reported that there were three Roman Catholic missionary priests in the city. There were also reports that a Catholic school had been opened and was so successful by 1688 that the community was hoping to be able to purchase a larger and more prestigious property.

But such hopes would be soon dashed. As soon as news reached Lincoln in December 1688 that King James had fled the country, fearing for his life, and that his son-in-law, the Protestant William of Orange, had landed in England and been offered the throne, a mob attacked both chapel and school. Fortunately, the three priests had been alerted beforehand and had fled. The mob wanted blood and would probably have carried out their threats to tear the priests limb from limb had they caught them. As it was, they satisfied themselves with razing the two buildings to the ground and burning the books and furniture. The attitude of the city's voters was demonstrated in the elections for a new Parliament in January 1689. Sir Thomas Meres, who had been returned in every election since 1659, polled a derisory nine votes, while the two successful candidates each polled over two hundred. While the latter had clearly declared their support for William's accession, Sir Thomas would seem to have had too many scruples about the legal niceties of this 'Glorious Revolution' (as its supporters called James II's removal) to be able to join the winning side.

Although anti-Catholic sentiment was clearly still very strong in the city, toleration of dissenters was gradually becoming more widely accepted. When the Toleration Act was passed in 1689, allowing dissenters to have their own places of worship, the Lincoln Quakers soon felt able to begin building the Meeting House that still stands today. The land had been purchased as a burial ground in 1669, but until now services had to be held in secret in private houses. To be a Quaker was still to court danger, however. In designing their Meeting House the city's Quaker leaders made sure that there was an emergency exit at the rear of the women's gallery into the graveyard, in case of a mob attack or in the event of a raid by the magistrates.

The attitude of the exclusively Anglican common council to Lincoln's Quakers was well illustrated by the problems encountered by one local Quaker who wished to become a freeman of the city. Shortly after James II had issued a Declaration of Indulgence in 1687 (hoping to win dissenter support for Catholic emancipation), a local Quaker mercer, Abraham Morrice, applied successfully to the king for a letter that he could present to the council, ordering the mayor and corporation to grant him the freedom of the city, to which he was entitled having served his apprenticeship. The king's letter also expressly exempted him, as a Quaker, from having to swear the usual oaths. Thus armed, he presented himself to the council and, grudgingly, it felt obliged to comply.

90   *The Quaker Meeting House as it appears today.*

As soon as James had fallen from power, however, the following year, the council seized the opportunity to declare that the late king's Declaration of Indulgence was no longer valid in this case and the town clerk was directed to remove Morrice's name from the city's list of freemen. Here the matter might have stayed but, seven years later, in 1696, a statute was passed by Parliament that allowed Quakers in certain circumstances to make a solemn affirmation instead of taking an oath. Morrice again sought admission to the freedom of the city. The mayor, however, refused to let him make the solemn affirmation. The case then went to the Court of King's Bench, where Morrice sought a judgement ordering the mayor to admit him. Chief Justice Holt dismissed the case, but only on a technicality, and the mayor had to admit that Morrice had served his apprenticeship. Finally, in July 1698, with his application correctly worded so that all legal obstacles had been removed, the mayor was obliged to let him make his affirmation and he was re-admitted a freeman of the city. Another Quaker was also re-admitted at this time, and Morrice's son, Abraham, was admitted soon after this, as his apprentice.

The Toleration Act, inflation and high taxation to pay for the wars against France combined to ensure that William's reign was not popular with many in the city, and Sir Thomas Meres was far from alone in his doubts about the legality of William's title. One of the two MPs elected to represent the city in 1689, Sir Henry Monson, found that he could not swear the oaths of loyalty to the new king after all and gave up his seat in Parliament. The city nevertheless managed to give William a warm welcome when he visited in 1695, with the recorder making the customary loyal address on his knees at Bargate, and the mayor presenting the sword of state as a symbol of loyal submission to royal authority. It was later reported, however, that the king himself was in no state to enjoy his visit. He had spent the previous night drinking heavily as the guest of Sir John Brownlow of Belton and was now suffering the uncomfortable effects of his indulgence. At the grand banquet to which the common council and their wives were all invited to dine with the king, William was able to eat nothing but 'a mess of milk'.

For the city, however, the visit was a success, and not least because the king agreed to the request for the right to hold another fair, for three days, at whatever time it was felt most suitable, for horses, beasts and goods. The royal visit and the new fair could later be seen as marking the beginning of a new, more optimistic era in the life of the city. The plague had not returned for more than half a century, the population was once again growing rapidly, buildings damaged or destroyed in the Civil War were being repaired or replaced and trading opportunities for the city's merchants were improving. A long period of economic decline and decay – stretching back for more than three and a half centuries – was at last coming to an end.

Economic Revival

The revival of the city's fortunes can probably be dated from the 1670s, when efforts to dredge and deepen the Foss Dyke between Lincoln and Torksey were finally successful, thereby making it navigable for larger vessels. Any revival in the city's fortunes was not at first apparent to visitors, however, for the most striking aspect of the town's appearance would long remain the sad, decayed and neglected state of many of its medieval churches, walls and gates, and other medieval buildings. Moreover, although its population was rising, Lincoln was still far smaller at the end of the 17th century than it had been in the 12th and 13th centuries, when its wool trade had been so important. For many years it would remain essentially a one-street town. When the diarist Abraham de la Pryme, visited the city in 1690 he was prompted to note: ''Tis a strange thing that great towns should so decay and be eaten up with time ... there is scarce anything worth seeing in it but the High Street.' Early in the 18th century Daniel Defoe found little improvement. His description of the city has often been quoted: 'an ancient, ragged, decay'd and still decaying city'.

Lincoln was expanding by the 1690s because its hinterland was beginning to enjoy greater prosperity. Improvements to the Foss Dyke enabled it to benefit from the increasing demand for Lincolnshire wool from Yorkshire wool-and-worsted merchants, and from an expansion in trade in other bulk goods as well, such as coal, timber, lead and, above all, corn. A French visitor to the town, whose account was published in 1672, described how 'barks bring their lading to Lincoln by the canal, which enters that town with the river of Whitham', but unfortunately, he added, due to the sad state of the canal, they could do so 'but seldom and with little success'. By 1672, however, improvements were already beginning to be made. No doubt encouraged by the success of other river navigation schemes elsewhere in recent years, the common council had agreed in 1670 to ask its representatives in Parliament, Sir John Monson and Sir Thomas Meres, to obtain an Act of Parliament allowing them to undertake improvements both to the Foss Dyke and the Witham, to make both waterways navigable from Torksey on the Trent to Boston. The Act was passed the following year. It appointed the mayors of Lincoln and Boston to be commissioners for the project, along with three of Lincoln's more senior aldermen and a large number of local nobility and gentry. Their responsibilities were to appoint the engineer to plan and undertake the task, to settle problems and disputes with local landowners whose lands would be affected, and to fix the tolls to be charged. The common council then agreed that it should make itself – at least initially – the undertaker responsible for the improvements to the Foss Dyke and for the little stretch of the Witham from High Bridge to the Sincil Dyke, and agreed to mortgage numerous properties in its possession to raise £900 to begin the work. Samuel Fortrey, an authority on water engineering from Cambridgeshire, was appointed as joint undertaker on the understanding that once the council had spent £500 he would bear a third of the remaining expenses and in return receive a third of the remaining profits.

Fortrey promised to offer his 'best advice, direction and assistance' and it seems that he was as good as his word. Work began at once and as early as August 1672 it was found necessary to pay compensation to a farmer at Torksey for damage done to his land by the workmen depositing dirt and silt on it. During the next few years sufficient progress was made to prompt numerous complaints that the water in the Foss Dyke was so high that it was causing flooding of adjoining fields. In 1680 the problems of flooding were such that some local farmers even took the extreme (and of course illegal) action of opening the sluice gates at Torksey.

Now, at last, quite large craft could pass along the canal throughout the year, and Lincoln could benefit from the expansion of the Yorkshire wool trade and the growing demand for Lincolnshire corn. The completion of the Aire and Calder Navigation at the end of the century completed the process, making possible direct water communications between Lincoln and both Leeds and Wakefield. Unfortunately, the accounts of the Foss Dyke Navigation for the late 17th century have not survived, but when they begin, in 1714, the chief exports from Lincoln were wool, corn, ale and poles for pit props, while the main import was coal.

The growth in trade that followed communications improvements brought more tradesmen and craftsmen into the city and helped swell a population already steadily increasing as baptisms in most of the city's parishes began regularly to outstrip burials. It has been estimated that between 1661 and 1714 the population grew from 3,500 to 4,500, approximately. In the poorest, low-lying and overcrowded parishes, such as St Peter's at Gowts, in Wigford, population growth may have come rather more slowly, for the parish registers show burial rates outstripping baptisms in this parish in most years up to 1699, when the trend is reversed.

Another indication of economic revival at the end of the century was the increase in building activity and, in particular, in the use of brick in building. The new Quaker Meeting House built in 1689 was one such brick building. Church repairs, the building of a new house of correction, road-building activity and a notable improvement in the size and fortunes of both the Bluecoat School and the grammar school were all indicative of a healthier economic climate. The earliest signs of revival were in the Upper City, the home of most of the city's wealthiest inhabitants. Rebuilding and repair work, both to houses and churches, began here soon after the Restoration. But better employment opportunities and rising wages meant that the city as a whole was beginning to prosper by the end of the century. The survival of more than 600 probate inventories from this period confirm this picture, showing the wide variety of occupations to be found in the city and the lists of furniture and other valuables owned by the recently deceased. During the 1650s a shortage of coinage had forced a number of the city's tradesmen to resort to issuing their own trade tokens, but this had ceased to be a problem by the 1660s and the government was able to ban the practice in 1674.

The Restoration also brought about a revival of the system of parish poor relief, which had also been badly disrupted during the Civil War. When Major-General Whalley arrived in the city in 1655 he found the poor were not being set to work, that the Jersey School had been 'set aside and wholly neglect[ed]', and that only the poorest classes could be found to take the office of parish constable. He told Cromwell the following year that he was 'taking order that in all places under our charge the poor may be set a work'. The Jersey School was only re-established in 1661, however, when a new master was appointed and given the stock of wool needed to employ spinners and knitters, plus a set of pay scales: 5d. apiece per week for spinners and 4d. apiece for knitters for their first six months and then to pay 'agreed rates'. It would survive well into the 19th century, and in the late 17th and 18th centuries became a model for other similar institutions throughout the county.

TEN

The Georgian City, 1714-1837

ECONOMIC REVIVAL CONTINUES

The economic revival that had begun in the last two or three decades of the 17th century would continue in the new century. With economic growth came a rise in the city's population, to equal and then surpass the levels last known in the High Middle Ages of the 13th century. The improvement made to the Foss Dyke, coupled with growing demand in Yorkshire for Lincolnshire wool and corn, was an important reason for continuing growth. By the 1760s and 1770s, however, developments in agriculture in the surrounding region and improvements in road transport were both additional factors, while population growth was both a cause and consequence of continuing economic success. By the time of the first national census, in 1801, the population had risen from approximately four thousand in 1714 to almost seven thousand, and housing was once again appearing in areas that had lain waste and empty for the previous 500 years. Moreover, in the last years of the Georgian era, the city's population – like that of the country as a whole – grew at an unprecedented rate, and by the time of the young Victoria's accession, in 1837, it had passed twelve thousand.

In the first decades of the 18th century it would seem that the common council, as undertakers for the Foss Dyke, found the costs of constant maintenance an increasingly onerous burden, which they were not always willing to meet. Consequently, by the 1730s the canal was once again in a poor state of repair and the common council was keen to find an investor willing to take over the responsibility of maintaining it. In September 1740 the council transferred its two-thirds share in the Navigation to a Yorkshire merchant, Richard Ellison, who already had considerable experience in schemes to survey and improve waterways in Yorkshire. For a fixed rate of £50 per year Ellison received a lease for 999 years, and for an additional £25 per year obtained the remaining third of the shares.

When Ellison died three years later the costs of deepening and scouring the canal far outweighed the benefits, but for his son and later successors the Foss Dyke would prove an exceptionally profitable investment, and the common council would long rue its short-sighted decision. By 1744 the canal was again fully navigable for coal barges

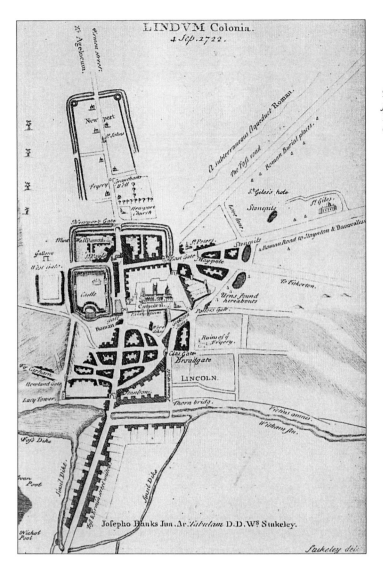

91 *Lincoln, 1722, from Stukeley's* Itinerarium Curiosum.

and coal was on sale in Lincoln for only two-thirds of its former price. Between 1746 and 1750 annual receipts varied between £450 and £600, and the common council found itself accused of not only a lack of foresight but also of corruption, a charge it vigorously denied. Richard Ellison Jnr built a new wharf in 1747, and as trade increased in the following years further wharves, river walls and warehouses were constructed both beside the Brayford Pool and along the River Witham, to the east of High Bridge. A Bill 'for restoring and maintaining navigation' of the Witham, between Boston and Lincoln, was passed in 1762. This also helped boost the city's trade, but Lincoln's links with the rapidly expanding industrial centres of south and west Yorkshire remained the principal source of profit for the city's merchants. By 1767 at least one vessel loaded with wool was leaving Lincoln for Leeds every fortnight. Annual toll revenues were £1,370 in 1764, but by 1789 they were over £2,000. After this, revenues were hardly ever below

£2,000, and in 1814 reached £6,000. By this time the Brayford was a busy port and large vessels, up to 50 tons, could now sail up the Foss Dyke. In *Georgian Lincoln* Sir Francis Hill describes the changing appearance of the Brayford Pool in the second half of the 18th century and in the first decades of the 19th:

> Brayford had been a pool of mud and sand without wharves or warehouses on its banks, surrounded by gardens and orchards. As traffic grew, the gardens turned into coal yards or were covered by warehouses, and the pool became an inland port.

The number of boats using the Witham was also increasing. Trade between Lincoln and Boston was much boosted in the first decade of the new century by improvements to the Witham in the short stretch of the river between Stamp End, at the eastern edge of the city, and High Bridge. As a result of this, through-traffic could be established from the Witham to the Foss Dyke. Sir Joseph Banks, an energetic supporter of the Witham improvement scheme, noted that large quantities of oats were soon being shipped up the Witham via the Brayford

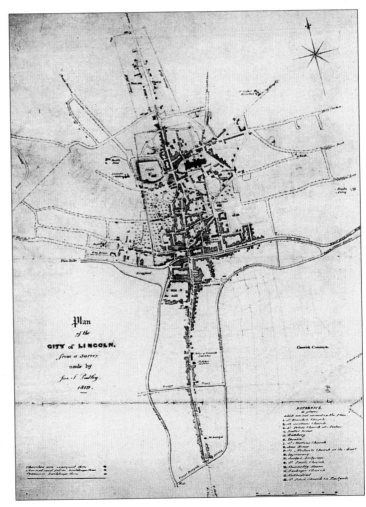

92 *Plan of Lincoln, from a survey made by J.S. Padley, 1819.*

93   *Richard Ellison Jnr.*

and the Foss Dyke to Chesterfield, and from there on to Manchester. The increase in tolls on the Witham between Lincoln and Boston was dramatic. In 1790 they were let for £300, but in 1810 for £3,000. In 1832 the Steam Packet Company began a regular service to Boston.

Economic growth and risk-taking were also encouraged by the expansion of credit facilities, made possible by the development of banking, a venture that Richard Ellison Jnr was also well placed to invest in. He was already a partner in a bank in Doncaster when, in 1775, he helped open Lincoln's first bank in partnership with Abel Smith, a Nottingham banker, and John Brown, a Lincoln mercer and a former mayor of the city, in whose house the bank was at first established. Each invested £1,000, but by 1786 the bank had almost £55,000 in circulation and by 1799 this had doubled again, to approximately £116,000. When Richard Ellison Jnr died in 1792 his personal estate was almost £36,000.

Another stimulus to the city's economic revival was the gradual improvement in road transport, brought about by turnpike trusts. The appalling state of the main roads running into Lincoln had long attracted comment. In his *Tour through the Whole Island of Great Britain*, written between 1724 and 1727, Defoe described the difficulties of a journey along the Old North Road, running south to London. A large section of the road, where it ran through heavy clay, was constantly cut up by herds of bullocks being driven to the London market. The road would regularly become impassable for wheeled vehicles, while the poor animals exhausted themselves and lost valuable weight wallowing through the gooey mud.

The first road in the immediate vicinity of Lincoln to be turnpiked was the road from Wragby. Enterprising farmers who made a living from fattening Scots cattle on the Wolds and selling the beasts in Yorkshire were keen to cut the time taken for the journey, and part of their route lay along the 'foundrous' Wragby-Lincoln road. The road was said to be particularly bad at Langworth, where it was known for a coach and six horses to be stuck fast in the mud. Without gravel cheaply or readily available, repairs made by the local parishes, using wood and other locally available materials, were of only temporary benefit. The Act authorising the turnpiking of the road was passed in 1739 and was one of the first in the county. Further improvements were slow in coming, but in 1755 the common council agreed to invest £500 in a scheme to improve the road from Lincoln to Peterborough and obtained the necessary legislation in the following year. At the same time, permission was also gained to set up turnpikes and improve the roads linking the city to the ferry crossings over the Trent at Dunham and Littleborough.

The ending of the wars with France in 1763 ushered in a new spate of turnpikes across the country and it was now that most of the remaining roads into Lincoln were improved. An Act passed in 1765 authorised the turnpiking of the road to Barton, where a ferry could be taken to Hull, Selby and York. Another Bill was passed the same year making possible improvements to the road to Bawtry, improving access to the towns of the West Riding. Plans were also drawn up in 1772 for improvements to the Lincoln-Newark road, but disputes between the two sets of trustees prevented the scheme from ever coming to fruition. The Lincoln trustees only improved the road as far south as Potter Hill, where the road crossed the county boundary into Nottingham.

The turnpike movement also brought notable improvements to communications within the town. The northern section of the Lincoln-Peterborough turnpike involved the making of a new road up Lincoln Hill, along the line now followed by Lindum Road and Pottergate. When completed, in 1786, the New Road (as it was for long known) became the main road linking the upper and lower cities and opened up the Close as the principal thoroughfare through the city. The common council co-operated closely with the trustees in this project, and the local gentry, led by Sir Joseph Banks, contributed generously to offset the costs. An earlier project, to improve the High Street in the Lower City, from St Mark's parish to Great Bargate, was almost entirely the initiative of the council. This had previously been regarded as the responsibility of the parishes through which the road ran, but by the 1730s it was becoming abundantly apparent that the parish inhabitants could not on their own be expected to maintain the road in a state appropriate to the growing traffic now to be found on the High Street. In 1738 the common council took the decision to pave the road with 'coggles', a Lincolnshire version of cobbles:

> Forasmuch as the repairing of the said highway tends to the welfare, trade and advantage of this city, and to the intent that the same may be with all convenient speed amended.

It was said that in the winter months the road was so deep in mud that wagons and carriages could not get through and the conditions were dangerous for all travellers. The council agreed to spend up to £200 a year in repairing and maintaining the road. It was reported in 1752, however, that the road was again 'excessive bad' and another £400 was voted for repairs, but this time using gravel, and over 7,000 tons were ordered for the purpose.

THE CHANGING APPEARANCE OF THE CITY

Transport improvements reflected the demands of a growing, thriving market town. Large-scale industrial development lay in the future, and throughout the Georgian era the city remained what it had always been: a market town and an entrepôt serving a wide area. But with growing prosperity and an expanding population the appearance of the city was slowly changing, and not only around the Brayford Pool.

One of the first visitors to spot the improvements and record them for posterity was William Stukeley, who visited the town in about 1722. As well as noting the city's surviving Roman antiquities (a topic of growing interest by this time), he also commented on how he found the city flourishing again. A few years later another traveller, John Loveday, noted the new buildings in brick that were to be found, and Thomas Sympson, writing in 1743, remarked that new houses were 'daily building' and noted the great improvements being made to improve the Foss Dyke. Sympson also found that such was the demand for brick by this time that a brick kiln had been recently established on the site of a former churchyard near Carholme, and ancient stone coffins had been dug up and put to use as horse troughs. A year earlier, in 1742, the council had agreed to allow clay to be dug on the south common for brick and tile-making.

Among the better, new brick houses that impressed Sympson were the so-called 'Number Houses' in Minster Yard, which had recently been built facing the west front of the cathedral and were probably the first houses in the city to be given numbers. Another fine house from this period that still stands today is D'Isney Place on Eastgate, built in 1736. Sympson would also have seen the new butter market, built just to the north of the Stonebow, near St Peter at Arches, in 1736-7. The façade can still be seen, although no longer in its original position. It is now incorporated into the Central Market on Waterside South, with the 19th-century Corn Exchange behind. Many other new brick houses may also have already begun to extend down the High Street south of the Stonebow by the 1730s. Many of the houses were shown in the watercolour painting of the High Street made by the French painter Augustus Pugin, in about 1800, and in the sketches he made, suggest that the rebuilding of this part of the city was well under way by this time, and probably extended as far down the High Street as the church of

94 *Nathan Drake's depiction of the Roman and medieval East Gates, c.1740.*

95   *Nathan Drake's depiction of the Roman South Gate, c. 1740.*

St Peter at Gowts. Here were to be found the houses and shops of many of the city's leading citizens: to quote Sir Francis Hill, 'the drapers and mercers, the grocers and tallow-chandlers, saddlers, ironmongers, cabinet-makers and liquor merchants (and) among them ... the growing class of merchants concerned with agricultural products: millers, brewers, maltsters, tanners'.

96   *The 'Number Houses' in Minster Yard.*

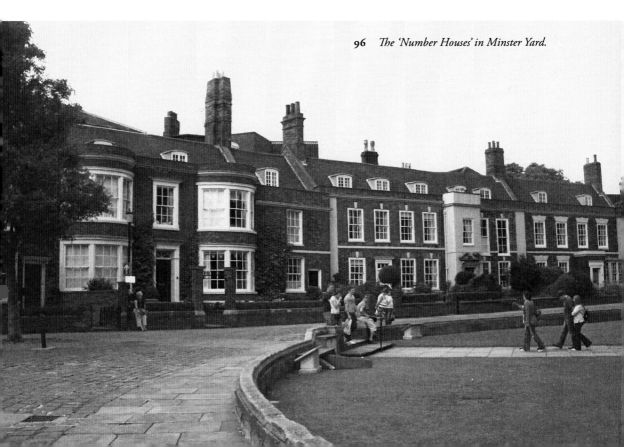

97   'Lincoln', by A.C. Pugin, c.1800. This is a view looking north along the High Street, towards the obelisk on High Bridge and Stonebow.

New churches were also being built to meet the demands of a growing population. The once grand medieval church of St Botolph, on the southern edge of the city, was rebuilt in 1721-3, but the church we see today is largely 19th century and only the west tower dates from the 18th-century church. St Peter at Arches, one of the largest and most important churches in the city, was also rebuilt in 1724 by the council, at a cost of £70. St Michael, on Christ's Hospital Terrace, just below the cathedral, was rebuilt in 1739-40, and in 1740 a new St Mark's was built. Both of the latter were small, unpretentious, rectangular boxes, just large enough for their congregation. Both have long disappeared, but drawings of them, together with a sketch of St Botolph's, were made by the Swiss artist Samuel Hieronymous Grimm about forty years later, and these have happily survived. Rapid population growth prompted

98   St Peter at Arches, rebuilt in 1724; this was the 'Corporation church', the largest and most important of the city's churches in the 18th and 19th centuries.

99 *St Mark's, built in 1740, by S.H. Grimm, c. 1784-6.*

the rebuilding of St Paul in the Bail in the 1780s and of St Swithin in 1801, both of which had remained largely unrepaired since the civil wars. Much necessary repair work was also being undertaken at the cathedral. The western towers were successfully underpinned in the 1720s and further extensive repairs were made to the exterior in the 1750s and 1760s. Interior repairs then followed, including the restoration of the choir screen, a new altarpiece and a new bishop's throne. Proposals to remove the spires on the western towers in 1727, as part of the repairs to the towers, had to be abandoned when local people threatened to riot in their defence. In 1807 the spires were finally taken down.

The improvements to the city's roads already referred to were also changing the appearance of the city. By the 1760s the High Street was no longer the dangerously muddy highway that had impeded travellers in the early part of the century. So successful was the new gravel and coggle surface that this improvement was extended in 1769 from St Mark's parish northwards to St Mary's. Moreover, the completion of the New Road up Lincoln Hill in 1786 necessitated the removal of the medieval Clasket Gate. Other gates and other parts of the Roman and medieval walls would also succumb to road improvements made by the turnpike trusts in the late 18th and early 19th centuries.

Even by the 1730s the increasing number of wagons and carriages coming into the city on market days was prompting complaints about the narrowness of the streets, and the dangers consequently faced by those frequenting the markets and by stall holders. The decision to build a market hall for the women who sold butter, cheese, poultry and eggs in the High Street by St Peter at Arches, just to the north of the Stonebow, was prompted by just such complaints, as the common council admitted in 1736. The road, it acknowledged, was too narrow:

Not only by reason of carriages and loaded horses frequently passing that way to the indangering of people's lives or maiming of them, but also by hindering a free communication of the other markets and persons going backward and forward, and frequent complaints have been made of the same.

Just to the south of the Stonebow, and also in the street, could be found the fish market. On Wednesdays the fishmongers' stalls were set up between the Stonebow and High Bridge, and they groaned under the weight of sea fish, caught mainly off the Yorkshire coast. On Fridays they were up again, but this time full of the fresh-water fish caught mainly in the Witham, especially carp, tench, pike and eels. Here the High Street was rather wider and the dangers less, but in 1769 the fish market was also moved to a new fish shambles in the old St Lawrence churchyard. At about the same time the council also demolished the houses it owned that had until now lined the east side of High Bridge. It had been recognised more than 10 years earlier that, with houses also on the west side, the bridge was inconveniently narrow for the growing volume of traffic passing over it.

At the end of the century, however, and in the first decades of the new one, the most significant change in the city's appearance was the rapid growth of tenements and small, ill-built houses for the city's burgeoning poor. In the first 30 years of the 19th century the number of houses in the city doubled, but most were only two-up, two-down or even smaller. They also lacked either water supplies or any system of sewage disposal other than a common earth closet and cess pit.

A Growing Population

Estimates of the number of families in each of the city's parishes were made by the clergy in 1705 and again in 1721, in response to surveys conducted by the bishop. In 1705 it was reported that there were 735 families in the 15 parishes that comprised the city, including the Bail and Close. If we assume an average family size of about 4.33, this being the average found in the first official census in 1801, then there was a total population of about 3,183 at the beginning of the century. By 1721 the number of families stood at 981, suggesting a total population of 4,248, an increase of more than 1,000 in 16 years. The chief cause was probably immigration, particularly from nearby villages and smaller country towns, for the total number of burials recorded in the separate parishes in the first 20 years of the century exceeded the number of baptisms recorded. In 1701-10 there were 42 more baptisms than burials (1,452 compared with 1,410), but in the following decade the number of baptisms recorded fell to 1,426 and was comfortably exceeded by the number of burials, which rose to 1,496. The baptism figures may well understate the true number of births, but it is unlikely that any shortfall was large enough to account for the apparently quite rapid growth in population.

The number of burials recorded also exceeded baptisms in 1721-30, and were exactly equal in 1741-50, but thereafter the baptisms consistently outstrip burials, and the gap also tends to widen. Although immigration remained a very important cause of growth, a rising birth rate and a falling death rate became increasingly important in the last decades of the 18th century, and also help account for the acceleration of the city's growth in the

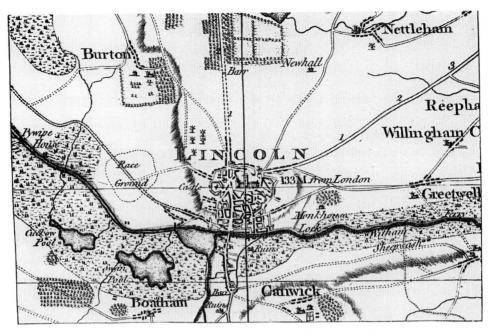

100   *Lincoln in 1779; enlarged from a map of Lincolnshire by Andrew Armstrong.*

first decades of the 19th century. In the 1770s there were only 98 more baptisms than burials recorded, and in the 1780s there were 127 more. In the 1790s, however, the gap jumped to 423, and it rose again to 621 in the first decade of the new century. In 1811-20 it reached 1,003 before falling back a little to 643 in the 1820s.

A rising birth rate reflected the impact of the immigration of young people of marriageable age from the surrounding districts, seeking work wherever they could. Young women worked as domestic servants in the households of the city's expanding 'middling class' of mercers and drapers, grocers and shopkeepers, and young men as apprentices and labourers. By the early 19th century the poorest inhabitants were to be found congregating especially in those parishes that lay close to the warehouses and boatyards of the Foss Dyke and Brayford Pool and the wharves beside the Witham. Consequently, the two largest parishes by the 1830s were those of St Martin and St Swithin, lying just to the north of the Foss Dyke-Brayford line and the Witham respectively. Here, in the 1820s and 1830s, could be found many tiny houses, built in long rows and with little sanitation, paving or lighting, housing the families of watermen, navvies, porters and labourers. A writer who saw the St Swithin area in 1827 clearly believed he had entered into a dangerously alien and disturbing environment:

The houses are old and ruinous; the ground rough, broken and almost impassable; these when united with the dirty coal-lighters, in a canal of the most impure water, with the watermen and other idlers constantly grouped on the turn-bridge, the haling-horses, boatmen's wives, and other accompaniments of a canal, give a study worthy of Hogarth, or of any artist skilled in delineating the lower grades of human life.

He might have been equally disturbed by the filth and overcrowding that could also be found in the courts and alleys growing up by the 1820s behind the High Street in the parishes at the southern end of Wigford. The situation was similar on the northern edge of the city, north of the Bail, where enclosure of the common fields had allowed speculators to invest in cheap housing to be let to the poorer classes. In 1801 the parish of St Nicholas, just to the north of Newport Arch, was one of the smallest in the city, with only 34 families and a population of 147 people. By 1831, however, the population had tripled to 442 and in the next 10 years grew to over a thousand.

Just as important, however, in explaining the growth in the city's population was a decline in the death rate. The decennial totals of burials in the city's 15 parishes did not rise nearly as rapidly as the rate of population increase. Although the city's population more than doubled between 1721 and 1821, the number of burials in 1811-20 was only a little higher than it had been in 1711-20 (1,816 compared to 1,496), and the 1721-30 burial total had been almost as high (at 1,804) as the 1811-20 figure. The slow rate of increase in the burial totals during the second half of the 18th century, and in the first few decades of the 19th, is perhaps the most striking aspect of all the parish population statistics assembled by Hill. The burials' total rose in the first 40 years of the 18th century, as the population grew, from 1,410 in 1701-10 to 1,854 in 1731-40. It then fell sharply to 1,592 in 1741-50, and further still to 1,404 in the next decade. As the city grew again from the 1760s the burial totals picked up again, but only very slowly, and the decennial total did not exceed the 1731-40 figure until 1821-30.

For all the horrors and hardships of the life of the poor in the early 19th century, conditions were still apparently better in most years than they had been for their forebears 100 years earlier. Housing was woefully lacking proper sanitation and clean water supplies, but it was no worse than the damp and cold mud and thatch cottages of the early 18th century. Except in years of very poor harvests, most people were now probably better fed, cleaner and better clothed, and certainly less prone to infectious diseases. There is also some evidence from the late 18th century that conditions for the poor in the city were generally better than they were for the rural poor. Slightly higher weekly wages and more opportunities for wives and children to find work meant that the Lincoln labourer's family was more likely than his country cousins to eat butchers' meat. Moreover, his bread was more likely to be made of wheat, or a mixture of wheat and rye, while the Lincolnshire villager had to make do with barley bread and looked forward to wheat cakes as an occasional luxury to be had at weddings and funerals.

Pauperism and the Poor Law

The growth in population brought with it increasing problems of both criminality and pauperism, and the two were, as always, closely related. The treatment of both in many cases was very similar. At the beginning of the 18th century the system of poor relief had changed little since the passing of the Elizabethan Poor Law a hundred years earlier, and in many respects it would remain largely intact until the passing of the New Poor Law in 1834. The poor rate was fixed by the city's justices: the mayor for that year and those aldermen who had already been 'through the chair'. The poor rates were collected by the overseers in each parish and it was also their task to distribute poor relief; handing out small sums of money to the worthy poor. These sums would usually be just 1s. or 1s. 6d. and were intended only to supplement other meagre incomes. Occasionally food and clothing would also be distributed. The recipients were required to wear a parish badge to identify their right to receive their 'dole', lest others without this right might try to obtain poor relief fraudulently.

The overseers would also try to find apprenticeships for poor children or enrol them in the Jersey School, where they would learn to comb, spin and knit wool and could earn a small weekly income. Once they were sufficiently skilled they would earn, according to Thomas Sympson, 'the customary prices in proportion to the goodness of the work'. Vagrants and beggars from parishes outside the city would be dealt with by the parish constable: they would usually receive a whipping and be lodged in the city gaol in the Stonebow before removal to their place of settlement. However, a new law, passed in 1723, gave the parishes the power to also open workhouses for their poor. These would be very different from the Lincoln Jersey School, for the conditions inside the workhouse had to be sufficiently unpleasant so as to deter all but the most desperate from applying for relief there. Those seeking relief from the overseers would only receive it if they were willing to go into the workhouse, suffer its indignities, privations and punishments, and do whatever work was required of them. This was the infamous 'workhouse test'.

This new power was not at first taken up, but in 1729 the mayor and aldermen who formed the ruling inner circle on the common council agreed that a house should be acquired for the purpose in St Martin's parish. This would be a workhouse for the whole city, to be known as Corporation House, to which the poor could be sent from all the parishes, and to which all the parishes would contribute. Progress was slow, however, and by the time a house was obtained, in 1731, some of the parishes were beginning to have 'second thoughts'. One parish, St Mary Magdalene, had already decided that it would prefer to have its own workhouse, and it was in operation shortly afterwards. The council's plans were abandoned therefore and Corporation House never opened. St Swithin's parish vestry then voted to follow St Mary's lead, and their house opened in 1736, and the two smaller but adjoining parishes of St Benedict and St Peter at Arches agreed to open a joint workhouse in 1739.

There was still support among the aldermen, however, for the original idea of having a general workhouse for the town, but the next proposal proved extremely controversial. In 1741, a group of aldermen, led by William Johnson, managed to persuade a majority of their fellow councillors that the Jersey School should be converted into just such a general workhouse. The proposal was agreed in December, and by the following March the workhouse was established, serving all the parishes that had not yet opened their own. The master of the former Jersey School, who had been receiving £35 per year for training the poor, and the poor combers, knitters and spinners themselves, petitioned the Secretary of State, the Duke of Newcastle, to have the decision overturned. Money to pay the master and equip the school had been left in the will of a local squire, Henry Stone of Skellingthorpe, in 1693, and he had made the governors of Christ's Hospital in London the trustees of his will. The petitioners could claim that the will had been ignored and that the trustees had a duty to act to restore the 'rights and privileges of our Jersey School':

101   *Paupers breaking stones for road-making, by J. Walker, 1813.*

And for want of our Jersey School, we poor Wool Combers And us poor people in general are almost ready to starve, And our Children which usually was taught to spin Jersey now wanders up and down the streets like vagabonds.

The common council was deeply divided. William Johnson himself became a figure of hatred. Some members of the council may have helped the wool combers with their petition and others were not slow to show where their sympathies lay. In 1746, while Johnson was mayor of the city, his house was robbed. Among the items stolen was the mayor's ring, but when a motion was proposed that he should receive £50 to help compensate for his loss, it was defeated by 16 votes to fourteen.

The petitioners won their case and succeeded in forcing the council to re-establish the Jersey School and to close down the general workhouse. The idea never went away completely, however, for the councillors were constantly made aware of the costs of poor relief, and the workhouse was seen by many as a means of cutting costs and weeding out the lazy and unworthy poor. The separate parish workhouses seem to have survived during the next few years. In 1754 the churchwardens of the little parish of St Peter in Eastgate were in discussions with their counterparts of the rather larger parish of St Swithin, just down the hill, to see if their poor might be placed in the St Swithin's workhouse. Proposals for a general workhouse were made again in 1762, a year of exceptionally high food prices and distress, but they again came to nothing, and the Jersey School survived until 1831. Other measures were taken, however, to relieve distress in particularly bad years. After poor harvests in 1756, when grain prices reached starvation levels in the following winter, the council suspended the collection of tolls on grain being brought to market. The tolls were not re-introduced until prices fell again in the summer of 1759. Money was also given to public subscriptions to help the poor; £21 in 1757 and £21 again in 1762, and help was also given to the Jersey School in 1765 so that it could take in and train more children.

The parishes sought to keep down their costs by farming out their poor to any who would undertake to employ them. Any who sought relief but could not prove they had a 'right of settlement' would be removed to wherever they could be traced, unless compensation could be obtained from the latter place. The overseers of St Peter in Eastgate are recorded as employing a formidable Mrs Mompesson to track down the origins of those who applied to the parish for relief, and then to remove them personally to their place of settlement herself. She is recorded as travelling to Gainsborough, Boston and Horncastle for this task.

Conditions in the parish workhouses were grim indeed. The paupers were encouraged to bring with them any goods they might possess, for the parish would provide only bedding and the materials and equipment needed for work. Paupers were likely to be as hungry in the workhouse as they had been before they went in, and in winter the conditions were especially miserable, as overseers were usually unwilling to spend money on coals for heating. Beatings were commonplace and those whom the overseers felt needed additional punishment or restraint would be locked in a 'strait waistcoat' or in chains. The only property recorded belonging to St Margaret's workhouse in 1782 were three bedsteads with beds and bedding, a worsted wheel with reel, a straitjacket to restrain the mentally ill, and lock and chains.

Attempts were also made to set up workshops to employ the poor on similar lines to the Jersey School, although none seem to have had much success. In 1774 it was reported that a small factory had been opened, employing the poor in making camlets – a coarse cloth of wool and goat's hair – but no more is heard of this. Greater hopes were entertained for the philanthropic Rev. Bouyer's proposals for opening a series of spinning schools across the county, including one in Lincoln. A broadsheet appeared in 1783 canvassing support for the idea and promising that the new spinning school would 'certainly keep from idleness and beggary most of the children above eight years old who now loiter in the streets'. Bouyer was a wealthy and well-connected man, but in Lincoln his scheme does not seem to have attracted as much support from other wealthy gentlemen as it did in some other towns, such as Louth. A school seems to have been set up, probably in the winter of 1785-6, but by 1787 it was reported to be suspended due to lack of wool and no more is then heard of it.

As well as money raised from the Poor Rate, the parish officials also had various sums to dispense, left for the purpose in the wills of the more affluent. In 1786 it was calculated that the numerous legacies were together worth a little over a thousand pounds a year. This must have helped keep down the cost of the poor rate, but the overseers of St Swithin's parish complained that the numerous donations that they were able to make every year, under the terms of the will of John Smith, a 17th-century merchant, only attracted more of the poor to try and establish a right of settlement in the parish so that they could benefit from Smith's will.

The quickening pace in the rate of population growth in the city in the 1780s and 1790s, together with a sharp increase in the cost of living, caused the cost of the poor rates to nearly triple in the same period, reaching over £3,000 in 1803. This increasing burden prompted fresh thoughts of a general workhouse. Moreover, an Act passed by Parliament in 1782, known popularly as Gilbert's Act, made it possible for large groups of rural and urban parishes to come together to form Unions and pool their resources to support a common workhouse, which would be under the supervision of the justices. The initiative was taken by a group of residents in the Close. A former glue factory was leased and converted into a workhouse and by 1789 it was full, with just over 80 inmates, mostly from surrounding rural parishes. All but the youngest and eldest were set to work, the women mostly in spinning flax and wool while the men were often hired out for gardening or breaking stones. Rules drawn up in 1797 stated that all female inmates had to wear a uniform consisting of a black bonnet, a white cap, a dark gown, black stockings and a blue neckerchief. When the inmates left the workhouse they had to wear a badge inscribed 'Lincoln House of Industry'. Any instances of drunkenness, swearing or profanity would be punished by up to four hours in the stocks. Other offences could lead to a whipping, and it was later claimed by the Whig MP, Sir Robert Heron, that the workhouse was 'ruled with an iron rod, and chains and dungeons were in constant use for trivial faults, and at the will of the governor'. In one notorious case an inmate was confined in a cell for four weeks for leaving the workhouse without permission.

In some respects, however, conditions were better than they had been in the earlier small parish workhouses. When Sir Frederick Eden visited in 1790 he found the house clean and 'very healthy'. The rules stipulated that meat should be served every day and that children who were too young to work had to be educated. A schoolroom was opened in 1798 and a schoolmistress appointed, but after a National School was opened in 1813 the children were sent there instead. Allegations of brutal treatment may have been exaggerated. Sir Robert Heron was a political opponent of Richard Ellison, the Lincoln MP who had championed the establishment of the workhouse, and although the punishments for rule-breaking were harsh, the workhouse authorities could also adopt a more humane attitude. When, for instance, it was learnt that the National School master had flogged one of the workhouse boys extremely severely, the subscription to the school was stopped, the children withdrawn and the workhouse school was started up again. Similarly, when complaints were made that a Nottinghamshire framework knitter had ill-treated one of the boys who had been sent to him as an apprentice, the man was sent for to answer the allegation and receive a warning about his behaviour. When children were apprenticed it was clearly on the understanding that they would be treated humanely, and when boys were hired out to local brick-makers (a particularly unpleasant and laborious employment) it was always agreed that they could be withdrawn at any time to be apprenticed.

CRIME AND PUNISHMENT

Lincoln had three prisons: the county gaol, located in the castle, the city gaol in the Stonebow, and the House of Correction, to be found in the sheep market, just to the south of the Greyfriars' Grammar School. Those who left a record of Lincoln's prisons make it clear that they were as grim as any 18th-century felon might expect to find. John Howard, the prison reformer, visited Lincoln county gaol in 1774 and 1776. As was normal at this time, he found that the conditions endured by both debtors and felons were determined to a large extent by their ability to pay the gaoler for privileges. Those who could afford their own rooms in the prison certainly lived rather better than those who could not. Felons who could not afford this luxury had to suffer the horrors of the castle dungeons. There were two dungeons: one for those who had been condemned to death, and the other – known as the pit – for those awaiting trial or transportation. Both were reached by a trapdoor, set in the floor of the debtors' 'free ward', immediately above them. The dungeons were reached by a set of ten steps. There was no water and no sewer and the prisoners had only a little straw on the floor to sleep on. The stench would have been appalling; Howard described it as 'offensive'. There was neither an infirmary nor a chapel but both debtors and felons were taken to attend religious services in the shire hall. The sermons of the chaplain were probably appreciated rather less by his unfortunate congregation than the fresh air and sunlight that might be enjoyed in the brief walk to the hall.

Conditions in the city gaol were not much better. John Howard described it as having:

One large room for men-debtors, one smaller for women, both upstairs: in each a fireplace. The rooms for criminals are two dungeons down three steps: with bedsteads, that they may not sleep on the damp earth floor. In one of them is a cage for closer confinement when necessary. These prisoners are sometimes taken into the keeper's house. No courtyard: no water accessible to prisoners: no straw.

The dampness of the dungeons was believed to have helped to cause the death of a female prisoner a few years later, and they were described by the *Gentleman's Magazine* in 1805 as a sepulchre for the living. Other contemporaries noted that felons and debtors alike were often drunk because the gaoler could make extra money by selling them ale, and passers-by also often passed ale to the prisoners through the bars of the prison.

Ironically, drunkenness was one of the more common reasons for a person being locked up in the Stonebow. Other common offences included sheep-stealing, robbery, violent behaviour and 'keeping a disorderly house', which usually meant a brothel. Vagrants and beggars were also sometimes lodged in the city gaol while awaiting removal to their place of settlement. In 1805 it was reported that the inmates of the House of Correction were mostly employed in spinning and carding wool and were allowed a plank bedstead with straw plus two blankets and a rug.

Howard's criticisms of the state of both the county and city gaols may have been partly responsible for the decision taken a few years later by the county magistrates to build a new county gaol in the castle. An Act of Parliament was needed, however, and this was not obtained until 1784. Work only began two years later. The city magistrates were perhaps less susceptible to Howard's arguments, however, for a new city gaol was only begun in 1804, and the urgent need for more space was probably the main reason for this advance. The number of cases before the magistrates was increasing sharply in the 1790s, and continued to rise in the new century. The rise in the city's population was probably partly to blame, but the French Wars were also driving up the cost of living, and poverty was turning hungry, desperate men to crime. In November 1808 the local newspaper, the *Mercury*, reported that there had been more robberies and petty thefts (particularly of poultry and linen) throughout the city that winter than had ever

102   *The Castle Gaol, built 1787, as it appears today.*

been known before. When the new city gaol opened, in 1809, a tread-wheel was soon installed in the hope of adding to the deterrent effect. Some of the magistrates also proposed that a ducking stool should be re-introduced, it being felt that this might be a particularly appropriate punishment for women accused of keeping a disorderly house. This suggestion was not acted on, but the existing pillory and stocks had probably never before been used as frequently as they were now.

An increasing crime rate had also helped prompt the introduction of street lighting in 1794, when a Lighting and Paving Commission was established, and 250 street lamps were soon after set up in the main streets. There was also clearly a need for a more adequate police force than that which the parish watchmen could hope to offer. A Bill to give the city a permanent force, as well as better lighting and paving, was passed in May 1828. Under the Act Lincoln was now policed by a force of 10 watchmen (as the new police were at first still called) and two superintendents, under the authority of commissioners who also had the power to recruit extra constables when there was particular need, such as for the races, when an extra 50 could be raised.

CHURCH, CHAPEL AND SCHOOL

Although a number of churches were repaired or rebuilt during the century, there remained much to criticise in the response of the Established Church to the challenge of a rapidly growing population in the city. Throughout the century there were only two churches 'below hill' at which there were services every Sunday: St Peter at Arches and St Mary le Wigford. In the rest there were either only occasional services or, where the church was in an especially poor state of repair, none at all. Following the destruction of the bishop's palace during the civil wars the official residence of the Bishops of Lincoln had been at Buckden in Huntingdonshire. This would remain his residence until 1836, when Buckden became part of the new diocese of Ely, and Bishop Kaye moved his residence to Riseholme, just two miles outside Lincoln. Kaye would prove an able and dedicated bishop, but this cannot be said of his more immediate predecessors, some of whom seem to have been principally concerned to further the material interests of themselves and their families. One example was George Pretyman, who became bishop in 1787, and owed his appointment entirely to his friendship with William Pitt, whose tutor he had been at Cambridge. He was also Dean of St Paul's and rarely visited Lincoln, but he did ensure that his brother became precentor and archdeacon. He also ensured that one of his sons became the chancellor of the diocese as well as prebendary of Winchester and rector of three livings, and that another son was also precentor, had four livings and received the wardenship of the Mere Hospital.

Such an example of pluralism and nepotism was not likely to encourage high standards among the clergy of the city, and pluralism among some of the clergy had indeed become a scandal by the 1820s. The Rev. George Davis Kent, the vicar of St Martin's, was also a canon of Lincoln and held three other Lincolnshire livings and one in Kent. The Rev. William Hett, who was famous for his hatred of Methodists, was the Rector of St Paul's in Lincoln, Vicar of St John's and a prebendary and vicar choral of the cathedral. He was also Vicar of Dunholme, Rector of both Mavis Enderby and Thorpe on the Hill, minister to two chapelries in Greetwell and Nettleham and chaplain to the Marquis of Stafford.

In spite of the failings of the Established Church, however, such was the power of clerical influence and authority in this cathedral city that John Wesley's Methodist movement could make only slow progress. Wesley himself recognised this and said of the city's clergy that they had created a soil 'ungrateful to the tiller's toil'. Wesley first came to the city in 1749 and preached 'the word of life' (to quote his journal) to a large crowd 'on the Castle Hill'. He was received politely and even allowed to use the court house when a thunderstorm interrupted his preaching, but no local society was formed and Wesley did not return to the city until 1780, although he made a great many visits to other towns and villages in his native county in the years between. His visit in 1780 was again met with polite indifference, and a third visit in the following year was equally unproductive. In 1787, however, a Methodist supporter from Great Gonerby, near Grantham, acquired a house near Gowts Bridge, at the southern end of the city, and a small group began to meet in the lumber room. Wesley visited in 1788 and two years later, when he made his last visit, the group had grown sufficiently to justify opening a preaching house on Waterside South capable of seating up to 600 people.

The movement faced considerable opposition in the city, made worse by patriotic sentiment stirred up by the French Wars, when any criticism of the established order might be interpreted as little better than sedition. There was therefore little sympathy for the Methodists in 1802 when a squib of gunpowder was thrown into the meeting house during a service. A man was arrested but the magistrate dismissed the case on the grounds of lack of evidence. The common council then chose to demonstrate its opinion on the matter by passing a unanimous vote congratulating their fellow magistrate on his creditable behaviour and judgement. The despairing Methodists sought legal redress through an appeal to the King's Bench, but with no success. In 1812 the movement faced further official obstacles when the magistrates in the city quarter sessions refused to grant preaching licences to Methodist preachers. They may have been influenced by the pamphlets written by the local pluralist vicar, the Rev. Hett, who claimed that boys as young as 16 were applying for preaching licences so that they could avoid the militia.

103   *The 'Big Wesley', for many years the city's largest Wesleyan Methodist church, built 1836.*

The virulence of Hett's attacks on the Methodists at this time probably partly reflects the success they were now beginning to enjoy, in spite of such opposition. The first Methodist Sunday School was opened in 1806, teaching children to read and write for five hours on Sundays, and two other schools followed soon afterwards. A large chapel was opened in 1815, in St Swithin's parish, capable of holding 700, and in 1820 it was reported to be regularly full. And such was the success of the movement that by 1836 it had been found necessary to build a still larger chapel, on Clasketgate, which could seat 1,400 people. This would remain the principal Methodist church in the city until its closure in 1961, prior to demolition two years later, and today is still affectionately remembered by some of the city's older inhabitants as the 'Big Wesley'.

The success of the Methodists seems to have also given encouragement to older dissenter groups, all of which had rather dwindled in the century following the Restoration. Growing numbers prompted a group of Baptists to build a little chapel in Mint Lane in 1818, and a congregation of Independents opened their chapel in Tanners Lane shortly afterwards. A small group of Quakers still met regularly in the city, but from about 1770 had ceased to occupy the meeting house they had opened in 1689. The Primitive Methodists, who had only recently broken away from the Wesleyan Methodists, also opened a little chapel in 1819, with a congregation of about 150 people. The little community of Roman Catholics, whose chapel had been attacked and burnt by a mob in 1688, had recovered from this blow and opened a new chapel near the river in St Swithin's parish, before moving, in about 1750, to a house in Bank Street, where they met in a locked garret.

Rivalry between church and chapel helped stimulate support among the Lincoln clergy and the common council for the establishment of a National School in the city to educate poor children. The National Society for the Education of the Poor in the Principles of the Established Church was set up in London in 1811. In the following year the bishop and the lord lieutenant together called a meeting to raise subscriptions to launch a National School in the city. Children of dissenters were not excluded provided they attended an Anglican Church service at least once a week and at the school learnt the catechism of the Church of England. Land was acquired from the common council in Silver Street and by 1813 the school was established with about 250 children attending, both boys and girls, each paying a penny a week for their instruction. In the next 12 years the numbers doubled. In 1825 it was reported that there were 307 boys and 202 girls attending. This was a triumph for the Established Church to which the dissenting churches, lacking the necessary financial resources, could as yet make little response, except to enlarge the number of their Sunday Schools. The rival to the National Society, the British and Foreign Schools Society, did not establish its first schools in the city until 1840.

The National School could offer only the most rudimentary education and was intended only to civilise the children of the poor and prepare them for their lowly station in life. In this respect it shared a common aim with a number of small charity schools established in the city, and with the more venerable Bluecoat School, which at the beginning of the 19th century still educated about thirty boys each year, preparing them for apprenticeships to local tradesmen and craftsmen. For the city's growing middling class of merchants, lawyers, clergy and doctors there was either the ancient grammar school or one of the city's numerous private schools to choose from by this time. It is an indication of the poor state of the boys' grammar school that so many were choosing the latter. White's *Gazeteer* of 1826 names 17 day schools and six boarding schools that also took day pupils. When commissioners inspected the grammar school in 1837 they found that there were only about thirty boys on the school roll. The curriculum had barely changed in the previous 100 years. A few years before the inspection the usher and master had both been obliged to resign following allegations of brutal treatment of the boys, and their replacements had also proved unsuitable.

The fortunes of the school had always varied with the reputation of the master. In 1724 it had been reported to be in such a decayed state that the common council had resolved to increase its contribution towards the master's and usher's salaries in the hope of obtaining competent and learned candidates for the posts. A salary of £50 per year plus a house and a share in the fees chargeable to boarders attracted the Rev. John Goodall, a graduate of St John's College, Cambridge, and under his care the school seems to have enjoyed a revival, sending numerous boys to Cambridge. With the council taking a close interest in the school, many of whom were themselves former pupils and the fathers of pupils, the school's reputation survived Goodall's early death in 1742, but later in the century it was again in decline. The master appointed in 1765, the Rev. Mr Hewthwaite, remained in post until his death 37 years later, at the age of 73, and it would seem that the school's reputation gradually sank with his advancing years. His ability to fulfil his responsibilities was also not helped by his insistence on also holding numerous country livings. Throughout this time the curriculum remained extremely classical. The great majority of the boys' time was spent being drilled in the Latin and Greek authors. Hewthwaite's successors failed to improve the school, however, and it was only with the adoption of a more liberal curriculum, from the middle of the century, that it began to regain the confidence of the city's middle classes.

SOCIETY AND LEISURE:
UPHILL AND DOWNHILL

For the gentry and nobility of the county
Lincoln offered two principal occasions
for jollity: the races and, from 1789,
the Stuff Ball. At the beginning of the
18th century horse racing had taken place
both to the north and south of the city,
and the first racing calendar, published
in 1727, mentions both flat racing and
steeplechasing. Very large sums were
wagered and large crowds gathered for
these occasions. In 1716 the king himself
gave 100 guineas to be run for. By the
1740s most races were being run on a
round course of four miles on Waddington
Heath, to the south of the city, but the

104   *The 'Harlequin' on Castle Hill.*

enclosure of the heath caused the venue to be moved, first to Welton Heath in 1770 and
then three years later to the Carholme. The leading gentlemen acted as stewards and
subscribed to the purses, but a stand was not erected until 1806.

During race week, which was always in the autumn, the gentry of the city and county
could enjoy plays, balls, concerts and assemblies. In the first decades of the century these
were always held in the great room of the *Angel* in the Bail, but at a meeting of gentlemen
at the races in September 1742 it was agreed to build an assembly room and this was
completed two years later, the subscription list being headed by the Duke of Ancaster.
The races reached the zenith of their popularity in the first years of the 19th century
when John George, the 4th Lord Monson, presided over the entertainments, but with
his early death in 1809 they began to fall out of fashion. The races had always been
notorious for attracting pickpockets and thimble-riggers, but the problem increased
in the 1820s and 1830s. In 1831, when it was estimated that there were possibly 500

105   *Lincoln
Races, from a
postcard of 1905.*

pickpockets and thimble-riggers on the course, riots broke out, gamblers' booths were
destroyed and carriages burnt.

By the end of the 18th century the high point of the social year was the Stuff, or
Colour, Ball held at the Assembly Hall late in October or early November, when there
was a full moon to assist parties travelling up to 15 miles or more. The patroness would
choose the colour of the year and the purchase of woollen ball dresses was supposed to
encourage the manufacture of cloth in the county. The ball was first held in Alford, in
1785, but moved to Lincoln in 1789. It immediately became the principal opportunity
for the upper echelons of Lincoln society – chiefly the clergy, lawyers and doctors of the
Cathedral Close, uphill society – to mix with the county social elite. Other events were
organised around it, perhaps a play before the ball, a race meeting, and a meeting of
Lord Monson's Burton hounds the following day.

Plays might be performed in private houses or in the Assembly Rooms, but a small
theatre did exist in 1732, in a lane under the castle wall that subsequently became known
as Drury Lane. As the lane was too narrow for carriages, ladies were taken to the plays
in sedan chairs. In 1744 a rather larger theatre was opened at the *Harlequin*, on Castle
Hill, under the actor-manager William Herbert, who led a 'Company of Comedians'. In
1763 the theatre moved downhill, to the *King's Head* on the High Street, and came under
the control of the Robertson family. The support of the gentry remained crucial to the
theatre's success, however, and Race Week was especially important. It was during Race
Week in 1806 that Thomas Robertson opened a new Theatre Royal in the city, on the site
of St Lawrence's Church, with two rows of boxes (for gentlemen and their ladies), and a pit
and a gallery supported by iron columns (for downhill society). Programmes were usually
very varied, to suit all tastes. An evening might begin with a play by Shakespeare, or with
extracts from Shakespeare, but this would often be followed by a comic song and a farce.

A similar social mix might also be found enjoying the entertainment of a cockfight.
Nearly every public house in the city organised a cockfight on Shrove Tuesday and at
Christmas but the chief centres for this very popular sport were the cock pits of the *King's
Head* and the *Reindeer*. Among the numerous gentlemen patrons were the Monson and
Heneage families. Very large stakes were sometimes gambled on the birds; one member
of the Heneage family was said to have lost such large sums at the Lincoln cockfights in
the 1740s that he endangered the family's control of their estate.

For the majority of Lincoln's population the chief means of relaxation was provided
by the sale and consumption of alcohol. In 1826 White's *Gazeteer* listed 66 licensed
premises in the city and in 1842 there were 73 listed. By the latter date, however, there
were in addition 39 beer houses in Lincoln, set up following the Sale of Beer Act of
1830, which established a free trade in beer and beer houses. Alcohol was also always an
important constituent of merry-making at village feasts, which the younger members
of the city's population were said to particularly enjoy, and of the celebrations of Guy
Fawkes' Night and the great Christian festivals of Christmas, Easter and Whitsuntide.
The magistrates' supervision of licensed houses could be extremely lax, especially when
a fellow magistrate was the owner of the house in question. In such circumstances even
the conviction of a tenant for keeping a disorderly house frequented by thieves and
prostitutes did not necessarily prevent a license from being renewed.

106   *The* Lion and Snake, *on Bailgate, in 1905. This is one of many of the city's Georgian inns that still survive today.*

Concerns regarding social problems associated with alcohol, and in particular drunkenness, gambling, criminality and prostitution, were behind the first attempts to establish a Temperance movement in the city in the 1830s. There were, however, some indications that society was becoming more humane and more civilised. One cruel sport that had been extremely popular for most of the 18th century, bull-baiting, was certainly in decline early in the 19th century and by the 1830s had apparently died out. Moreover, among the most popular causes supported by the ladies and gentlemen of uphill society were a new hospital (later the Lincoln College of Theology), which opened in 1777 at the top of Steep Hill, and an asylum, later known as the Lawn, opened in 1820 on Union Road near to the hospital, and now a city council conference centre.

107   *The Lawn Hospital, Union Road, built as a lunatic asylum, 1819-20, from a postcard of 1908.*

ELEVEN

The Victorian and Edwardian City, 1837-1914

THE COMING OF THE RAILWAY

When the first steam train came into Lincoln in June 1846 it heralded a truly new age for the city. The first line – George Hudson's Midland Railway from Nottingham – was opened for regular service two months later, on 3 August, amid scenes of considerable celebration, attended by the 'Railway King' himself. Within four years three further lines had been completed and the city had two railway stations – it was at the hub of a system that radiated in all directions. Almost overnight the city's communications with the rest of the country had been enormously improved. The city was unfortunate not to be included on the Great Northern line that bypassed the city and passed instead (as it still does) to the west of Lincoln, through Newark and Retford. The Great Northern 'Loop' line, however, was built in 1848, linking the city both to Gainsborough to the north and to Boston and Spalding to the south, and joining the main line at Peterborough. Lack of co-operation between the rival companies resulted in not only two stations but also two level crossings on the High Street, and this remained the case until the closure of the Midland Station, St Mark's, in 1985.

In 1849 the much-maligned Manchester, Sheffield and Lincoln Railway completed a line linking Lancashire and the West Riding with Lincoln. It was later better known to passengers as 'Mucky, Slow and Late' and to investors as 'Money Sunk and Lost'. But this was much later and these were not the sentiments that would have been appreciated by Prince Albert, who travelled to the city by train on 18 April 1849 and went on to Grimsby to lay the foundation stone of the dock. With road, river and canal transport as yet unable to compete, it proved profitable for at least a few years for yet further lines to be built during the next half century, and by 1900 seven lines radiated from the city's two stations.

The city's failure to secure the GNR's main line route north from London to York was due partly to vigorous lobbying by the Member of Parliament for Doncaster, who feared that a Lincoln route might exclude his town. But Lincoln also had itself to blame. Two public meetings held in the city in April 1845 to resolve the matter ended in chaos and recriminations, with the local pro- and anti-GNR parties each accusing the other

108 *The last days of long-distance coach travel: a coach and four passing through the Stonebow, 1836. A detail from 'The Stonebow, Lincoln', by Thomas Allom.*

of hiring labourers to pack the meetings and shout down their opponents. Matters were also not helped by the attitude of the Lincoln MP, Colonel Charles de Laet Waldo-Sibthorp, who had a strong dislike for all railway schemes and said that he would vote for only one railway; that which would carry ministers to hell.

Ironically, the city was mentioned in more railway schemes – at least 80 – than any other city in the country. As early as 1821 a proposal had been made and a route surveyed for a railway to run from London to Lincoln via Cambridge, and in 1827 the Rennie brothers surveyed a route from Cambridge to York via Lincoln. More schemes were proposed in the 1830s and during the railway mania of 1845 so many schemes were drawn up involving the city that several brokers opened offices in Lincoln for the sale of shares. In November that year, with railway mania reaching hysterical proportions, a stock exchange was opened in a room next to the city Assembly Rooms.

However, lacking either large centres of population or industry, Lincolnshire was relatively late in witnessing the arrival of railways, and the 33 miles of track from Nottingham to Lincoln was the first in the county. But the impact of the railways was already being felt before this. In 1838 a new coach service, appropriately called 'the Railway', was inaugurated to take passengers from the city to the nearest railway station on the London-Birmingham line near Northampton. A few years later another stage coach was taking travellers from the city to Wansford, where the LBR's branch line to Peterborough crossed the Great North Road. Once the railway reached the city, long-distance coach and goods wagon services quickly disappeared and water transport came to specialise only in heavy goods such as grain for the flour mills and the raw materials required by fertiliser manufacturers. Business for the local carriers, however, grew considerably, and their number continued to increase throughout the rest of the century. Pickford and Co. established an office at St Mark's station almost as soon as the first railway arrived. Additionally, the continuation of water traffic on the Foss Dyke guaranteed the survival of a number of small boat-building yards in the city right up to the start of the First World War.

A WORLD-RENOWNED CENTRE FOR ENGINEERING

The impact of the railway on the development of Lincoln was enormous. The physical appearance of the town changed, for the stations, tracks and sidings occupied a considerable area, but, more significantly, the railway also made possible the creation of a large-scale engineering industry of international importance. The railways were the catalyst, for they gave the city access to cheaper coal and iron and greatly improved access to markets both in Britain and overseas. The initial demand from the 1840s was for agricultural machinery, but a number of inventive Lincoln engineering firms were able to diversify into many other areas of engineering and therefore survived agricultural depressions and changing demands.

The foundation for Lincoln's engineering industry was provided by the growing demand from the 1840s for steam-driven thrashing machines. In 1845 Clayton and Shuttleworth was the first Lincoln firm to build a portable steam engine, at its Stamp End Works to the east of the city. The partnership of Nathaniel Clayton, the owner of a steam packet on the Witham, and his brother-in-law, Joseph Shuttleworth, a boat builder on the river, had begun just three years earlier when they acquired one-and-a-half acres of marshy land on Waterside South. They had begun with 12 men, two forges and a lathe, making pipes, fire grates and doing a variety of work for the railways. In 1848 the firm was boasting that it was selling its steam engines and thrashing machines in other

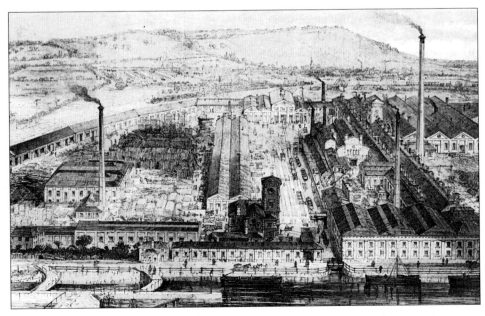

109   *The Stamp End ironworks of Clayton and Shuttleworth, beside the River Witham, 1869.*

counties as well as Lincolnshire, and in 1852 it won first prize for its thrashing machine and steam engine at the Royal Show at Lewes. As demand grew, other firms were also set up and expanded, but Clayton's was able to quickly establish itself as the largest and most successful engineering firm in the county. By 1848 they were already employing 100 men and producing a few dozen thrashing sets a year. By 1854, however, they were employing 520 men and 80 boys and output was being considerably expanded. By now the thrashing sets had reached a standard design that changed little for the next half-century, and they were being sold not only in England but throughout Europe. The firm claimed in 1857 that it had made 2,400 sets, and by 1862, when it employed 940 men, production had reached 15 per week. The journal *The Engineer* described the Stamp End Works at this time as the greatest manufactory in the world.

This success was only possible because the firm was able to find markets abroad. As early as 1851 it was selling its thrashing sets to Austro-Hungary, and today a Clayton and Shuttleworth engine dating from this time can still be seen in the museum of agriculture in Budapest. Steam engines were also sent to the Crimea, for use in the war against Russia. In 1856 the *Stamford Mercury* noted that large quantities of the firm's products were seen 'passing through Berlin on their way to Vienna for Hungarian grandees and landowners'. Once the Crimean War was over the Russian market was also opened up and the firm opened branches across Eastern Europe; in Vienna, Prague, Budapest, Cracow and Lemberg. During the 1860s new markets opened up in the other great cereal-growing areas of the world, in Canada and the USA, and also in South America, Egypt and Australia. By 1870 Clayton's were employing 1,200 men and were making 900 thrashing machines and 1,000 steam engines a year. By virtue of foreign markets and diversification, expansion continued, in spite of the agricultural depression of the 1870s and 1880s. In 1885 Clayton's was employing 2,300 men, and five years later the firm could report that it had produced over 26,000 portable steam engines and 24,000 thrashing machines.

Clayton and Shuttleworth's success was also partly due to the position of their Stamp End Works. The watery strip of cheap land purchased in 1842 proved an inspired choice and more land was acquired as the business grew. Placed between the river and the railway, it enjoyed ideal communications. The illustration of the works (*see* Fig. 109) drawn in 1869 also shows both a navigable stretch of water extending from the river into the centre of the works and, running alongside, railway sidings connected to the MSLR railway in the background.

Other engineering firms soon followed Clayton's to this part of the city to enjoy the same benefits. One of the fastest-growing firms of the second half of the century was Ruston, Proctor and Co., led by the young Joseph Ruston. When the 22-year-old joined the partnership of Proctor and Burton in January 1857 it was a small firm with a workforce of just 25 men. Ruston, however, was a young man in a hurry with a burning ambition to be a great entrepreneur. He soon bought out Burton, who was unwilling to invest in building engines for stock and, by enormous efforts and the most energetic salesmanship, quickly established the firm as a rival to Clayton and Shuttleworth, not only in this country but also abroad. Already by 1870 the company's Sheaf Ironworks

110 *A Clayton and Shuttleworth steam wagon, as shown on a postcard, c. 1905.*

employed over 700 men and was exceeded in Lincolnshire only by Clayton's and the Grantham firm of Hornsby's. His ability to find new markets was prodigious. By 1870 he had established agencies in India, Japan, Chile, Argentina, USA, Russia and Hungary. The export of thrashing machine and traction engine sets was again at the heart of the business, but Ruston was also extremely successful in diversifying into other lines.

During the 1870s his firm developed steam excavators, for instance, to replace the pick- and shovel-work of major civil engineering projects. The first one was sold in August 1875, made entirely of wrought iron, instead of the cast iron and timber used in earlier models. They were used in building the Albert Dock in London, which began in 1875, and in constructing the Manchester Ship Canal in 1887. When his firm became a limited company in 1889 the most important products, apart

111 *Joseph Ruston, 1835-97.*

112 *A Ruston-Dunbar steam navvy at work on the Manchester Ship Canal. This project used 71 of these machines.*

from thrashing machines and steam engines, were electric lighting machines, centrifugal pumps and sugar mills. When Joseph Ruston died in 1897 his firm had already overtaken Clayton's to be one of the largest agricultural engineering firms in the country. In 1911 the firm occupied three large sites, covering 52 acres, employed over 5,200 men in the city and was producing over 6,000 items a year.

The success of the city's engineering firms in the last two decades of the 19th century led to the development of a second major industrial area to the south-west of the city centre, on the banks of the upper Witham and served by railway sidings from the Midland

113 *(Left) A Ruston-Proctor traction engine designed for export to Argentina, c.1880. Note the extra-wide rear wheels, which had been requested to cope with soft ground.*

114 *(Opposite) A traction engine built by William Foster & Co. Ltd, c.1900.*

Railway. In about 1885 Ruston's established their sawmills, wood works and boiler works here, and at about the same time the city's third major engineering firm, Foster's, established a factory for making thrashing machines. Like Clayton's and Ruston's, Foster's were already established on the east side of the city, close to the river, but unlike their two rivals their site – the Wellington works – did not have ready access to the railway. Consequently, after a serious fire in 1898, the entire works was moved to the new site.

William Foster, from Manchester, had established his foundry in 1856, investing the profits made from his flour-milling business beside the Witham. He built his first portable steam engine to drive a thrashing machine in 1858. Although his business did not grow as rapidly as either Clayton's or Ruston's – he employed 200 men in 1885 – he also soon came to rely heavily on the export market, and particularly on trade with Eastern Europe. A branch works and repair depot were opened in Budapest and his engines won prizes at exhibitions in Moscow in 1864, Hungary in 1869 and Vienna in 1873. Also, like his larger rivals, the ability to diversify proved essential for survival. The Budapest branch, for instance, produced torpedo boats for use by the Hungarian navy on the Danube. Foster was also a pioneer in the development of self-moving traction engines, building his first in 1861. In the 1890s the firm also became a major producer of light steam tractors and with the outbreak of the First World War it would achieve its greatest fame as the manufacturer of the first tanks.

The success of Clayton and Shuttleworth's business encouraged many firms to attempt to follow in their wake. Ruston's and Foster's were two of the most successful; another was the ironworks established nearby by a Nottingham man, Robert Robey, in 1854. Together, the enterprise and inventiveness of these four firms, congregated so near to one another between river and railway, quickly transformed an ancient cathedral town into a rapidly growing major industrial centre, and one of the most important producers of agricultural machinery in the world. Like the others, Robey made his first fortune by building thrashing machines and steam engines and selling them well

115   *The Ruston steam roller factory, c. 1900.*

beyond these shores, particularly to South America and Australia. He was also, together with William Foster, one of the first engineers to develop a successful traction engine, winning a prize for one of his first models at the Great Exhibition of 1862, and was also a pioneer in building steam-ploughing machinery. When the agricultural depression struck in the late 1870s, and order books started to look rather empty, Robey's firm moved into the market for mining machinery, and particularly for winding engines and pit-head towers. The new developments in electric power also offered opportunities that Robey's (like Ruston's) were quick to grasp. During the 1880s the firm began to import the first Edison dynamos from the USA and linked them with their high-speed steam engines for electric power stations. A little earlier, in 1882, a Robey steam engine had also been used to drive the dynamo for the first electric lights in Cleethorpes.

These four firms were the largest and most successful heavy engineering firms in the city, and all four survived well into the 20th century, but there were many other enterprising individuals who also attempted in these years to enter this growing and profitable market. One who did not succeed was a local man, Michael Penistan, who had manufactured horse-driven thrashing machines before attempting to move into production of the new steam-powered machines. He sold his foundry in St Rumbold's Lane in about 1870 to William Rainforth, an owner of keel boats, who used it to manufacture agricultural implements, including corn screens, harrows and potato diggers. More successful was the Lindum Plough Works, founded in 1851 by John Cooke, from the nearby village of Eagle. He was a blacksmith who had invented an improved plough that was suitable for all soils. He moved to Lincoln in 1857 to expand his business and was soon selling 2,000 ploughs a year. When he died in 1887 he was employing 70 men. Other agricultural implement makers included Penney and Porter on Broadbank, and Harrison's Malleable Ironworks, established near St Mark's Church in 1874.

Such was the extent of the growth of heavy engineering that a number of relatively small firms were also able to set up as specialist suppliers to the major engineering works. Edward Clarke, for instance, started making crank shafts for other firms in 1859 and from 1872 James Dawson supplied belting for power transmission. William Singleton, who had started out as a rope-maker, moved into the manufacture of oil cloths and waterproof covers for engineering firms and railway companies.

The most successful entrepreneurs, such as Nathaniel Clayton, Joseph Shuttleworth and Joseph Ruston, also came to play a dominant role in the political and social life of the city in the second half of the century. The old order had been represented by the city's ultra-conservative MP, Colonel Sibthorp, who died in 1851. As well as loathing the railways, he had opposed every reforming measure of the 1830s, including Catholic Emancipation, the Reform Bill, Municipal Reform, and the New Poor Law. He had also incurred the undying hatred of Queen Victoria by also opposing the Great Exhibition (Prince Albert's pet project) and successfully arguing in Parliament for a reduction in Prince Albert's grant. It was later said that it was because of this that the Queen refused to leave her carriage when the royal train stopped in Lincoln some years later. Ruston became an MP for Lincoln himself in 1884, after Clayton had declined to stand for the Liberals, believing he was by now too old. By this time these wealthy Liberal industrialists had become the great benefactors of the town, supporting schools, hospitals, charities, parks and gardens, and later it would be Ruston's private art collection that would form the nucleus of the Usher Gallery.

116   *Singleton & Flint's workmen outside the Newland Tarpaulin and Brush Works, on Newland Street West, 1916.*

OTHER INDUSTRIES

Other industries that grew up in the city in the Victorian era were also usually closely related either to the needs or the products of agriculture. They included chemical manure manufacturers, oil millers, flour millers, maltsters, brewers, tanneries and a glue factory.

Lincoln had always been a centre for the sale, slaughtering and processing of sheep and cattle and the first large-scale tannery was established beside the upper Witham during the first half of the century. From the 1860s Galsworthy's Tannery was established to the south of the Midland Railway station, with sidings running into the works. Bernard Cannon took over an existing skin yard when he set up his leather processing and glue works in Gaunt Street in 1863, but in 1874 he also moved to a site beside the upper Witham, south of the Brayford Pool. This was the beginning of a new industrial district for the city, referred to already. A few years later both Ruston's and Foster's also moved into the vicinity, as did another large-scale leather works, that of James Dawson and Son Ltd, who established their new tannery in Beevor Street in 1886.

The stench from the glue works was notorious, but at least as noxious were the smells that emanated from the chemical manure factories, sited along the banks of the Foss Dyke between Lincoln and Saxilby, but close also to the GNR loop line. The first was the business established in about 1856 by John Jekyll and William Gresham on Carholme Road, on a site now occupied by Fisons. The demands of High Farming meant that this was a steadily growing industry in the second half of the century, and 25 manure manufacturers were listed in the county directories by 1882. Jekyll's was probably one of the largest, however, for it was one of only two also described as sulphuric acid manufacturers. The other was also a Lincoln firm, located further along the Foss Dyke at Skellingthorpe, the Kesteven Chemical Manure Company, founded by Edward Toynbee of Lincoln in 1874, on the site of an earlier chemical works established about twelve years before. The chemical manure works set up by the oil-milling firm of J.G. Doughty and Sons at Burton Lane End in the early 1860s was probably on a slightly smaller scale, but in 1920 this firm would take over Jekyll's Carholme chemical works.

The expansion of flour milling meant at first a growing number of windmills,

117 Hobbler's Hole windmill on Green Lane, c.1905. St Mathias' Church can be seen in the background. This was one of many mills that lined the escarpment to the west of the city throughout the 19th century. Only one, Ellis Mill, survives today.

118 *The Brayford Pool and warehouses, from the south, c. 1900. G.H. Pacy's 'Corn, Coal, Cake, Salt & Seed Warehouse' can be seen in the background.*

particularly along the northern edge of the city, but steam-driven roller mills also appeared early in the century. By the 1870s there were several to be found around the Brayford Pool and the days of the windmills and the old-fashioned grinding stones were fast fading. Some steam mills, including Le Tall's Crown mill, were built on the same sites as the windmills they replaced. The Le Tall mill retained the original tower to support a water tank.

Other industries simply grew as the city expanded. An example was the brick and tile industry. The rapid growth of the city's population prompted the opening of new brickworks, especially along the western edge of the city, along the line of the escarpment. The railways, however, opened up the Lincoln brickworks to competition from outside the county, and by the end of the century their numbers were in decline. A brickworks that flourished at Stamp End in the middle decades of the century, meeting the demands of that rapidly growing industrial district, had disappeared by 1872, and the amalgamation of four brickworks in 1889, to form the Lincoln Brickworks Company, could only delay their eventual closure.

Similarly, the small maltings and breweries that grew up in the city in the first half of the century also gradually succumbed to the competition of larger producers in the latter decades. One firm that survived, however, was that of Dawber and Co., founded in 1826, which soon became one of the largest breweries in the county, owning 60 public houses by the turn of century, most of them in the city. In the 1990s the remains of former maltings could still be found near the Brayford, and work at St Mary's Guildhall in 1982 revealed the remains of a brewery here too, which had probably been enlarged by Dawbers in the late 19th century.

The growing demand during the latter decades of the century for organs to be installed in churches, to replace the old village bands, led to the creation of a new industry in the city. J.R. Cousans established his organ manufacturing business in 1877, and a second was set up early in the next century.

Lincoln was, of course, once famous as a centre of woollen cloth production, but there could be no attempt to relaunch this industry. The only example of large-scale textile production in the city came with the establishment of a silk mill in 1871, beside the Brayford, using steam power and employing 200 female workers in the 1880s.

POPULATION EXPANSION, NEW HOUSING AND NEW SHOPS

The growth of industry, and particularly the creation of a large-scale engineering industry, did more than anything else to draw migrants into the city at an unprecedented rate. We have seen that the population was already growing at a rapid pace in the first 30 years of the century. During the next 40 years, however, the city's population grew by 150 per cent and in the 1870s it grew at the unprecedented rate of 39 per cent, before the depression of the 1880s caused the rate to slow. At the time of the first census in 1801 the city had reached its medieval high of about seven thousand, but by 1851 it had more than doubled in size, and by the beginning of the 20th century there were almost 50,000 people in Lincoln. Much of this increase was the result of immigration. Just over two-thirds of the adult population in 1851 were reported by the census to have been born outside the city. Most had only come from nearby villages or from other towns in the county, and most had come while still in their twenties, unmarried and single, and had started their families after they had settled. Consequently, the birth rate was also rising rapidly, far outstripping the death rate, and as a result as many as two-thirds of those under 20 in 1851 had been born in the city.

119 *'Lincoln High Street Two Years After The Coming Of The Railway', by John Fearnley.*

120 *Workmen from Clayton & Shuttleworth's foundry at Stamp End leaving work and returning home across the footbridge that linked the works to the new housing to the north of the river, c. 1900.*

Rapid population growth inevitably meant problems of housing and insanitary living conditions. Most of the newcomers were very poor and could afford only the lowest rents. The city's streets were filthy, there was no system of underground sewage disposal for many decades, and as the city grew its drinking water became increasingly contaminated. The waterside parish of St Swithin's was already growing rapidly in the first decades of the century, and by 1841 its population had almost tripled in 40 years,

121 *Eastfield Street, c. 1905. This was one of many rows of small houses built in the second half of the 19th century to house the families of workmen employed at the engineering works across the river.*

122   *Mr Tye, the milkman, making his deliveries in St Nicholas Street, in Newport, c.1903. This was another part of the city that grew rapidly in the 19th century.*

to over 2,600 inhabitants. Following the opening of Clayton and Shuttleworth's factory, however, the parish grew even more rapidly. A bridge was put across the river and long terraces of small houses began to fill the hillside to the north of the river, opposite the factory. By 1881 the population of the parish had almost tripled again, to well over 7,000, and about a thousand new houses had been built. Consequently, throughout the century it remained one of the largest parishes in the city and in 1901 numbered almost 9,000 people.

Robey's workers were also housed close to his factory, south of the river, in the Wigford area to the west of Canwick Road, and the Wigford parishes were consequently also among the fastest growing in the second half of the century. St Mary le Wigford, for instance, had doubled in size in the first half of the century, to just over 1,100, but in the next half-century its population rose more than five-fold, to almost 6,000, and the increase in St Peter at Gowts was even more spectacular. The draining of the land to the east of the Sincil Dyke and the building of the Canwick road opened up a new area for cheap housing from the 1850s, as the population figures for the parish make clear. The census records just over 1,400 people living in the parish in 1851; this was 1,000 more than there had been 50 years earlier. By the end of the century the numbers had increased seven times, to almost 10,000, over-taking St Swithin's to be the largest parish in the city. Here was to be found some of the poorest housing of all, described by the *Stamford Mercury* as 'kennels' and 'mere dog-holes' in the 1850s. Houses in Canwick Square were said to have been built on a swamp and houses erected near to the Primitive Methodist chapel in this area were described as 'fever holes' by the *Mercury* in 1856.

Not all those who found employment in the city's engineering works, however, lived close to their place of work. One area outside the city that grew particularly rapidly – and unhealthily – was the village of Bracebridge, to the south. Poorer workers walked

123   (Above) One of the last horse-drawn trams of c.1903, close to the terminus at the Brant Road corner in Bracebridge. Bryant and May matches are advertised on the side of the tram.

124   The first electric trams arrive in 1905 pulled, ironically, by a horse.

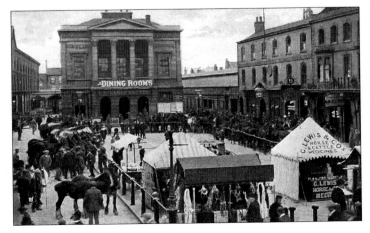

125   The horse fair in the Corn Hill market, c.1910, with the Old Corn Exchange in the background, built in the classical style in 1847, with a projecting Corinthian portico. By this time the building had long ceased to be a corn market and a new Corn Exchange, just visible in this picture on the extreme left, had been erected in 1879, necessitated by the rapid expansion of the city as an agricultural centre.

to work, but a horse-drawn tram began operation from Bracebridge in 1883, and was replaced by an electric version in 1905.

The second half of the century also saw a rapid growth in the retail trade. The cattle market was moved to a more convenient location on Monks Road in 1849 and the corn market was moved to its present site in 1846 and was rebuilt on a much grander scale in 1880. Consequently, the adjacent Sincil Street soon developed as a retail area and by 1860 it housed a row of shops. A new retail industry developed as shopkeepers benefited from a rapidly growing population and rising living standards. Among the first new shops were the Co-operative Stores, which opened its first outlet in the city on Silver Street in 1861, Boots the Chemist, and a number of department stores.

PUBLIC HEALTH

The need for improved systems of water supply and sewerage was pressed by many in the city, and particularly by local doctors, long before any determined action was taken by the city council. The dangers to health of the overcrowded and damp state of much of the housing let to the poorest classes, of pig-sties, cowsheds and dunghills in such areas, and of over crowded burial grounds were well recognised, especially after the cholera alarm of 1831. Reports made by local doctors on the unhealthy state of housing in numerous parishes were frequently reported in both the *Lincolnshire Chronicle* and the *Mercury* from the 1840s, and public discussion of the issue was also encouraged in 1848 by the passing of the Public Health Act. This gave the city council the power to levy a rate to meet the cost of an underground sewerage system, and in the following year an expert drainage engineer was commissioned to come up with an appropriate scheme. However, his proposal for a scheme costing almost £30,000 was met with a storm of protest. The Paving and Lighting Commissioners were quite sure that they were capable of dealing with any nuisances and there were many who were certain that the rate payers could not be expected to meet so great a cost, a rate of 8½d. for 30 years.

For many years the political unpopularity of levying a rate paralysed any plans for improvements, in spite of recurrent outbreaks of disease. The city council was dominated in the second half of the century not by the great industrialists, who might have taken a more progressive view, but by small-scale businessmen, who would have been hurt much more by the imposition of a rate than would the very rich. Small manufacturers and traders suffered constant insecurity and the fear of bankruptcy was never far away. Hostility to rates and council expenditure was strong enough to lead to death threats to councillors. The strongest opposition was said to come from small landlords who owned a few working-class houses, sometimes holding them effectively as pensions. For this group a substantial rise in rates would be disastrous. In some larger cities it was the great industrialists who dominated local government and forced through innovation, but in Lincoln men such as Clayton, Shuttleworth and Ruston preferred to move into rather more prestigious public roles, as MPs and JPs.

The frustration and anger felt by many of those who urged reform, especially in the medical profession, was expressed in the words of the coroner, James Hitchens, as reported in the *Lincolnshire Chronicle* in October 1857:

… in Lincoln we have a corporation, and typhus fever; a Board of Lighting, Paving and Cleansing, and scarlet fever; a Sanitary Board and diarrhoea; all more prevalent than has been known for years. We have also a water company, and streets stinking in our nostrils for want of flushing the channels.

The year before, the annual report of the Lincoln Dispensary had drawn attention to the link that it perceived between the state of the housing of the 'humbler classes' and the prevalence of disease. The houses were now generally better built, it reported, than they had been 20 years earlier, but there were still three major problems:

First, they are much too small for the large families of many of the occupiers, if they are to enjoy health, decency and comfort, in many cases there being only one sleeping room for a family consisting of two parents and six or eight children; secondly, all proper means for ventilation seem to be neglected; and thirdly, the solitary privy appropriated to several cottages (with perhaps an open cesspool or ashpit) is permitted to remain uncleansed for months, or even years, exhaling constantly a noxious effluvium, and polluting still further the confined atmosphere of the dwellings.

It then went on to express its incredulity that:

… habitations are allowed to be yearly built in this corporate city without any provision being required by the authorities to carry away the dirt and filth which necessarily collect around any habitation. In too many instances the surface water even is unable to make its escape, and, therefore, collects close to the cottage, becomes loaded with suds, urine and dung, as well as decayed vegetable and animal matter, and sends forth the seeds of disease.

126   *A Corporation water cart delivering water during the typhoid epidemic of 1905.*

127   *A postcard of 1911 celebrating the completion of the new water supply that year.*

The Public Health Act of 1858 gave further powers to city councils to install effective sewerage systems, but the Lincoln councillors again felt unable to ask their electors to make the necessary financial sacrifice, and they were probably right to believe that the great majority of the ratepayers would not have supported them had they done so. A petition against introducing a rate to pay for a new sewerage system was presented with 2,550 names on it, more than the number of voters in the city.

The campaign for reform continued in the 1860s, through occasional public meetings and letters to the press, but only direct pressure from central government, backed by the threat of legal action, finally compelled the city council to take the necessary measures. A group of enlightened employers, including Joseph Shuttleworth, and a number of the city's doctors, supported an appeal to the Home Office in 1870 to send an inspector to enquire into the sanitary state of the city. At the inquiry two local doctors gave evidence that leaking cesspools were increasingly contaminating water supplies. Shuttleworth described the appalling state of the river near his factory – it was so filthy that it could not be used for any industrial purpose in the engineering works – and his manager told the inspector that the stench made many of the employees ill. The council's attempts to defend itself were dismissed by the inspector. He did not, for instance, accept that the state of the river was due mainly to an exceptionally hot, dry spell of weather. Another petition against underground drainage that the council had collected, with 2,560 names on it, also had little effect. The inspector concluded that 'there is not a town in England which offers a more flagrant instance of the dereliction of this duty than the city of Lincoln.'

Even the inspector's conclusions did not lead to rapid action, as most members of the council favoured delay, but a threat of legal compulsion in the high court was effective, and in September 1876 the contract for building the new sewerage system was signed. It would take almost five years to complete the work, connecting almost every house in the city to the main sewer, and it was at a cost of almost £64,000 to the ratepayers.

The lack of clean water supplies, however, remained a major problem. Under the authority of further public health acts the council took over responsibility for water and gas, as well as sewage disposal. Its legal powers were further strengthened by reforms in 1888 and 1894, under which it became a county borough, a status that it retained until 1974. However, it was only a devastating outbreak of typhoid in the winter of 1904-5 that finally prompted the council to take decisive action to improve the city's water supplies. Complaints about the quality of the city's drinking water had been common for many years. In 1867 two doctors condemned the city's main source of drinking water, the conduit beside the church of St Mary le Wigford, as unfit to drink and the worst they had come across outside London. During the 1870s and 1880s the medical officer of health repeatedly called attention to the contamination of the upper Witham, the main source of the water supply, and called for the water to be filtered and for public notices to be issued telling people to boil the water if diarrhoea broke out. The council took no notice of this, however, even though diarrhoea was prevalent in the city. In 1885 the cathedral precentor,

128   *The water tower, nearing completion in 1911.*

Edmund Venables, wrote to the Local Government Board to add his voice to the calls for improvement:

> Water supply is in the hands of the Corporation, who are hoodwinked by their manager. The water professes to be taken from certain meres and large ponds to the south west of the city, but the greater part of it is really drawn from the Witham, at a point where it is liable to pollution by manure works, gas works etc. existing on its banks.

The letter was referred to the council but it was dismissed with derision as the opinion of the ill-informed.

The typhoid outbreak of 1904-5 killed about 130 people and the cause was clearly pollution of the water supply with sewage, as intestinal bacteria were found in a sample of water taken from a domestic tap. Condemnation of the city council's neglect was soon forthcoming. In February 1907 the *Lincolnshire Chronicle* published a copy of the judgement made by the British Medical Association:

Taking into consideration the history of the nature and conditions of Lincoln water supply during the last twenty years, it might safely have been predicted that – sooner or later – an epidemic of typhoid fever would occur in the city with extensive and sudden violence ... It is difficult to understand how the Corporation of Lincoln can have ignored for so many years the obvious and continuous risks to which the citizens have been exposed through using a water supply constantly liable to dangerous contamination. They have turned a deaf ear to the repeated warnings given to them by their medical adviser, by the experts who corroborated his views, and by the Medical Society of the city.

In the same year a chastened council agreed to seek a Bill authorising a scheme to bring water from Elkesley, 22 miles away in Nottinghamshire. It would cost £180,000, but there was now clearly no alternative. Work began in October 1908 and was completed almost exactly three years later. It involved the building of the tall water tower that still stands today in Westgate.

Poverty and the New Poor Law in Lincoln

National concerns in the 1830s regarding the growing number of the destitute, vagrancy, and the cost of poor relief were to be found also in Lincoln. Many of the city's newcomers were labourers earning only 12s. a week, who could afford only the poorest, most over-crowded housing, and lived mainly on a diet of bread and potatoes. The new Poor Law passed in 1834 made it clear that in future conditions in workhouses had to be 'less eligible' than conditions for the poorest outside their walls; in short, only the most desperate must be encouraged to apply for relief. The Lincoln Union was constituted in November 1836 and a new workhouse, on a site adjoining the old House of Industry and close to the Lawn Hospital, was completed three years later. It served the city and 63 surrounding country parishes. Outdoor relief for the able-bodied poor was forbidden by the London commissioners. Even in the winter of 1838, when there was exceptional distress, the Lincoln commissioners did not seek permission to give relief out of the workhouse, and even the sick and elderly poor could be left to starve if they were unwilling to enter it. Tasks provided for inmates were invariably unpleasant. They included picking oakum, grinding corn by hand, breaking stones in the quarry and emptying cess-pools. As in previous generations, the poorest would still be treated as if they were criminals.

For the children born or brought up in the workhouse, life was just as brutal. An education of sorts was provided, but it was made clear that it was designed to prepare the children only for the lowliest stations in life, and they were put out to service at the earliest opportunity. The children also had to have their heads shaven and wear distinctive workhouse garb. From 1870, as a result of voluntary initiative, workhouse children were boarded out, but they continued to attend the workhouse school until 1893 when it was closed down and the children transferred to other schools in the city.

The application of workhouse rules became a little more humane as the century wore on and it was reported in 1890 that the Lincoln Union was one of the most expensive in the region. The chairman of the Lincoln Board of Guardians made it clear, however,

129   *The Union Workhouse, opened in 1839 to house 360 paupers. It was demolished in 1965.*

that they would not economise if it meant greater suffering for the poor. Nevertheless, desperately poor families continued to prefer to face starvation at home and reliance on charity rather than enter the workhouse. The workhouse rapidly came to stand for an abandonment of all self-respect and all hope. It also meant the splitting up of families, and for men who were desperately looking for work the probable loss of any prospects of real employment. Instead they faced the humiliation of labour otherwise associated only with the prison. A report on poverty in Lincoln in 1885 in the *Lincolnshire Chronicle* concluded that:

> ... amongst many of the poorest classes there is a feeling of pride – and a very admirable one too – which no matter how keen may be their sufferings, causes them to have a wholesome dread of anything that savours of parochial relief, and (they) would rather endure unheard of privations than end their days in the workhouse.

To help keep the unemployed and their families out of the workhouse during the winter months, when outdoor work ceased and unemployment rose, soup kitchens were regularly set up, both uphill and downhill. In January 1881, on one day alone, 1,150 quarts of soup and loaves of bread were distributed in the city. In times of slack trade, when men were laid off in the engineering works, the situation was much worse. Particular cases of starving families, where the man had been laid off but had refused the workhouse, were described by a correspondent in the *Chronicle* in February 1885:

Amongst other cases a man with a wife and five children, the man out of work for eight weeks, and no food in the house; another with a family of three children; another with nine children, and, when we called, entirely without food ... Another family of six children had had no work for nine weeks. Another family, where there were six children, had not a mouthful of food in the house of any description, and the little ones were famishing ... (They) are all respectable hard working men who have been paid off from the various foundries, and they do not like to make their trouble known: they would rather suffer starvation.

To avoid the workhouse, some families who could not pay their rent shared accommodation, and whole families could be found occupying a single room. Some resorted to begging and even to hiring their infants out to beggars standing in the streets, as beggars with infants invariably attracted more sympathy. In 1857 it was reported that infants could be hired for 8d. a day.

For many girls born into destitution, Lincoln's numerous brothels had long offered at least the prospect of better earnings than could be had as domestic servants, seamstresses or laundresses. In the 1830s, and for most of the century, numerous tenements in the Castle Dyke district were well known to the police as 'houses of ill-fame' and it was claimed that some had been built specifically to be brothels. The district was just outside the area of the council's authority, or of any of the city parishes, and until the 1840s the city magistrates paid the matter little attention. In 1841, however, a local clergyman, the Rev. Richard Garvey, began a campaign against immorality and stirred up the magistrates to action. A number of brothel keepers were indicted and the police were urged to bring offenders to justice. The *Mercury* undertook its own investigation and in 1846 reported that in the previous two-and-a-half-years, 13 girls and women from the Castle Dyke district had been taken into the workhouse in a diseased state, many suffering from syphilis. One was only 13 years old and the average age was eighteen. It was also said that at least half the women working in the city as prostitutes would end their lives as parish paupers, if not in the lunatic asylum, and suicide among prostitutes was also common. Garvey's campaign prompted a group of local ladies to open a home for 'fallen women', but while there was so much poverty little could be done to prevent the continuing growth in the number of women resorting to prostitution. In 1865 a local doctor claimed that there were 58 prostitutes working openly on the streets and known to the police and also much secret prostitution. There were, he said, 22 brothels and 10 common lodging houses where prostitutes could be found.

For many Victorians, prostitution was one of two great social evils afflicting the poor; the other was drunkenness. Bishop King's view that beer was the gift of God was appreciated by many poor working men, but not by the local Temperance movement led by the dissenters and evangelicals. A Temperance society was established in 1833, and later a Temperance hall and a working men's hall, but the number of beer houses and public houses continued to grow throughout the century. In 1842 there were 112, but by 1863 there were 150, and 183 only six years later. In 1876 the police reported that the number of cases of drunkenness had greatly increased in the previous 20 years, and a police report of 1877 had no doubt about the links between excessive drinking, poverty, vagrancy and crime:

In the gross and increasing abuse of strong drink lies the source of the enlarged total of offences. It cannot be doubted that by indulgence in this vice, is stimulated the frequent assaults, and that the poverty resulting from drunken habits is the origin of much of the vagrancy and begging which have now assumed such formidable proportions, while to vagrants may be largely attributed the frequency of petty larcenies.

Although excessive drinking certainly caused much misery and destroyed families, the very detailed investigations into poverty later undertaken by Charles Booth in London and Seebohm Rowntree in York showed that it was a relatively minor cause of poverty. Their investigations showed that it was far less important than low wages, unemployment, sickness, the death of the chief bread-winner or old age.

CHURCHES, CHAPELS AND SCHOOLS

When Horace Mann conducted his national census of church and chapel attendance on Sunday 30 March 1851 the results were keenly awaited in Lincoln. The enormous success enjoyed by Methodists and other dissenters in recruiting adherents and opening ever-larger chapels was well known, but the Anglican Church in the city had also begun to stir itself by this time. A new church had recently been completed for the parish of St Nicholas, with 800 free sittings, St Peter at Gowts had been enlarged, other churches were being repaired and renewed and in 1840 St Peter at Arches – the principal church for the Lower City – had set up a committee of local inhabitants to support weekday evening services. When the results of the census were published, however, they proved doubly disappointing for Anglicans. The number of attendances on Census Sunday at the 13 parish churches plus the cathedral was 4,242; at the 11 dissenting chapels 5,670; and 374 at the Roman Catholic chapel. It could be argued that the dissenter figures were boosted by having more adherents attending twice in the day, but it could not be denied that at least half the worshipping population in the city were dissenters. In Lincoln, as in the nation as a whole, the Church of England was no longer truly a national church. More disturbing still for many, however, was the second revelation: that about half the population of the city attended no place of worship at all.

The challenge facing Anglicans and dissenters over the next few decades would prove even greater than seemed apparent in 1851. The city's population had grown by just over 10,000 in the previous half-century, but it would grow by more than 30,000 in the next half-century. And as the population grew, so did the number of churches and chapels, but by 1901 only around a third of the population would be attending any place of worship. This was a reflection of a national trend. Before the First World War Britain was already fast becoming a secular society.

At the time of Mann's census the Wesleyan Methodist church was in the process of dividing in two. The 'Primitives' had broken away to form their own organisation in the city in 1818, and had opened their first chapel in the following year, but by 1851 another split had occurred. Wesleyan Reformers, seeking a more democratic system of church government, had recently broken from the Wesley chapel on Clasketgate and were holding separate services in the Corn Exchange. But these secessions did

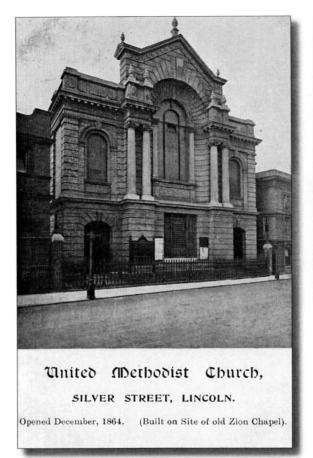

United Methodist Church,

SILVER STREET, LINCOLN.

Opened December, 1864.   (Built on Site of old Zion Chapel).

ROSEMARY LANE WESLEYAN DAY SCHOOLS, LINCOLN.

130   (Left) The Free Methodist Silver Street Chapel, c. 1910.

131   (Above) The Rosemary Lane Day Schools, c. 1905. They opened in 1858 to meet the demands of this rapidly growing part of the city.

nothing to hinder the growth of dissent. In 1864 the Reformers, or Free Methodists, built themselves a fine white brick chapel on Silver Street, complete with Corinthian columns, and 1,000 people sat down for tea at the opening services. The previous year, the Free Methodists had also opened a chapel on Saxon Street in Newport, in the north of the city; a third chapel followed in 1870 in the south of the city (Fairfax Street chapel), and a fourth in 1904, in Portland Street.

The Wesleyans also recovered quickly from the secession. A large Wesleyan Day School was opened on Rosemary Lane in 1858 and the expansion of Wesleyan Methodism in the south of the city was marked first by the opening of a little chapel on Alfred Street, just off the High Street, in about 1864, and then by building a much larger one in 1875, the Hannah Memorial Chapel in the High Street, with seating for over 1,000 people. In 1887 another new chapel was being built a little further south, at St Catherine's, although the tower was not completed until 1908. Expansion in the north of the city also prompted the building of a new chapel on Bailgate in 1880, replacing a little chapel opened in 1842 in Newport. The Primitive Methodists also found that their chapel in Portland Place, which had been built in 1839 and enlarged in 1854, was not large enough and in 1874 built a larger one, which would also have to be replaced by a yet larger one in 1905. Before 1914 five smaller Methodist chapels had also been built on

132   *The Hannah Memorial Chapel, High Street, c. 1905.*

133   *The Mint Street Baptist Church, c. 1905. A Band of Hope Temperance procession is just about to begin from the Baptist church, which was always a firm supporter of the city's Temperance movement.*

the edges of the city. The Baptists built two new chapels, in Mint Street in 1871 and in St Benedict's Square in 1886, and the Congregationalists found that they needed to build a new, larger chapel in Newland in 1876, capable of holding 1,100, and also built smaller chapels in the south and east of the city.

The Anglican revival also continued, and the building of new churches was its outward and visible manifestation. In 1867 the newly appointed Bishop Wordsworth laid the foundation stone for a new church in Sheep Square for the rapidly growing industrial suburb of St Swithin. By this time the parish contained over 7,000 people, but the little Anglican church had room for only 260 worshippers. The cost of the new, much larger church, was met by Nathaniel Clayton and Joseph Shuttleworth, whose engineering works lay just across the river. They could well afford to give it a fine tower and spire, designed by the Louth architect James Fowler and modelled on the magnificent spire of Louth parish church. During the next eight years many more Anglican churches would be built or rebuilt, as the bishop himself pointed out as he laid the foundation stone for a new church at St Paul's in 1875:

> At the north, on the side of this old Roman road, is the Training School new chapel; here is St Paul's; a little to the east is St Peter in Eastgate, which, I am glad to find, has an overflowing congregation, fruitful in good works; to the south are the spacious new churches of St Martin and St Swithin; further to the south is the new church of St Mark … and further (south) is the church of St Andrew, now still rising from its foundations. There is also the restored church of St Mary le Wigford with its new aisle. And to return to the neighbourhood where we are, we have also the prospect of a chapel of ease in the parish of St Nicholas and St John.

However, as the city continued to expand rapidly, both Anglicans and nonconformists alike were running hard to stand still. In 1903 a count of church attendance was organised by the *Lincoln Leader*. It reported finding 7,103 attending an Anglican service and 9,046 attending a nonconformist service. The total population in 1901, however, was 48,784, and, as in 1851, many of those attending a service would have been counted twice. The great majority of the city's population would still seem to have seen themselves as adherents of some place of worship, however, even if only for purposes of baptisms, marriages and funerals. When the Free Church Council undertook a house-to-house visitation to over 9,000 houses in 1896, only 1,223 households – about thirteen per cent – described themselves as non-attendants.

Although this was a Free Church initiative the bishop asked his clergy and parishioners to co-operate with it, and one of the questions asked in the survey was whether or not the household would like a visit from either a clergyman or a minister. Although rivalry and sharp differences could still arise, especially over questions of educational provision, relations between Anglicans and nonconformists were generally far more cordial at the end of the century than they had been in the first few decades. The church rates issue had led to disputes in a few city parishes where there were large numbers of dissenters and where church rates were an important source of income, but 10 years before the church rates were abolished, in 1858, the issue was defused by the archdeacon advising

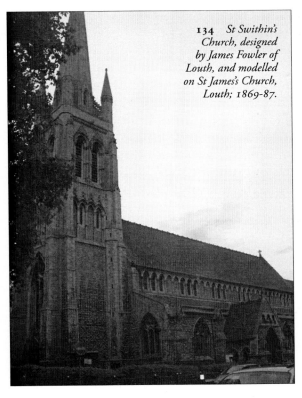

134 St Swithin's Church, designed by James Fowler of Louth, and modelled on St James's Church, Louth; 1869-87.

parish officers not to even try to collect the rates if this was likely to arouse hostility.

Rivalry in providing elementary education began in earnest in the 1840s. Until the Independents opened a non-denominational British Society School in Newland in 1840 the Anglicans' National School had had the field largely to itself, challenged only by a few private schools and the Methodist Sunday Schools. Although the British School charged 2d. or 3d. a week and the National School only a penny, the numbers on roll almost immediately overtook the numbers at the National School and it was followed very shortly afterwards by a second British School opened by the Baptists in Mint Lane. The Methodists opened their first day school in about 1840, with about twenty to thirty children, in the Wesley Rooms of the 'Big Wesley' chapel on Clasketgate. So great was the demand for

135 The Rosemary Lane Wesleyan Day School infants' department, c. 1900.

places, however, that a new school was opened in October 1859, on Rosemary Lane, and within two years it had 662 pupils on the register.

But the Anglicans were not slow to respond. A Lincoln Diocesan Board of Education was set up with plans to co-ordinate the work of all church schools and to open a training college to prepare young men for the challenges of the schoolroom. The college did not open until 1846, in Newport, and then struggled to attract young men willing to be trained. It was soon converted instead into a training college for female teachers (later becoming Bishop Grosseteste College). The National School had been in decline for some years, partly because many of the city's clergy showed little enthusiasm for it and it was not easy to drum up the money needed to pay an able master. The Archdeacon of Stow, H.V. Bayley, voiced the views of many of the clergy when he said that he saw much danger in educating the poor, fearing that it would 'take their minds … from the manual employment and necessary labour' that was their destiny in life. With friends such as this it was hardly surprising that the Anglicans would find it hard to compete with their dissenter rivals.

It was said in 1849 that there had once been 500 children in the National School but there was only between 160 and 170 at this time. There were also numerous private schools in the city run by clergymen but, according to the *Lincolnshire Chronicle*, the majority of children who went to an elementary school were found to be attending schools run by dissenters. The Board, however, had plans to open seven new schools, if sufficient funds could be raised, and in April 1852 they succeeded in opening the first: the Lincoln North District National School, in St Paul's parish.

The following year the Board received valuable assistance with the appointment of John Jackson as Bishop of Lincoln, but his views surprised those who believed themselves to be locked in a struggle with dissenter rivals. Bishop Jackson was not just an ardent supporter of education for all children. He saw education as having an importance that transcended rivalry with the dissenting churches. Indeed, he preferred to welcome the schools and chapels they had opened because they had met a need that the Established Church had failed to meet. At his first visitation, in 1855, Bishop Jackson told his listeners that he thought it an act of justice to their nonconformist brethren:

> To acknowledge the service they have rendered to religion by stepping into the void which the retreating vigour and discipline of the Church had left, and keeping alive the flame of piety which might have been extinguished in the damp of indifference and neglect.

When opening a new school in January 1868 Bishop Jackson noted that for all the progress recently made there were still about nine hundred children in the city who were receiving no education at all, and expressed agreement with a government inspector who had recently stated that he had not visited a town where so little had been done by the Church to educate its people.

The means to 'fill the gap' left by the churches was soon to be made available by the new Liberal government. Under the Education Act of 1870 the city council was given the opportunity to set up a school board that would have the power to levy a rate to pay for the extra schools required. The council, however, was ever mindful of the unpopularity of any additional burden on the rate payers and preferred to rely on the continuing efforts of the

136   *The grammar school, 1861, outside the headmaster's house.*

churches and private individuals. The Anglicans launched an appeal for £5,000 to build schools in five parishes, and the Wesleyans and Congregationalists each announced plans to convert one of their chapels into schools and to build new chapels. Lincoln, however, was now growing faster than ever and the 'gap' could not be filled. In 1897 the Lincoln Public Elementary Church Schools Association, which had been set up to defend the voluntary system, had to admit that the city still needed another 1,000 school places. In 1902, however, another Education Act effectively saved the voluntary system while also obliging the council to take responsibility not only for elementary schools in the city but for secondary schools

137   *The School of Art, on Monks Road, as it appeared in c. 1903. The school opened in 1886, financed partly by local industrialists; it later became the City School.*

138 *The Christ Hospital School for Girls building on Lindum Road, designed by local architect William Watkins and opened in 1893; it is now part of Lincoln University.*

as well. The managers of the voluntary schools would continue to provide buildings and appoint the teachers, but current expenses would be met out of the local rates and the schools would be either free, or charge not more than 3d. a week. Alternatively, managers could hand their schools over to the council completely, and two did: the girls' school in Free School Lane and St Peter at Gowts Wesleyan School. New council schools were also now planned, and the first opened in 1905, in Monks Road, to serve the east of the city. But the city was still growing too fast for the pace of school provision and even in 1914 there were still many children obtaining very little education at all.

The ancient boys' grammar school moved to a new site on Wragby Road in 1907 and at first opted to remain a fee-paying school, but the city's middle classes now had two other high-quality secondary schools to choose from, and these were already threatening the survival of some of the city's private schools. The School of Art and Science, established on Monks Road as a night school in 1886, became the City School. It had a good reputation for the standard of its science teaching and charged only £1 a year for boys from a Lincoln elementary school. Moreover, since 1894 there had been a girls' grammar school in the city: the Christ's Hospital Girls' High School, on Lindum Road, established partly by money raised by the closure of the Bluecoat School, amid much controversy, in 1883. The boys' grammar school would later merge with the girls' school.

139 *A meeting of one of Lincoln's cycling clubs in the forecourt of the Central Station in 1898.*

RECREATION

Reductions in the working week, the creation of Bank Holidays, rising living standards and the introduction of cheap rail fares all helped boost the range and opportunities for recreation. As well as the annual fairs, races and the theatre, there was by the end of the century a music hall, railway excursion trips to the seaside and to larger cities including London and Manchester, cricket matches, cycling clubs and football. Lincoln City Football Club was established at Sincil Bank in 1884 and there were at least three cycling clubs in the city by 1895, each organising 'spins' into the nearby countryside on Saturday afternoons to coincide with the engineering workers' half-day holiday.

Between 1870 and 1900 vast numbers of Lincoln's inhabitants enjoyed a day excursion on the last Saturday in July, many having saved all year for their treat, often by contributing to a savings club organised by the factory foreman. Others worked

140 *A charabanc outing to a football match, about to depart from the* Blue Anchor *on the High Street, c.1900.*

overtime or pawned their valuables to pay for the day out. Most trips were organised by committees of the workers in the various engineering works. In 1871 the railway companies sold almost 10,000 tickets on 'Trips Saturday' (equal to a third of the city's population). During the next 30 years the numbers tended to increase, reaching a peak in 1899, when 18,537 tickets were sold, but a sharp increase in rail fares in the early 1900s caused numbers to fall dramatically. By the mid-1870s the habit of taking a trip on the last Saturday in July had become fixed for many of the

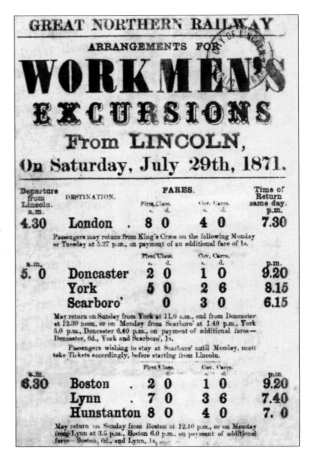

141   (Right) Poster advertising excursions on 'Trips Saturday', July 1871.

142   (Below) Lincoln Fair, c. 1903. By this time the fair was being held on the Cattle Market on Monks Road. A carousel can be seen at the left-hand edge of the photograph, with a large steam engine nearby to drive it. Donkeys and the 'donkey boy' wait patiently for their customers.

143 *The Arboretum, c. 1903. The pavilion on the left is no longer to be seen but the Arboretum's other features have been recently restored.*

city's families, and so great were the numbers that many shops and businesses closed on that day. The first trains would leave as early as 3 a.m. and by 8 a.m. the last train had left and the city's streets were deserted.

The health-giving properties of parks were also now well appreciated, and the Arboretum, or People's Park, was opened on the hillside north of Monks Road in August 1872, consisting of 12 acres of ornamental gardens, complete with fountains and a pavilion. A huge crowd celebrated the opening, with bands playing as they led a procession that included Miss Lizzie Gilbert's Lilipudlian Ladies, Professor Banzo's performing dogs and representatives of all the city's trades. The Arboretum, it was hoped, would not only help improve the physical well-being of the people; there was a moral purpose, too. It was hoped that men would be

144 *The statue of a lion erected for the opening of the Arboretum in 1872.*

145   *The original bandstand of the Arboretum, recently restored.*

induced to spend more time with their families 'in preference to accepting the pleasure of the public house'.

Opportunities for self-improvement through evening classes and libraries also increased during the century. A Mechanics' Institute was founded in 1833 in rooms in the Greyfriars' building that were not being occupied by the grammar school. While rooms upstairs were used for lectures and exhibitions the crypt was fitted out as a library. By the end of the century its library contained 20,000 books and the institute's activities included a gymnasium, cricket, football and shooting. The Co-operative Society also provided a library and newsroom for its members long before the first public library was opened in 1894 in a room over the Butter Market on Silver Street. It moved to its present site on Free School Lane in 1913. By this time, however, the international situation was becoming increasingly uncertain and very soon many working men would be forsaking the comforts and recreations of home for the appalling conditions of the trenches of the Western Front.

146   *The fountain and lake of the Arboretum. This was a feature added as part of the celebrations of the city's new, clean water supplies in 1911. The fountain is constructed from cores extracted in drilling for water at the Elkesley pumping station.*

TWELVE

The Twentieth Century

Sopwith Camels, Lewis Guns and 'Big Willie'

Almost 1,000 men from Lincoln lost their lives in the First World War. A war memorial was erected in their memory in 1922, outside St Benedict's Church, and is today still a focus for remembrance services. The city was emptied of young men as many thousands rushed to do their patriotic duty and enlist in one of the battalions of the Lincolnshire Regiment. Before the war most of the city's shops had only employed men as assistants, but this would change very soon, and as the men left, women also began to pour into the great engineering works, all of which were soon converted to munitions factories.

Lincoln's contribution to the war effort was unique for it was in the engineering works of William Foster Ltd that the first tanks were built, while one of their rivals, Ruston & Proctor, quickly became the largest producer of aircraft engines in the

147 *Lincoln High Street in 1912, looking south. This photograph was taken just in front of St Benedict's Church, to be used as a postcard. Ten years later a crowd would gather at this spot to witness the unveiling of Lincoln's war memorial.*

148   *A sign of the times: women are now driving the trams. A female driver and conductor pause briefly to have their picture taken.*

country. The arrival of women to take over many of the jobs previously only thought suitable for men was not without difficulties. The unions insisted that the more skilled jobs be reserved for men and the appointment of women inspectors was especially resented. Partly in response to the introduction of female workers, shop stewards' committees soon developed in all the engineering works, and sit-down strikes became an effective and frequently used means of enforcing their will.

The idea of developing an armoured, mechanised vehicle capable of traversing the muddy trenches of Flanders exercised a number of minds from the beginning of the war, and won the enthusiastic support of Winston Churchill, the First Lord of the Admiralty. A chain-tracked tractor had been designed and built by David Roberts of Hornsby's of Grantham, in 1907, and demonstrated to the military at Aldershot. Although the press had been enthusiastic, senior military figures, many of

149   *Ruston workers, both men and women, during the First World War with three of their engines.*

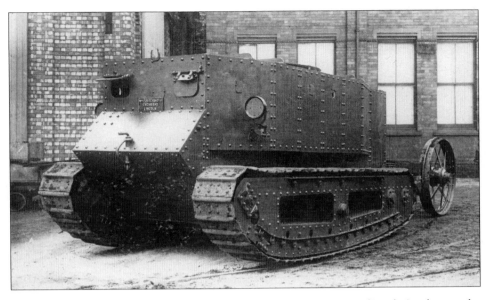

150 *'Little Willie'. This design was soon made obsolete by the development of 'Mother' and was used mainly for driver training.*

whom were cavalrymen, found the idea of mechanised transport distasteful and nothing came of the project. When, in July 1915, the managing director of Foster's, William Tritton, received a request to build the first British tanks, he borrowed from Hornsby's the drawings of Roberts' chain-track system. Churchill had requested that Foster's should build 'small armoured shelters, holding men and machine guns, mounted on caterpillar tracks'. The first prototype, known as 'Little Willie', was tested in Burton Park, near Lincoln, in December 1915. A much improved and quite different machine, nicknamed 'Big Willie', or 'Mother', was also tested at Burton just six weeks later. Shortly afterwards, demonstrations of 'Big Willie' were organised in great secrecy at Hatfield Park for Lloyd George and Lord Kitchener. These proved very successful and

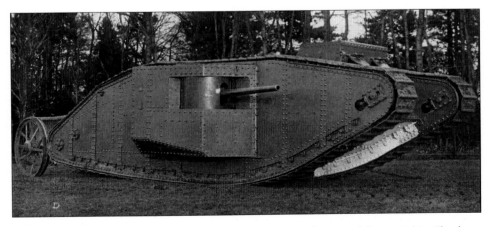

151 *'Mother', built by Foster's at their Tritton Road Works. It is being tested during trials in Clumber Park in Nottinghamshire in 1915.*

152 *Sir William Tritton, managing director of William Foster & Co. Ltd, 1904-40.*

a fortnight later the government placed an initial order for a hundred 'Big Willies'. For reasons of security they were officially referred to as water carriers, or 'tanks', for use in Mesopotamia.

The first tanks arrived in France in August 1916 and on 15 September went into battle for the first time at the Somme. During the next two years they came to play an essential part in the Allied war effort. They frequently caused panic among the German troops, greatly boosted the morale of British troops, proved particularly effective in destroying machine-gun posts and in-village fighting, and, in spite of heavy losses, played a key role in breaking through the German lines at Amiens in August 1918. For his part in their development William Tritton received a knighthood in 1917. Today, the area once occupied by Foster's Wellington Works, where the tanks were built, is part of a retail park, but the road crossing through is named Tritton Road. One of Sir William's Mark IV tanks can still be seen in the Lincolnshire Life Museum.

Six months before Foster's had begun work on the first tanks, their larger rival, Ruston's, had received their first order for 100 two-seater bi-planes. Ruston, Proctor & Co. were soon the largest producer of aircraft engines in the country, helping Lincoln to become, between 1915 and 1919, one of the largest centres of aircraft production in the world. In 1916-17 Ruston's produced 350 of the Sopwith 1½ Strutters, and 1,600 of the famous Sopwith Camels in 1917-18. This was more than any other manufacturer.

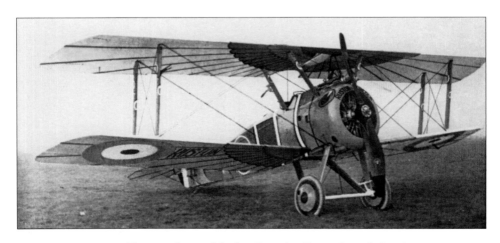

153 *The 1,000th aircraft built at Ruston's: a Ruston Sopwith Camel.*

By 1918 they were employing 3,000 men and women on aircraft production alone, building 2,000 aircraft, over 3,000 engines and spare parts for a further 800 engines. Women fitted and painted the textile coverings to the fuselage and wings while men made the engines and assembled the finished aircraft.

Over 500 Sopwith Camels were also built by Clayton & Shuttleworth, together with Sopwith Triplanes, at their Titanic Works, near the Witham, from 1917. From 1916 they were building tail stabilisers for airships at their nearby Stamp End Works. The firm also constructed 46 large Handley Page bombers in 1917-19 in aircraft shops built by German prisoners at their Abbey and Tower Works. The city's fourth largest engineering firm, Robey's, mainly concentrated on building sea planes, particularly the Short 184s, and built more of these – 256 – than any other firm in the country. It also built an aerodrome on Bracebridge Heath, near the county lunatic asylum, which was used also by other firms for test-flying aircraft, including Clayton's Handley Page bombers. The seven large brick hangars built for the bombers still exist and are now used as factories and vehicle workshops.

154   *(Above) A section of the Wing Erection and Covering Bay at the Ruston Aircraft Factory.*

155   *(Right) The Ruston Sopwith 1½-Strutter assembly plant.*

156   A squadron of soldiers lined up in the Old Barracks square, on Burton Road, about to depart for France. The building is now used by the Museum of Lincolnshire Life.

157   A familiar wartime sight: a soldier, perhaps on leave, outside the fruiterers and fishmongers, Smalley and Son, at 373 High Street. It is thought that the soldier was a member of the Smalley family.

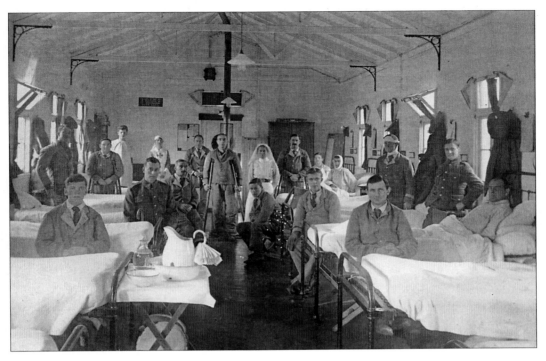

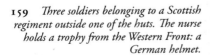

158   *The grammar school on Wragby Road was converted into a military hospital and wooden and corrugated iron huts were erected on the school grounds behind the main building to provide extra wards.*

Other munitions were also manufactured in Lincoln. Ruston's produced 8,000 Lewis guns and Clayton's built crawler tractors at one end of their Titanic Works while Sopwith Camels were built at the other. As well as building tanks, Foster's also built 12-inch heavy howitzers, and most of Lincoln's engineering firms also won orders for general service wagons, field kitchens, gun carriage limbers and other equipment.

159   *Three soldiers belonging to a Scottish regiment outside one of the huts. The nurse holds a trophy from the Western Front: a German helmet.*

THE GREAT DEPRESSION

Lincoln's engineering firms did not easily adapt to the ending of war contracts, which in some cases came quite suddenly and left businesses with materials but without orders. Overseas markets had absorbed a very high proportion of production before the war, but these markets had in many cases now been lost and could not be won back. Russia had been an important market, but the Revolution ensured that old contacts were now lost forever, along with any outstanding debts. The doleful consequences of peace were not at first apparent, as the war was followed by a re-stocking boom. But this proved short-lived. By 1920 order books were beginning to look decidedly thin and the depression that now set in was to last for almost 20 years and cause enormous suffering for many thousands of families that had once depended on the engineering works.

The difficulties of re-establishing overseas markets were compounded by economic and political difficulties, and particularly by the break-up of the former empires of eastern and central Europe. At the same time, British goods were made less competitive abroad by the return to the gold standard in 1925. The consequences for Lincoln were dire; bankruptcies, closures and unprecedented levels of unemployment. In 1922 unemployment rose to 6,600 as more firms laid off workers. Demand then rose again for a few years and unemployment fell back to a mere 1,000 in 1927-8, before rising rapidly again as the city's firms felt the chill effects of worldwide depression and protectionist policies. By 1933 there were nearly 8,000 men and women registered as unemployed, out of a total population of just over 66,000. For many families the soup kitchen offered the only prospect of any sort of meal.

Perhaps the greatest disaster for the city was the closure of Clayton and Shuttleworth in December 1936. Founded in 1842, this was one of the largest and most prestigious firms in the county, but the ending of the war dealt it a blow from which it could not recover and in February 1930 it was obliged to call in a liquidator. Between 1910 and 1920 the firm had grown rapidly, erecting the Titanic, Tower and Abbey works close to the original Stamp End Works, but this level of production could not be maintained in peacetime. The Stamp End Works were used from 1924 to 1932 by a Scottish firm, Babcock & Wilcox, to build enormous mooring masts for an airship route linking England, Egypt and India. Clayton's found themselves heavily reliant on building steam wagons, however, and when this market ceased in the late 1920s it was unable to find alternatives. The name did not entirely disappear, however, as both Marshall's of Gainsborough and Babcock & Wilcox bought up Clayton & Shuttleworth's patent rights so that they could continue to produce thrashing machines and other products using the Clayton name. The firm's motor engineering works also continued to operate, under the control of a new company, Clayton Dewandre Co. Ltd, set up in 1928. It occupied the Titanic Works and survived until 1988.

The much smaller firm of John Cooke & Sons Ltd also went out of business in 1937, and most of Lincoln's other engineering firms survived only after take-overs and radical restructuring, which invariably meant a marked reduction in scale and a much-reduced workforce. The only firm to survive the 1930s Depression largely intact was Ruston & Hornsby. Anticipating future problems, the firm of Ruston, Proctor & Co. Ltd had

160 *Almost all that is left of Clayton and Shuttleworth's Stamp End engineering works today. These office buildings are now used by the City Corporation.*

agreed to a merger with Hornsbys of Grantham as early as September 1918. Their attempts to adapt their wartime aircraft-building skills by moving into high-quality car production proved unsuccessful, and in 1924 the last Ruston car was produced. Moreover, the production of Ruston steam engines and thrashers was transferred to Ransomes of Ipswich, before Ruston & Hornsby sold their controlling interest in Ransomes in 1930. The firm continued, however, to supply engines for road rollers and expanded its mechanical excavator business after 1930 by setting up a new company with the American firm of Bucyrus-Erie.

The economic and financial problems of the city's great engineering firms in the post-war era had grave consequences for all those who had hoped that, with the ending of war, the living conditions of the great majority could be considerably improved. Lloyd George's boast that the coalition government he led would build 'homes fit for heroes' was taken up with great enthusiasm in Lincoln, and for about two years – while the re-stocking boom lasted – optimism seemed well placed. Among the most ambitious private housing projects in the country in

161 *A Ruston & Hornsby Class 'HR' single-cylinder horizontal engine, c.1930.*

1919 was Lincoln's Swanpool Garden Suburb scheme. This was a plan to build 2,000 houses to the north-east of Skellingthorpe Road, drawn up between 1917 and 1919. The garden city idea pioneered by Ebenezer Howard had caught the imagination of Colonel J.S. Ruston, one of the directors of Ruston, Proctor & Co., and with his energy, money, connections and enthusiasm behind it the project seemed likely to succeed. He bought 25 acres of the Boultham Hall estate, formed the Swanpool Co-operative Housing Society and engaged the architect A.J. Thompson, who had worked on the designs for Letchworth, one of the first 'garden cities' in the country.

The plans drawn up by Thompson in 1919 were ambitious and exciting, and featured in two articles in the *Architects Journal* and in a book on contemporary housing published in 1924. The new suburb would now be much larger than originally planned. It would cover 340 acres, with the central axis provided by a wide avenue that would link the Swan Pool itself to a central square. Curving avenues, cul-de-sacs and quadrangles radiated from this; each house would have generous garden spaces and it was intended that a great many trees would be planted to provide a taste of the countryside. The houses themselves would have complex, steeped hip roofs and much care was taken to ensure attractively designed doors, chimneys and windows.

In a rapidly deteriorating economic climate, however, expectations for the scheme's success were soon in decline. It was intended that all tenants would be shareholders in the scheme, and to attract maximum interest the minimum stake was set extremely low – a mere £5. But in spite of this, few shares could be sold, a government loan could not be raised and the council refused to take the scheme over. Consequently, only 113 houses were ever built and the undeveloped land was bought up by Colonel Ruston. Moreover, the houses that were built could not be sold quickly to the tenants and about half were still tenanted in 1945.

162 *A postcard showing the Swanpool Garden Estate shortly after the first houses had been built.*

163 *Corporation refuse collectors with a Clayton electric wagon, on the recently built St Giles Estate, c.1920.*

The optimism that lay behind the garden city movement in the first post-war years also inspired much of the thinking behind the Addison Housing and Town Planning Act of 1919, and the opportunities for better public sector housing for working people that the Act made possible were taken up with enthusiasm by Lincoln Council. As recently as 1905 it had taken a serious outbreak of typhoid, killing over a hundred people, to prompt the council into financing improved water supplies, but after this the council's attitude to public services changed dramatically. In December 1913 it approved a scheme for the council to buy 65 acres of land beside the Wragby Road to provide 900 low-cost homes. Among the most vociferous supporters of the proposal was Arthur Taylor, the city's first socialist councillor and later Labour MP for the city. The Lincoln Trades and Labour Council, which he represented, had long campaigned for more working-class housing and in 1914 it collected 600 signatories in favour of the council's proposals. The outbreak of war prevented the scheme going ahead, but the council nevertheless gained permission to purchase the necessary land, and did so.

Following the introduction of the Addison Act the council appointed the architect Alfred Hill to work on the Wragby Road housing scheme, soon to be known as the St Giles Estate. When financial aid was withdrawn in July 1922, only 234 council houses had been built, but the Ministry of Munitions had also bought some of the land from the council to build a further 200 houses. Unlike Swanpool, much of Alfred Hill's plans for the nascent estate would eventually be completed, following further building from 1935. The design followed similar principles to those of the Swanpool development: a geometrical road pattern incorporated cul-de-sacs and quadrangles, and a circus and a large space was reserved in the centre for two schools. In 1936 St Giles' Church was built, mainly from materials taken from the early Georgian St Peter at Arches, which had been taken down earlier that year.

164 *Housing on the St Giles Estate today: Goldsmiths Walk.*

The development of the St Giles Estate represented a very considerable improvement in the quality of housing available to poorer families. At the same time some of the worst slums were being demolished and the city council was also creating another new estate to the south-west of the city, at Boultham. Thus, in spite of the depression, by 1939 the built-up area of the city was increasing, and in Lincoln, as in the country as a whole, house-building was one of the major reasons for the reduction in unemployment levels in the late 1930s. Another was the creation of new industries and in Lincoln the most significant example was the new Smiths crisp factory, which opened in Bracebridge in 1938.

The continuing growth of the city, and the growth of surrounding villages, such as Bracebridge, meant also that public transport facilities were becoming increasingly important. The first motor bus service in the city began in June 1900, with two vehicles running from the Arboretum to West Parade, but this was abandoned after only a year. One of the first services linking local villages was a bus that ran from Scunthorpe to

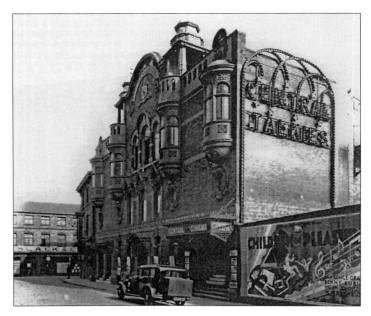

165 *The Central Cinema,* c. *1938.*

Lincoln on market days and began in 1914. After the war a number of the traditional country carriers switched over to motors and the Silver Queen Company was established in the city in 1922 to run buses linking numerous villages and country towns across the county. In 1928 it was renamed the Lincolnshire Road Car Company. A regular city bus service was re-introduced in November 1920, at first serving the Burton Road area in the north of the city, and a service for the new St Giles Estate began just four months later. The trams, however, could not compete, and they made their last journey in 1929. Moreover, high levels of unemployment kept down the number of bus passengers between the wars. Whereas in 1939 Lincoln City Transport carried 9.7 million, just six years later, with the demands of war having long banished unemployment, the annual figure was 16.3 million.

The fall in prices brought about by a depressed economy meant that, for many of those in work, living standards improved between the wars and this partly explains the growth in the popularity of both the cinema and football in these years. The city's first cinema had been opened in St Hugh's Hall on Monks Road in 1909, running hourly shows on Saturdays between 2 p.m. and 9 p.m. using portable equipment, and charging between 2d. and 4d. In the same year the New Central Hall in St Swithin's Square was converted into a cinema – the Central Cinema – and boasted 'flicker-free and rock-steady pictures'. The Cinematograph Hall opened in the Corn Exchange in May 1910; the Grand – later the Grand Electric – opened on the High Street (at number 262a) in 1911; and a fifth cinema, known as the Picture House, opened near the Stonebow in 1915. This was a 'state of the art', purpose-built cinema, able to charge 9d. for its most expensive seats. When refurbished and renamed the Regal, in 1931, it seated 1,200 and boasted a café lounge so that patrons could drink tea while watching the films. This was the 'golden age' of Hollywood, and such was the demand that four other large cinemas soon followed: the Plaza in 1931, the Savoy in 1936, the Ritz in 1937 (with parking spaces for 250 cars) and the Radion in 1939. The last three were all purpose-built, but the Plaza, in Newland, was a converted musical hall, the Palace Theatre, which had closed down in 1930, killed off by the rise of the cinema. A young Gracie Fields appeared here in 1918, and

166 *The Palace Theatre, c. 1905.*

other stars included George Formby and Harry Tate. In March 1939 (when the Radion opened) the city had eight cinemas.

Cinema-going was at its height in the 1930s, but there was one other entertainment that could come at least close to matching it in terms of popularity: football. Every other Saturday afternoon a few thousand flocked to Sincil Bank for eight months of the year, to see their football team compete in the northern half of the Third Division. In the 1920s and 1930s, as today, supporting the team required much faith and loyalty. Lincoln City FC had been a founder member of the Second Division in 1892, and since that time it had been a professional club, but in 1920 it had to seek re-election and was only saved from the loss of League status by the formation of the Third Division (North) in the following year.

The Second World War and After

In one way or another, the outbreak of war in September 1939 changed the lives of the city's inhabitants almost immediately. Two days before the war began, 4,000 children began to arrive by train, evacuees from Leeds, but there were not enough homes to take them all in. Shortly after the announcement of 'a state of war' the bells of the cathedral and the city's churches were silenced, with instructions to ring again only if invasion threatened; black-out curtains appeared everywhere, as did the obligatory gas masks; theatres and cinemas were closed down – only to open again after a few months; ration cards were issued and, by Christmas, shopping had long come to mean queuing, for two ounces of butter, possibly two small tins of fish, perhaps a tin of fruit. The city's newest cinema, the Radion, did not re-open. Instead it was requisitioned as a base for the Pioneer Corps for the duration of the war.

As the first few months of 'phoney war' ended, in the following spring, Anderson air raid shelters were erected, the Observatory Tower of the castle was adopted by the Observer Corps and the Local Defence Volunteers were formed (soon to be known as the Home Guard). A Toc H Forces canteen was set up in an old building at the bottom of Lucy Tower Street, and a week before the evacuation from Dunkirk began, the first bombs fell near the city – four high-explosive bombs falling on North Hykeham – but with no casualties.

During the rest of 1940 there were many more bombing raids, causing sleepless nights and doing much damage, and on 28 September a Hampden bomber crashed on St Mathias Church on Burton Road, killing the pilot. The first civilian casualties came in March 1941, when the Baggeholme Road area was hit by five high-explosive bombs. Seventy-two-year-old Alfred Medd was killed in Coningsby Street and six other people were injured. St Swithin's School was destroyed and 200 houses and shops were damaged. During the next four years more than 50 men, women and children, civilians and servicemen, would lose their lives in the city, or in the immediate surrounding area, either as a result of enemy bombing or due to planes crashing.

Not only the city, but also the numerous surrounding airfields were obvious targets. Just a few weeks after Lincoln's first civilian casualties, the airfields at Waddington and Scampton were hit. Scampton escaped lightly on this occasion, but seven of the ladies employed in the services' canteen and three servicemen were killed when the air-raid shelter took a direct hit. The local villagers suffered as well, with one fatality, numerous injuries and 19 houses completely destroyed. Two months later, on 22 July, a Hampden bomber crashed on Lindum Hill, killing all of the crew, destroying the high school building on Greestone Stairs, and killing the senior French mistress. And less than a week later, two pilots stationed at Kirton Lindsey staged a mock dogfight over the city, causing their planes to collide. They managed to bale out safely, but as the planes crashed

167 *One of the Luftwaffe's aerial photographs of Lincoln, 1941, with Ruston and Hornsby's works marked as targets.*

into the city four people were killed in Oxford Street, six more were seriously injured, and many houses were badly damaged.

One of the worst incidents of the war for the city occurred on the evening of 15 January 1943, at about 8 p.m. The city's streets, pubs and cinemas were full of local people and service men when a lone Dornier 217 appeared to the east of the city and flew down Monks Road, dropping its lethal cargo as it came, before turning sharply over the Stonebow, and continuing down the High Street, doing further damage and causing terrible panic. By the time it had been brought down by a pursuing Mosquito, seven miles south of the city, it had killed six people, seriously injured 30, totally destroyed 25 houses and damaged hundreds more.

The highest single loss of life occurred in the following June, when a stricken Lancaster crashed in the Swanpool area, killing six of the seven-man crew and five civilians. And just 11 days later a Handley Page Halifax crashed on the southern edge of the city, between Brant Road and the river, killing all seven crewmen. But these were among the last casualties of the war in the Lincoln area, and the city could consider itself fortunate not to have suffered more than it did. On Christmas Eve, 1944, V–1 flying bombs screamed over the city, just above the level of the chimney pots, but their targets were well to the west of Lincoln and none hit the city.

From the beginning of the war the city's engineering works had been geared to the war effort, with labour and raw materials allocated by the government. Not surprisingly, the city's largest employer, Ruston and Hornsby Ltd, was from the start a prime target for the Luftwaffe, as Fig. 167 reveals, although it was never hit. This aerial photograph of Lincoln in 1939 also gives us an excellent view of the housing of the families working in the city's engineering factories. The spacious pattern of the new housing estate of St Giles can just be seen in the top right-hand corner of the picture, but the great majority of the city's workers still lived in the dozens of rows of terraced houses that stretch east, west and south: along Monks Road, on the hillside above the Foss Dyke, and to the west of Canwick Road. From this height the cathedral is

168 *Sir Winston Churchill inspecting 'Nellie' during trials in Clumber Park, 1940.*

barely visible, but the city's more recent Victorian heritage as an industrial centre is very clear indeed.

Ruston and Hornsby produced many thousands of diesel engines for a great variety of wartime purposes. They drove refrigeration plants in the North African desert, electrical, hydraulic and compressed air machinery for guns and searchlights at the Singapore naval base, and were used in small naval vessels such as landing craft and minesweepers. They were also shipped to barracks in south-east Asia and through Arctic waters to Russia, to power Russian factories relocated east of the Urals. Closer to home they also provided the power for Churchill's underground bunker, and when the war was over it was found that the Germans had also been using a Ruston engine in their underground bunker near Paris. Diesel locomotives were also built to work in underground munitions dumps, coal mines and quarries. Ruston and Hornsby also built tanks and armoured tractors. They produced 400 armoured tractors to tow 17-pounder guns, and 400 'Matilda' tanks were built before the firm developed an improved version, the 'Cavalier', and built a further 220 of these. Other munitions produced by the city's factories included mines, warheads for midget submarines, parts for radar and searchlights, crankshafts and Bofors guns. A huge trench-digging machine, nicknamed 'Nellie', was also developed by Ruston Bucyrus. It was designed to help in the destruction of the German western defences, the 'Siegfried Line', but it was not yet ready for use when France fell to the Germans in 1940, and its effectiveness was consequently never tested.

POST-WAR CHANGE AND DECLINE IN ENGINEERING

Even before the war ended, a new era in the history of engineering in Lincoln was beginning. Late in 1944 the managing director of Ruston and Hornsby, Victor Bone, became convinced that there was a future for the gas turbine in industry. The firm began design work in the following year and by 1950 a successful prototype gas turbine engine had been built. Full-scale production began in 1952 at the Anchor Street works and the firm were soon recognised as the leading British manufacturer in this field. During the next 20 years more than 500 industrial gas turbines were built in Lincoln.

But while a new industry was being created an old industry was quietly dying. Lincoln's fame as a major centre for engineering since the 1840s had been built on the steam engine and its application to the needs of agriculture. Several Lincolnshire firms had ceased making steam engines before 1939, but in 1955 Robey's of Lincoln were still making some of the last stationary steam engines produced in the country, and in 1960 Foster's of Lincoln built the very last thrashing machine made in Britain. The numbers produced in Lincoln had long been in decline as more farmers turned instead to combine harvesters. Until the 1960s, however, engineering remained the dominant employer in the city. There are many in the city today who can remember a time when it seemed that most young men who left school went to work in one of the engineering factories, as one gentleman recently recalled. 'When I left school in the early 1960s, it wasn't so much of the question: "What do you want to do when you leave school?" as "Which factory are you going to work in?"'

The second half of the 20th century witnessed a long, slow decline of large-scale engineering in the city (as indeed also in the country generally), culminating in the final closure of Ruston's, the city's last great Victorian-founded company. Long before this, however, in 1961, Ruston & Hornsby had been taken over by the English Electric Co., which in turn was taken over by GEC (General Electric Co.) in 1966. The firm's gas turbine activities were then formed into a separate group, Ruston Gas Turbines, but continued to occupy the firm's original Sheaf Iron Works site, beside the Witham, sharing it with Napier Turbochargers. This then became part of European Gas Turbines, but far fewer men and women were now employed, and far less space was needed. Consequently, the firm's Anchor Lane Works and Boiler Works were demolished in 1983-4, along with Foster's Wellington Works, which stood nearby and had latterly been occupied by Ruston-Bucyrus. Engineering still survives on the old Sheaf Works site, at the north end of Pelham Bridge, but only as a relatively small offshoot of the vast German-owned Siemens Group. It is a pale shadow of the city's great engineering past, but at the time of writing, in 2008, the future of engineering in Lincoln does seem secure. The Siemens Group has acquired land near the A46 bypass junction with the Skellingthorpe Road to build a new factory. It will continue to produce here the relatively smaller gas turbine engines (up to 10,000 hp) which have for many years been the staple product of Siemens in Lincoln.

The City Today

The city, however, has diversified and continued to grow, in spite of the loss of so many of its largest employers, and in 2001 the population was well in excess of 80,000. Tourism, distribution, and other service industries account for much of the city's workforce today. The largest single employer is probably the university, which opened its main campus beside the Brayford Pool in 1996 (having gained university status in 1992). Large public housing schemes have resulted in the creation of the extensive Birchwood Estate to the west of the city and the Ermine Estate to the north, while private housing developments have also helped extend the built-up area of the city, especially to the east. The numbers

169 *The University of Lincoln and the Brayford Pool.*

170 *The Waterside Shopping Centre with the Millennium sculpture in the foreground.*

commuting into the city every morning has also continued to grow with the massive expansion in car ownership since the 1960s and the growth in communities surrounding Lincoln. Communications were improved by the opening of Pelham Bridge in 1958 and by the closure of one of the city's two level-crossings on the High Street in 1985. Most important, however, has been the building of the bypass, which was opened in 1985, although the continuing growth in car usage has meant that now, at the beginning of the 21st century, car journeys at peak commuter times can still be painfully slow, and the need for a complete ring road is now widely recognised.

The opening of the university has had a major influence on the life of the city. The university has about ten thousand students, whose spending power has had a major impact, particularly on the city's nightlife. It has also brought considerable investment. Over £100m has already been invested in the Brayford campus alone, the latest addition being a £6m student centre, the 'Engine Shed', providing space for nearly 2,000 students, and is now the city's largest multi-purpose entertainment venue.

The city's success as a retail centre for an ever-widening area has owed much to the development of a major retail park off Tritton Road, partly on the site of the former engineering works demolished in the 1980s, and also to a very successful pedestrianisation scheme, which has included almost the whole of the central shopping area. Four regular monthly farmers' markets have also proved popular and the city has become famous for its Christmas market, held early in December in the grounds of the castle and on Castle Hill, with over 300 stalls attracting many thousands of shoppers. The closure of St Mark's Railway Station in 1985 was also used as an opportunity to develop another small pedestrianised shopping area around St Mark's Square, keeping the grand classical façade of the station. The opportunity was also taken to re-erect, as a focal point, the obelisk that had stood on High Bridge since the 1760s but had had to be dismantled

171   St Mark's Station, built in 1846 as the terminus for the Midland Railway's branch line from Nottingham, closed in the 1980s but the façade has been preserved to house a new retail centre.

172   The obelisk, which once stood on High Bridge and was designed in 1762, was dismantled in 1939 but now stands in St Mark's Square, having been reconstructed in 1996.

in 1939 as part of restoration and repair work on the bridge. The obelisk is now a memorial to distinguished local people, including the historian Sir Francis Hill (to whom this writer, like so many others, owes a considerable debt).

Many of the new buildings erected in the 1960s and 1970s have been much criticised for lack of architectural merit. Michael Jones, for instance, refers to the 'brutalism' of both City Hall and the nearby Divisional Police Headquarters, and others have described the Pelham Bridge flyover, Deansgate House, the *Lincoln Hotel* and Co-op House in similar terms. But the Waterside Shopping Centre, opened in 1991, has met with more approval, as has the development of the market area and, more recently, the new Lincoln University building, on its very attractive site overlooking the Brayford Pool. The city's historic centre has been protected since 1967 when it was designated as a conservation area and recognised as an area of national historic importance. Other buildings have been listed and parts of the city have been scheduled as historic monuments. The enormous importance of the tourist industry and the city's potential as a regional arts centre are now also well appreciated, not least by the city council. The once rather drab Drill Hall has been converted into an attractive location for musical, literary and theatrical productions, including both a book festival and a beer festival, and the Theatre Royal was restored by the city council before being returned to private hands. The Arboretum was also enormously improved as a recreational area in 2003, transforming a rather neglected area of the city into a major asset enjoyed by thousands of city-dwellers and visitors.

Ambitious restoration programmes are also in progress at both the castle and the cathedral, backed by central government grants, and the medieval bishop's palace has been restored and re-opened to the public by English Heritage, with a helpful audio guide to assist the visitor interpret the remains of this once most impressive building. The opening of a new museum and art gallery, The Collection, in 2005, next to the Usher Gallery on Danesgate, has been another important step in the city's recent cultural revival. Through well-displayed artefacts, the museum tells many stories of archaeological discovery in both the city and the county since prehistoric times. One of the exhibits of the museum is a Roman mosaic floor, discovered on the site during excavations prior to construction. The city's other major museum, the Museum of Lincolnshire Life, is still located in the Old Militia Barracks on Burton Road and illustrates the more recent history of the county.

173   *The Collection, a new museum and art gallery, opened on Danesgate in 2005.*

Another major development in the services provided in the city came in 1980 with the opening of BBC Radio Lincolnshire, dedicated to providing local news and discussion of local issues, as well as music and entertainment. It is located appropriately in the former Radion cinema in Newport. The independent 'Lincs FM' followed a few years later. Of the city's former eight cinemas none now survive, the last to close being the Ritz. The building still stands but the ground floor is now occupied by a Wetherspoon pub. With the opening of the university, however, on the south bank of the Brayford Pool, the north bank has been transformed into a popular leisure area, lined with a variety of restaurants and bars and boasting a new multiplex cinema with nine screens, the Odeon.

The city's other major centre of entertainment of the first half of the century, Lincoln City FC, only manages to attract a faithful 2,000 to 4,000 fans every week to Sincil Bank – much depending on the opposition and the team's position in the League tables. In the years before television, however, numbers could be much higher, and in the 'golden years', immediately after the Second World War, between 10,000 and 20,000 could be expected, standing on the rain-sodden and windswept terraces. Unfortunately, at the end of the 2010-11 season Lincoln City were relegated to the National Conference. The only slight consolation was that their great rivals, Grimsby Town, had been relegated the year before.

The second half of the 20th century has also seen the closure and disappearance of many of the city's churches and chapels. The union of the three principal branches of Methodism – Wesleyan, Primitive and Free – in 1932 made possible the closure of all four of the Free Methodist churches by 1965, when the Portland Street chapel closed. The first to go had been the 'gem of the Connexion', the Silver Street chapel, which closed in 1940, although the building survived as part of the Co-operative store, but without the Corinthian columns. Perhaps the saddest closure, however, was that of 'Big Wesley' itself in 1961, exactly 125 years after it had opened. Demolished in 1963, it leaves not a trace. When it closed there were just 187 members; in 1865, at the peak of Methodist expansion, there had been almost 700 members, and congregations of well over a thousand.

Lincoln remains a relatively little-known city for most inhabitants of the United Kingdom, served neither by the motorway network nor on the main north-south railway line. It is still, however, a very beautiful and historic city, with the cathedral as its unrivalled crowning glory. A sound conservation policy, including a commitment only to allow new building where it improves on the existing, should ensure that this remains the case. And the city's communications are improving. Improvements made recently to the A46, linking Lincoln to Newark, have helped, and a direct train link to London has been established.

Select Bibliography

General Sources

Abell, E.I. and Chambers, J.D., *The Story of Lincoln* (Lincoln, 1949)
Antram, Nicholas (ed.), *The Buildings of England; Lincolnshire* (London, 1995)
Beckwith, Ian, *The Book of Lincoln* (Lincoln, 1990)
Jones, M.J., *Lincoln, History and Guide* (Stroud, 2004)
Jones, M.J., Stocker, D. and Vince, A., *The City by the Pool* (Lincoln, 2003)
Mills, Dennis and Wheeler, Rob (eds), *An Atlas of Historic Maps of Lincoln, 1610-1920* (Lincoln, 2004)
Owen, Dorothy (ed.), *A History of Lincoln Minster* (Cambridge, 1994)
Vale, D., *Lincoln, A Place In Time* (Lincoln, 1997)
Walker, Andrew (ed.), *Aspects of Lincoln; Discovering Local History* (Barnsley, 2001)
Yeates-Langley, Ann, *Lincoln, A Pictorial History* (Lincoln, 1997)

Chapter One: Roman Lincoln

Jones, M.J., *Roman Lincoln* (Stroud, 2002)
Jones, M.J., 'The Latter Days of Roman Lincoln', in Vince, Alan, *Pre-Viking Lindsey* (Lincoln, 1993)
Whitwell, J.B., *Roman Lincolnshire* (Lincoln, 1992)

Chapters Two, Three, Four and Five: Anglo-Saxon and Medieval Lincoln

Bassett, Steven, 'Lincoln and the Anglo-Saxon see of Lindsey', *Anglo-Saxon England*, 18 (1989)
Blackburn, Mark, 'Coin Finds and Coin Circulation in Lindsey, c.600-900', in Vince, Alan, *Pre-Viking Lindsey* (Lincoln, 1993)
Duke, Dulcie, *Lincoln, The Growth of a Medieval Town* (Cambridge, 1974)
Gem, Richard, 'The Episcopal Churches in Lindsey in the Early Ninth Century', in Vince, Alan, *Pre-Viking Lindsey* (Lincoln, 1993)
Green, Thomas, 'The British kingdom of Lindsey', *Cambrian Medieval Celtic Studies*, 56 (2008)
Hill, J.W.F., *Medieval Lincoln* (Cambridge, 1965)
Leahy, Kevin, 'The Anglo-Saxon Settlement of Lindsey', in Vince, Alan, *Pre-Viking Lindsey* (Lincoln, 1993)
Leahy, Kevin, *The Anglo-Saxon Kingdom of Lindsey* (Stroud, 2007)

Jones, S., Major, K. and Varley, J., *The Survey of Ancient Houses in Lincoln, I: Priorygate to Pottergate* (Lincoln, 1984)

Jones, S., Major, K. and Varley, J., *The Survey of Ancient Houses in Lincoln, II: Houses to the South and West of the Minster* (Lincoln, 1987)

Jones, S., Major, K. and Varley, J., *The Survey of Ancient Houses in Lincoln, III: Houses in Eastgate, Priorygate, and James Street* (Lincoln, 1990)

Jones, S., Major, K., Varley, J. and Johnson, C., *The Survey of Ancient Houses in Lincoln, IV: Houses in the Bail: Steep Hill, Castle Hill, and Bailgate* (Lincoln, 1996)

Owen, Dorothy, *Church and Society in Medieval Lincolnshire* (Lincoln, 1971)

Platts, Graham, *Land and People in Medieval Lincolnshire* (Lincoln, 1985)

Steane, Kate and Vince, Alan, 'Post-Roman Lincoln: Archaeological Evidence for Activity in Lincoln in the 5th-9th Centuries', in Vince, Alan, *Pre-Viking Lindsey* (Lincoln, 1993)

Stocker, David, 'The Early Church in Lincolnshire', in Vince, Alan, *Pre-Viking Lindsey* (Lincoln, 1993)

Vince, Alan (ed.), *Pre-Viking Lindsey* (Lincoln, 1993)

Yorke, Barbara, 'Lindsey: The Lost Kingdom Found?', in Vince, Alan, *Pre-Viking Lindsey*

CHAPTERS SIX, SEVEN, EIGHT AND NINE: TUDOR AND STUART LINCOLN

Hill, J.W.F., *Tudor and Stuart Lincoln* (Cambridge, 1991)

Hodgett, Gerald A.J., *Tudor Lincolnshire* (Lincoln, 1975)

Holmes, Clive, *Seventeenth Century Lincolnshire* (Lincoln, 1980)

Johnston, Jim, 'Getting Drunk in Seventeenth century Lincoln', in Walker, Andrew, *Aspects of Lincoln* (2001)

Wilford, John, 'Thomas Watson: The Last Roman Catholic Bishop of Lincoln', in Walker, Andrew, *Aspects of Lincoln* (2001)

CHAPTERS TEN, ELEVEN AND TWELVE: EIGHTEENTH-, NINETEENTH- AND TWENTIETH-CENTURY LINCOLN

Beastall, T.W., *The Agricultural Revolution in Lincolnshire* (Lincoln, 1978)

Clarke, George, 'Lincoln's Cinemas in the Twentieth century', in Walker, Andrew, *Aspects of Lincoln*

Hill, J.W.F., *Georgian Lincoln* (Cambridge, 1966)

Hill, J.W.F., *Victorian Lincoln* (Cambridge, 1974)

Hill, Kate, 'The Middle Classes in Victorian Lincoln', in Walker, Andrew, *Aspects of Lincoln* (2001)

Hurt, Fred, *Lincoln During the War* (Lincoln, 1991)

Hurt, Fred, *Lincoln War Diaries* (Lincoln, 1997)

Leary, William, *Methodism in the City of Lincoln* (Lincoln, 1969)

Mills, Dennis R. (ed.), *Twentieth Century Lincolnshire* (Lincoln, 1989)

Nannestad, Eleanor, 'Pleasure Excursions From Lincoln, 1846-1914', in Walker, Andrew, *Aspects of Lincoln* (2001)

Nowell, Terry, 'Remembering those in Lincoln's Prisons, 1774-1872', in Walker, Andrew, *Aspects of Lincoln* (2001)

Olney, R.J., *Rural Society and County Government in Nineteenth-Century Lincolnshire* (Lincoln, 1979)

Wright, Neil R., *Lincolnshire Towns and Industry, 1700-1914* (Lincoln, 1982)

INDEX

The index lists only principal subjects and selected persons and places
Note: Numbers in **bold** refer to illustrations